# *The* MANUAL
# *of the* HOLY FACE

# *The* MANUAL *of the* HOLY FACE

## A.M.P.

*The Manual of the Holy Face*
by A.M.P.

Second Printing, March 2021.
A. M. P., El Paso, Texas, U.S.A.
ISBN-13: 978-0-578-87439-5

First Printing, June 17, 2018.
Saint Paul Press, Dallas, Texas, U.S.A.
ISBN-13: 978-1-721-23849-1
ISBN-10: 1721238492

*Dedicated to the Sacred & Immaculate Heart*
*Their love for souls is unfathomable —*
*including for yours, dear reader.*

# PREFACE

"The audacity of impiety has increased, a clamor issuing from hell has been raised for the purpose of denying Thy Divinity and outraging the Church, a diabolical pact has been formed against God and against His Christ. It is for us, faithful Christians, to close our ranks under the banner of the Holy Face, to multiply our phalanx of reparation, to offer to Jesus, as did Veronica, the veil of our love and of our veneration. We need no longer, O merciful Face, envy the happiness of that heroic woman; by a redoublement of faith, of fervor and of zeal, we may, like her, wipe Thy tears away, staunch Thy blood, and solace Thy sufferings." – from the Act of Reparation prayer.

It may surprise the reader to know that this prayer of reparation, which is applicable to the times in which we live in the 21st century, was published in the 19th century in a book called *Manual of the Archconfraternity of the Holy Face*, by Reverend Abbé Janvier at Tours, France. While researching and becoming acquainted with the devotion of the Holy Face, copies of the *Manual of the Archconfraternity of the Holy Face* (published in 1887) and *Sister Saint Pierre and the Work of Reparation with an Appendix of Prayers and Devotions for the Confraternities of the Holy Face* (published in 1885) were obtained. Beyond the beauty of the prayers and meditations contained in these books, there was a realization that now more than ever, this is a devotion for our times. These times in which we live, where God and His laws are attacked and removed by the laws of man, where praying and mentioning the Name of God **with reverence** is ridiculed, but using the same Name as a statement of surprise, anger, or blasphemy is perfectly acceptable.

*The Manual of the Archconfraternity* from 1887 contains a special reprint of *The Little Office of the most Holy Name of God.* The explanation as to why it was being included in the publication was written as follows, "We first found it in a pamphlet entitled, *Association of prayers against blasphemy, etc.*, which went through several editions, the last being dated 1867; but since then it has not been reprinted. This portion of the pamphlet deserves to be saved from oblivion."

How appropriate those words, "deserves to be saved from oblivion." Indeed, the entire work deserves to be save from oblivion! If you worry about your family, friends, country, and countrymen, there are treasures within these pages to make reparation, to win graces, and to save souls. There are beautiful, loving prayers to God, meditations, and more!

In republishing this work, the two books have been consolidated into one. Only duplicate prayers have been omitted. This printing entitled *The Manual of the Holy Face*, contains the historical notices of the Confraternity and Archconfraternity of the Holy Face, prayers, meditations, and the Life of Sister Marie de Saint-Pierre. Any mistakes made in the consolidation, arrangement, and reprinting are my fault alone and not reflective of the original works.

Dear reader, if you have this work in your hands, it is no mistake or accident. Consider that you are being called to the spiritual battlefield for souls. *Knowing the season, it is now the hour for us to rise from our sleep. For now our salvation is nearer than when we believed. The night is passed, and the day is at hand. Let us therefore cast off the works of darkness, and put on the armor of light* (Romans Ch. 13, 11-12).

With the Golden Arrow ever at the ready, may the Holy Face be your shield, the rosary your sword, the Sacred & Immaculate Heart your banner, and your battle cry ever be "Jesus, Mary, I love Thee! Save souls!"

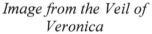

Image from the Veil of
Veronica

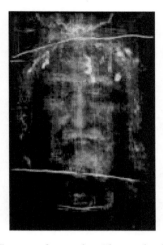

Image from the Shroud of
Turin

*I desire that My Face, which shows My Soul's deepest
anguish, My Heart's sorrow and My love, may be more
honored. Whosoever contemplates Me, consoles Me.*

*Every time that anyone gazes at My Face, I will pour My
love into hearts and by means of My Holy Face, the
salvation of many souls will be obtained.*

*It may be that some souls fear that the devotion and
veneration of My Holy Face diminishes that towards My
Heart. Tell them that on the contrary, it will be
completed and augmented. In contemplating My Face,
souls will share in all My gifts, and will feel the need for
love and reparation. Is that not perhaps the true
devotion to My Heart?*

— Our Lord to Bl. Maria Pierina de Micheli

# CONTENTS

## FIRST PART
### Historical Documents, Letters, and Notices

## SECOND PART
### Observations, Meditations, and Novenas

## THIRD PART
### Litanies and Forms of Prayer

## FOURTH PART
### Exercises of Devotion and Different Practices

15

## FIFTH PART
### Little Office

## SIXTH PART
### Supplement

## SEVENTH PART
### The Life of Sister Marie de Saint-Pierre

# First Part
# HISTORICAL DOCUMENTS, LETTERS, AND NOTICES

The following section is from the 1885 publication of *Sister Saint Pierre and the Work of Reparation with an appendix of Prayers and Devotions for the Confraternities of the Holy Face.*

*\*Note: The Discalced Carmelites are no longer in New Orleans and the Oratory of the Holy Face at Tours has a different address. The original addresses and locations are included for historical context only.*

# Conditions for being received into the Confraternity of the Reparation of the Holy Face

1. To be inscribed on the Register of the Confraternity where it is canonically established.
2. To obtain a copy of the Regulations, wherewith will be found the ticket of admission.
3. To wear at all times the Cross of the Confraternity.
4. Never to blaspheme, and to do all one can to prevent blasphemy.
5. When not possible to prevent these crimes, to make, at least, an interior Act of Reparation for them.
6. To recite daily a *Pater, Ave,* and *Gloria Patri,* "with the Act of Praise," in union with the Associates, in the spirit of Reparation.

Note.—The Most Reverend Archbishops, Right Reverend Bishops, and Reverend Clergy, also all pious laymen, are earnestly requested to use their influence in having exposed for devotion pictures of the Holy Face, and establishing everywhere the Confraternity of the Reparation for Blasphemy and Profanation of Sunday. All desired information *connected with this Confraternity may be obtained by addressing the Reverend Director of the Confraternity, Oratory of the Holy Face, 8 Rue Saint-Etienne, Tours, Indre-et-Loire, France; or the Reverend Mother-Prioress, Convent of Discalced Carmelites, 134 Barrack Street, New Orleans, Louisiana, in whose chapel the Confraternity of the Holy Face is canonically established.\**

# Historical Notice

Pope Pius IX, in an audience of July 30, 1847, approved the Confraternity for the Reparation of Blasphemy and the Profanation of Sunday. His Holiness greeted the petition with the most ardent enthusiasm, requested that his name be the first inscribed on the register of the Confraternity, and said that the "Reparation was a work destined to save society." Sister Saint-Pierre, on hearing this, exclaimed: "My mission here below is accomplished; I can now die!" She died a year later, July 8, 1848.

M. Dupont developed and continued her "work." On Wednesday of Holy Week (1851) he lighted a lamp (which has never ceased to burn night and day) before the image of the Holy Face, which is the sensible sign of the Confraternity of the Reparation. The miraculous graces obtained by the oil of the lamp were to his eyes as so many proofs that our Lord accepted the devotion rendered to His Holy Face as a means of repairing the outrages committed against the majesty of the Thrice Holy Name of God. He never ceased to recommend the Reparation. He said: "Pray that this work may spread. It seems from what is taking place that our Lord desires, and without delay, that souls devoted to Him should practice this salutary exercise. It is a necessity that those who comprehend what God wills should courageously walk in the way of Reparation."

The work has spread, and today the members in the different parts of the world are counted by hundreds of thousands. In transforming the Oratory of M. Dupont into a public chapel Monseigneur Colet, Archbishop of Tours, established a Confraternity of Reparation in honor of the Holy Face on June 2, 1876; he also established a society of priests who would devote themselves to it and extend its propagation.

"Our Lord," said Sister Saint-Pierre, "demands this work of Reparation of France which will be a rainbow of mercy." "Ah!" said she, "if it were established in all dioceses I would be without uneasiness, for God is faithful to His promises.... Oh! — how I would wish to make known to all bishops this consoling truth, and ask them with earnest supplication the establishment of this work of the Reparation! I have always said it, and I now repeat it, this work will disarm the anger of God, save France and the world." Happy are those who profit by this means of salvation.

(See Life of Sister Saint-Pierre, written by herself. This book and all others in English and French can be found at No. 134 Barrack Street, New Orleans, La., by addressing the Rev. Mother-Prioress of the Discalced Carmelites.)*

# Rules of the Confraternity of the Holy Face in Reparation for Blasphemy and the Profanation of Sunday

(Established at Tours in the Oratory of the Venerated M. Dupont, and in the Chapel of the Discalced Carmelites, New Orleans.)*

**Article 1.** The objective of the Confraternity of the Reparation in honor of the Holy Face is, first, to repair the outrages committed against the Divine Majesty of God by blasphemies, the profanation of Sunday and the feasts of the Church; second, to obtain the conversion and salvation of blasphemers and profaners; third, to preserve youth and the family from the fatal effects of these scandals. To obtain this triple end, so important in our day, it offers a special devotion of prayer, adoration, and love to the most Holy Face of our Lord, outraged and disfigured in His Passion.

**Art. 2.** It is consecrated to the adorable Trinity, to the Holy Name of Jesus, and to His sorrowful Face. It is placed under the patronage of St. Michael, St. Martin, and St. Louis, protector of France. In the devotion which the Confraternity renders to the Holy Face it takes for its models the Immaculate Virgin Mary, patroness of the United States; the apostle St. Peter, and the pious Veronica. Trinity Sunday is the principal feast; the second one is that of the Holy Name of Jesus (second Sunday after Epiphany); and for particular feasts those of the saints above mentioned or those who are proposed as models.

**Art. 3.** Catholics of all ages, of either sex, and of all conditions are exhorted to enter this Confraternity. Children who have not yet made their first Communion will be received as aspirants and placed most particularly under the protection of the amiable Face of the Savior, who so tenderly called little children to Him.

**Art. 4.** Each member, from the time of entrance into the Confraternity, devotes themselves for life and death to the worship of the merciful and compassionate Face of our Lord, and assumes the strict obligation never to utter blasphemies or imprecations, to hold no conversation, to read nothing written, and to take no part in any act which outrages God and our Lord Jesus Christ in His saints or through His works; never to perform any servile work on Sundays and holy days without necessity and without permission.

**Art. 5.** Those in authority over others, such as parents, public officials, proprietors, superintendents

24

works, patrons, workmen etc., should make a firm resolution as far as is in their power to promote the observance of the rules which are laid down in the preceding Article. They will take particular care that the aspirants of the Confraternity shall not receive scandal in this regard.

**Art. 6.** When the members hear a blasphemy or any impious word uttered, when they see Sundays and holidays profaned and cannot prevent it, they should offer up to God some Reparation, saying, for example, Sit Nomen Domini Benedictum — May God be praised; may His Holy Name be blessed; Our Father, hallowed be Thy Name; God our Protector, look upon the Face of Thy Christ. They may also add, Vade retro, Satana.

**Art. 7.** The Confraternity of the Reparation considers the adorable and sorrowful Face of our Lord the exterior sign and sensible object of the Reparation, as has been declared by the ordinance, dated June 2, 1876, of his Grace the Archbishop of Tours, who canonically erected the Confraternity in "the Oratory of M. Dupont. Since 1851 there has been honored a picture of the Face of our Lord, an authentic facsimile of the celebrated Veil of the Vatican, given to the servant of God by the Rev. Mother-Prioress of the Carmelites on account of his zeal for the Reparation and in remembrance of the pious relations he had with Sister Saint-Pierre, who died in the odor of sanctity July 8, 1848." This sign is represented by a Cross, on one side of which is an image of the Holy Face, bearing on the top the inscription of the cross, on either arm "Tours, 1876," at the base "Vade retro, Satana," on the reverse side the monogram of Christ encircled by these words, "Reparation, Pius IX, 1847," and upon the Cross, "Sit Nomen Domini Benedictum."

**Art. 8.** The members will receite daily a Pater Noster, Ave Maria, Gloria Patri, and the Act of

Praise in reparation for outrages committed against God by blasphemy and the profanation of Sunday; they will at least unite their intention to the prayers which are offered up daily in the oratories of Reparation, in the morning after the 7 o'clock Mass and in the afternoon at 5 o'clock. The Litany of the Holy Face, composed by Sister Saint-Pierre and approved by ecclesiastical authorities, is daily recited in the oratories, after which follow the different recommendations presented by the faithful.

**Art. 9.**  On the last Sunday of each month, in the afternoon, a solemn assembly takes place in the oratories of the Holy Face, in reparation for these same outrages, but more especially for those committed within the month. The Act of Reparation is recited with the invocations: St. Michael, pray for us; St. Peter, pray for us; St. Martin, pray for us; St. Louis, pray for us; O God our Protector! Look upon the Face of Thy Christ and we shall be saved. These prayers are preceded by an instruction and followed by Benediction of the Blessed Sacrament. Each member is exhorted to offer up these prayers every other Sunday of the month in reparation for the sins of each week. On the first Thursday of the month the evening assemblies, held at 5 o'clock, are especially devoted to the aspirants of the Work of Reparation. (Special prayers are also recited daily, weekly, and monthly in the chapel of the Discalced Carmelites for the Reparation of the evils of this country — namely, intemperance, gambling, immorality, etc.)

**Art. 10.**  The director of a canonically-established Confraternity admits as members those who ask to have their names inscribed upon the register. All are exhorted to habitually wear the Cross of the Confraternity and to read over the Rules from time to time. To share in the merits of the work their name must be inscribed in the register. A particular register is kept for the aspirants of the work who, after their first Communion, may desire to have their names inscribed in the grand register.

**Art. 11.** The Confraternity of Reparation established at Tours and in the Carmelite chapel, New Orleans, La., are conically affiliated to the Archconfraternity of St. Dizier, diocese of Langres, and enjoy the same privileges and spiritual favors.

**Art. 12.** The members may gain the following Plenary and Partial Indulgences:

Plenary: (1st) On the day of admission and putting on the Cross; (2nd) At the hour of death; (3rd) On the feasts of the Holy Trinity, the Holy Name of Jesus, St. Michael, St. Martin, and St. Louis, either on the day itself or on any day during the octave — Pope Pius IX, July 27, 1847; (4th) On the last Sunday of each month, if they assist at the monthly meeting and if the Cross of the Confraternity is worn habitually (applicable to the souls in Purgatory) — Pope Pius IX, Aug. 18, 1847. To gain the abovementioned Indulgences it is necessary to go to Confession and Holy Communion, visit an Oratory of the Confraternity (or, if this is impossible, one's parish church), and there pray for the intentions of the Sovereign Pontiff. — Pope Pius IX, Aug. 18, 1848.

Partial Indulgences: (1st) 100 days for each pious work of the Confraternity — Pope Pius IX, July 27, 1847; (2nd) 300 days for attending the monthly meeting (applicable to the souls in Purgatory) — Pope Pius IX, Aug. 18, 1848; (3rd) 100 days for every prayer offered before an image of the Holy Face (applicable to the souls in Purgatory) — Pope Pius IX, Dec. 11, 1876; (4th) 40 days for attending each of the Exercises of Reparation which are held morning and evening in the oratories of the Holy Face — Archbishop of Tours, Nov. 15, 1876.

These Rules of the Confraternity in Reparation for Blasphemy and the Profanation of Sunday, canonically erected at Tours and New Orleans in honor of the Holy Face, have been seen and approved.

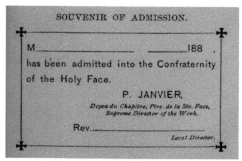

SOUVENIR OF ADMISSION.

M_____ _____188 ,
has been admitted into the Confraternity
of the Holy Face.

P. JANVIER,
*Doyen du Chapitre, Ptre. de la Ste. Face,*
*Supreme Director of the Work.*

Rev._____
*Local Director.*

Tours, Nov. 15, 1870.
✠ Charles, Archbishop of Tours.

New Orleans, March 12, 1883.
✠ N. J. Perche, Archbishop of New Orleans.

# Forms for the Canonical Erection of the Confraternity in a Parish Church or Chapel

Reverend Pastors, Chaplains, Almoners, Superiors or Directors of communities should:

1. Ask the permission of the ordinary and his approval of the Rules.
2. Adopt the Rules used by the Confraternity established at Tours, with any special modifications the ordinary may see fit to suggest.
3. Obtain a diploma of affiliation from the director of the Archconfraternity of St. Dizier, diocese of Langres (Haute-Marne), which is never refused, and which must be submitted to the ordinary before the inauguration of the Confraternity.

4. To hang in the church or chapel an image of the sorrowful Face of our Lord like the one in the Oratory of M. Dupont, and, if possible, to keep a lamp constantly burning before it.
5. To obtain a diploma of aggregation and union of merits and prayers from the director of the Confraternity at Tours, and in return assume the duty of propagating as zealously as possible the spirit of Reparation and devotion to the Holy Face.

# An Abridgement of Conditions for Membership

$1^{st}$ – To be inscribed on the register of the Confraternity.

$2^{nd}$ – To obtain the Rules containing the Certificate of Admission.

$3^{rd}$ – Recite daily a *Pater*, *Ave*, *Gloria*, and the *Act of Praise* in a spirit of Reparation.

$4^{th}$ – Avoid blasphemies and the profanation of Sunday, and to at least repair those evils by an interior act of Reparation.

$5^{th}$ – Wear at all times the Cross of the Confraternity.

$6^{th}$ – To zealously propagate the devotion to the Holy Face.

For further particulars apply to No. 134 Barrack Street, New Orleans, La.,* where these Rules of the Confraternity, the oil from the lamp of the Holy Face, scapulars, medals, pictures, photographs, crosses, books chaplets, gospels of the Holy Name, and all else connected with the Reparation can be obtained. The oratories of the Holy Face are open to pilgrims and visitors daily from

5 a.m to 6 p.m., where petitions can be sent by mail or left by visitors. It is earnestly requested that persons who obtain graces should send a written account of the same, and likewise have an ex-voto put up in thanksgiving for favors received through the Holy Face. These ex-votos can be procured on applying at the Oratory. During novenas, lamps and candles will be kept burning when requested.

*Note: The Discalced Carmelites are no longer in New Orleans. The original addresses or locations are included for historical context only.*

---

The following section is from the 1887 publication of the *Manual of the Archconfraternity of the Holy Face*.

# Conditions for being Associated to the Archconfraternity

$1^{st}$ – To be inscribed on the Register of the Oratory of the Holy Face.

$2^{nd}$ – To receive the rule, with the certificate of admission.

$3^{rd}$ – Everyday, to recite, for the intentions of the Archconfraternity, in Latin or in English, a *Pater, Ave, Gloria* and the invocation: *Domine, ostende Faciem tuam et salvi erimus* (Lord show us Thy Face, and we shall be saved).

$4^{th}$ – To wear a little effigy of the Holy Face, either on a cross, medal or scapular.

$5^{th}$ – To assist, in as far as may be possible, at the monthly meetings.

$6^{th}$ – To propagate, to the utmost of our power, the devotion to the suffering Face of Our Lord.

# Approbation of the Archbishop of Tours

Tours, 15th of April 1886.

We approve of and recommend to the pious faithful the *Manual of the Archconfraternity of the Holy Face*.

This collection of the special documents of the Archconfraternity, containing in addition, edifying reflections, meditations, and various pious and reparatory prayers, is very well suited for guiding the associates, enlightening them, and sustaining them in the practices which have relation to the worship of the Holy Face.

The venerated Mr. Dupont, known in France and in foreign countries under the designation of *the Holy Man of Tours*, was the restorer of the worship of the Holy Face in our midst. His cherished memory, the examples and the traditions he bequeathed to us have been the means of inspiring the author of this manual, who is continuing in our sight, the fruitful and salutary work of his holy predecessor, with a generosity of soul corresponding to our desires and to the exceptional favors granted by Leo XIII happily reigning.

✠ GUILLAUME-RENÉ
ARCHBISHOP OF TOURS

# Preface by Rev. Fr. Janvier

The new Archconfraternity of the Holy Face requires a new Manual. We therefore present to our associates one which is furnished with the characteristic features that appear to be most suitable to it.

We have preserved the excellent reflections, the beautiful forms of prayer and the pious practices extracted from the writings of Mr. Dupont and of Sister Saint-Pierre, constituting the basis of the former Manual which was drawn up solely for the use of a simple confraternity. We have however been obliged, in order to bring it into conformity with its present title, to subject it to important modifications required by the laws of our new rule; by the special object we desire to attain and by the new favors granted by the Sovereign Pontiff. Moreover, whilst reforming it, we have also considerably augmented it; for instance, we have added to it a Novena of Meditations which we have, for a long time past, been requested to give; a prayer entitled "An honorable amends to the Holy Face," intended to be used at the monthly meetings, acts of consecration and of reparation, and various other prayers on the same subject. Lastly, all the pious practices concerning the worship of the Holy Face, the leaflets of which are printed and distributed in a separate form, are united together in this Manual and placed before the reader, each in the place most suitable for it. Hence, we here possess a real "Manual of the Holy Face" in a complete form and adapted to the needs of all the associates. We also purpose to detach from the body of the work, under the title of *The Little Manual* everything that is essential under the various heads, and out of them to form a small book, costing very little, in order to be within the reach and to suit the convenience of all. In this way it will likewise be possible to procure in a separate form the *Little Office of the Holy Name of God*, which is so highly appreciated by many fervent Christians.

At the head of the present Manual, are a series of documents which may be termed official, and of which we have had it at heart to give the text in all its integrity. These documents consist of the three most precious Briefs of the Holy Father, the Ordinance of the venerable Metropolitan of Tours, the petition addressed to Leo XIII, and several other documents connected with the origin and the very basis of the Archconfraternity. Our associates will be glad to have them at their disposition and before their eyes; they will see therein an authorization which will increase their respect and confidence; moreover, in time of need, our members and our friends will discover in them a mine rich in instructions and in information with regard to our institution.

The erection of an Archconfraternity of the Holy Face by the Sovereign Pontiff has been, in the times in which we live, a providential event of which time alone will reveal all the fruits. Let us review the manner in which this important matter has been accomplished; it is well that our associates should not be ignorant of it and that they should never forget it.

According to the customs of the Roman Court, the favor which we solicited could not be granted, excepting successively and by degrees; that is to say the power of aggregation would have been conceded to us, at first for our own diocese only, then later on for France, and some of the neighboring countries, and finally, after a period of time, for the rest of the world. It would have been a prolonged period of waiting, during four or five years, that we would have had to submit to, and it was believed at Rome that no other course was possible. Now, on the 15th of last September 1885, the cardinal prefect of the Sacred Congregation of Rites was present at an audience given by the Holy Father. His Eminence, who was kindly disposed towards us, thought that he was bestowing upon us a great favor by making it the subject of his first request, that the title of Archconfraternity should be granted to the whole of France: *Pro Gallia*. The Holy Father listened and reflected. What was it, which at that moment, passed through the mind and the heart of the Vicar of Jesus Christ? Had he an intuition of the good which the worship of the Holy Face was destined to produce? Did the holy man of Tours, whose cause has been begun, exercise over him an invisible and secret influence? Did the name of Tours, the remembrance of Saint Martin, our *thaumaturgist*, inspire Leo XIII with an especially favorable interest in us? Therein lies the secret of God. What is certain is that the Sovereign Pontiff did not delay his decision; it was precise, absolute and plainly formulated: *Tam pro Gallia quam ubique,* "For the whole world as well as for France." These great words were uttered on the 15th of September, the Octave of the Nativity of the Blessed Virgin. The Brief was signed on the 1st of October, and arrived at Tours on Rosary Sunday. The promptitude with which we obtained everything at once, thanks to the unexpected benevolence of Leo XIII, was looked upon at Rome as a real miracle. It is easy to perceive some of the dogmatic and moral consequences resulting from so striking a fact.

# I

Firstly, in virtue of the new title of Archconfraternity attached to our Oratory, the city of Saint Martin receives by means of a species of canonical investiture, the privileged place appertaining to it in the order of works of reparation, belonging to our times; it enters into full and legitimate possession of a sacred inheritance which it derives from the "holy man of Tours" and from the celebrated Carmelite, Sister Marie de Saint-Pierre. This family inheritance can never be taken away from it, it is a domain which henceforth is assured to it; it is guaranteed forever by this sole fact that it has become the seat and the center of the Archconfraternity "of the Holy Face," so called.

An archconfraternity, according to the organization of the Church, is possessed of great importance. Archconfraternities occupy the first rank, after the ecclesiastical hierarchy, the religious orders and the different institutions approved by the Holy See. They are sacred institutions, springing from the Holy See, endued with their own individual life, and having their own special legislation. If we glance over the Collection of Papal Bulls, we shall find in them a number of constitutions, of decrees and of pontifical ordinances relating to them, establishing or explaining their statutes, or defending and maintaining their privileges and their rites. Such is our beautiful Archconfraternity of the Holy Face; it is erected in perpetuity, *in modum perpetuum*; it participates in the duration, in the immutability of the Church herself; it is derived in a direct manner from the Apostolic See.

It has, moreover, a characteristic which other archconfraternities do not possess, namely, a right of affiliation devoid of any restriction attached to it; its power of aggregating to itself similar confraternities embraces all the dioceses of all cities, all the different parts of the world: *ubique terrarum*. Let then the town of Tours, amongst all the glories which decorate and enrich it, congratulate itself and let it deem itself happy to have obtained still another through the Holy Face. Let it not forget that it is indebted for it to Sister Marie de Saint-Pierre and to Mr. Dupont!

## II

In the second place, the Pontifical Brief of the Archconfraternity casts a vivid illumination upon the devotion itself, it shows it to us in its true light. No longer can it be said of the devotion to the Holy Face, as some have formerly rashly insinuated, that it is a new devotion, that it is local and private, that it is not suited to any, except to devout persons and to Religious. For we now behold it blessed, encouraged, and solemnly recognized by the Head of the Church. Our Statutes, as submitted to Pope Leo XIII, are not conceived in vague and incomplete terms; they clearly affirm "the special worship of adoration and love, which has for its object the most Holy Face of our Lord Jesus Christ;" they declare "the veneration of this adorable Face to be the great means of preventing and repairing the impious outrages committed against the Majesty of God, the Divinity of Jesus Christ, and the authority of the Church": expressions which permit the crimes of free-masonry and of secret societies to be comprised amongst the objects of reparation; they adopt as their motto the invocation to which the Holy Father has attached sixty days of Indulgence: *Lord, show us Thy Face, and we shall be saved;* lastly, they oblige the associates: 1st to wear an effigy of the Holy Face; 2nd to propagate the devotion by all the means in their power.

Thus, by means of the special title which it bears, as well as by the essential particulars and the spirit of its rule, thanks to our Archconfraternity, we now possess what has never hitherto been seen elsewhere; that is to say, a pious Archconfraternity of the Holy Face, really and properly so called, which the Sovereign Pontiff has overwhelmed with signal favors, and has raised to the highest possible dignity.

Henceforth, each time that a public or private act of devotion towards the Holy Face is made, we may be sure of performing an eminently Catholic act of worship. You may then, pious associates, in all security and confidence, prostrate yourselves before this august picture; you may place yourselves, as it were, face to Face with It; you may look at the adorable Face, study It and contemplate It; you may by Its means become penetrated, little by little, with an intimate knowledge of the spirit of Jesus and of His Divine Heart, and you may descend into the depths of the different mysteries relative to His birth, His life, His death and His resurrection; in these exercises of faith and love, you will be guided, not only by a sentiment of personal piety, but by the will and, so to say, by the finger of the Vicar of Jesus Christ. Under such a Master, what treasures of light and of grace may you not draw out of this heavenly mine? What fruits of benediction may you not receive as the recompense of your fervent contemplations!

## III

In the third place, by virtue of the Apostolic Brief, the devotion to the Holy Face and the practice of Reparation are *united* in our Archconfraternity; they *complete* each other, and are, as it were, fused into one another. Henceforward, the two works no longer run the risk of being separated from one another in the mind of the faithful. The work of Reparation, for instance, ceases to be isolated, and therefore, in a certain sense, defective incomplete and subject to fall into disuse, as was the case formerly; it finds its life, its fecundity and its most certain success in the worship of the Holy Face, above all, in the sorrowful Face of the Redeemer, which, in accordance with the communication made to Sister Saint-Pierre, ought to be at once the symbol and the means of reparation.

It is evident that, separated from the Holy Face, the reparations we offer to God for contemporary blasphemies and the profanation of Sunday, are in themselves imperfect and very insufficient. What human tears, in fact, even if they were to flow in torrents from the most penitent and the purest eyes, would suffice worthily to weep over the frightful crimes that are committed against the sovereignty and the majesty of God? What humiliations and what voluntary sufferings on the part of the holiest souls would ever suffice to repair the sacrileges and other inexpressible outrages invented by freemasonry and modern impiety!

But in our Archconfraternity, appropriating to ourselves, in the name and through the authority of the Church, the merits of the Holy Face, and invoking it directly, we present it to the heavenly Father, we say to Him: "Look, O God, our Protector, behold our tears and our expiations, listen to our prayers and our sighs. *Protector noster, aspice, Deus.* But this is not enough. Are we worthy of ourselves to appease Thine anger? Look at the same time on the Face of Thy Christ. Behold the tears which flow from His penitent eyes; the wounds which cover His sacred cheeks! Listen to the cry for pardon which He addresses to Thee on our behalf, and forgive us! *Respice in Faciem Christi tui...*" We can understand how marvelously suitable this offering and this spectacle are to disarm the Divine Justice. Such then is the power of the Reparation obtained through the Holy Face; such is the work which Pope Leo XIII, in his profound wisdom, has approved and decorated with the title of an Archconfraternity.

## IV

Lastly, the Holy Father, by establishing the Archconfraternity in our midst, gives thereby to our work the character of a great *Catholic union;* and he converts our humble Oratory into a center of prayers and of reparatory adoration which extends its rays throughout the whole universe. This dear little sanctuary of the Holy Face! What a contrast with the modesty of its commencement and the simplicity of its original state! Formerly, within its narrow limits, we remember how some few of the faithful used to come and timidly gather round a fervent servant of God in order to unite with him in prayer offered half aloud at an hour which had previously been agreed upon; those who could not be present at the meeting united themselves with it in spirit; whilst those who were prevented by distance from visiting the august picture desired to have a similar one in their homes. Prayers were offered for an infirm person, for someone who was sick or who asked to be cured, for a sinner who had been recommended to them. It was not a Confraternity; it was not even an association, but a simple union of secret and spontaneous prayers. Behold, at the present day, this same union of prayers and of homage to the Holy Face, the beginning of which was so little and so obscure, which commenced in an ordinary room, in the parlor of a man of the world, attracts the notice and the benevolence of the Sovereign Pontiff! Through his apostolical authority, he, in a manner, adopts it, blesses it, sanctions it, consecrates it, and elevates it to the dignity and the preeminence of an Archconfraternity; he makes it a durable and permanent association to which he assigns no other limits than those of the extremities of the world, and the end of time!

Associates of the Holy Face, it is for us to derive for our own benefit all the consequences which result from so memorable an event. Let us respond to the intentions entertained by the Head of the Church, let us put to profit the favor which he offers us; let us fructify it by means of the zeal and fervor it requires from us. Oh! if we are only faithful, what hopes may we not conceive? Salvation is in question; yes, the salvation of society, the salvation of families, the salvation of souls! But the work of salvation is primarily a Divine and holy work; it is associated both with the power of God and the cooperation of man. Remember, dear associates of the Archconfraternity, that in giving yourselves up to this work you have for cooperator the God-Man Himself. You have in His Holy Face all that in Him is most personal, most merciful, most amiable, most touching; you have the riches of graces and of merits acquired during His Passion by the grief and the ignominy of His adorable Face. Make the most of them in union with your brothers and sisters of the association who multiply and will continue to multiply in all the different portions of the globe. Take this manual, read it over again and again; be penetrated with the doctrine which it contains; appropriate to yourselves the sentiments and thoughts which it suggests; follow the beautiful counsels and the rules of conduct which it prescribes; let every one of us often repeat in the fervor of his soul: *I have prayed to and entreated Thy Face, O Lord; have pity on me according to Thy promise, save me in Thy mercy; no, I shall never be confounded, because I have called upon Thee.*

Could the heart of the God-Man be insensible to such a concert of supplications, supported by so many acts of virtue? No doubt! His merciful Face will be our powerful Advocate; He will send us that grace of salvation of which, at the present day, society has so great need, and which the sacred Scriptures promise us: *O Lord, show us Thy Face, and we shall be saved.*

P. Janvier

# Official Documents and Observations

*Ordinance of Monseigneur the Archbishop of Tours, For the establishment of the Confraternity of the Holy Face*

GUILLAUME-RENÉ MEIGNAN, through the mercy of God and the favor of the Holy Apostolic See, Archbishop of Tours: To all the priests and faithful whom the present ordinance concerns, greetings and benediction in Our Lord Jesus Christ.

Considering that a picture of the Holy Face of our Lord, being an authentic facsimile of the veil of Veronica preserved at Rome, has been for the last thirty years exposed in a public chapel in our archiepiscopal city; that it is the object of an ever increasing devotion which attracts pilgrims from all parts of the world; that spiritual and temporal graces of every kind are being daily obtained in presence of it, by means of prayers, many of which graces are deemed to be miraculous; desirous of favoring this devotion, which we look upon as being a very suitable means for developing true and solid piety, by causing the person and the mysteries of the life and Passion of our Lord Jesus Christ to be better known and loved more ardently, and at the same time considering it to be a salutary and very efficacious remedy for the cure and reparation of the evils by which our contemporary society is afflicted, such as indifference in matters of religion, the profanation of holy things, the sacrilegious impiety of free thinkers and freemasons; we have resolved and decided upon the following measures:

I. That there shall be established at Tours a Confraternity of the Holy Face in the Oratory called by that name.

II. That the statutes of the Confraternity shall be approved according to the form in which they are registered in the accompanying document.

III. That the said Confraternity, or association, being thus canonically established, shall enjoy all the indulgences and other spiritual graces with which it may be favored, whether in virtue of our ordinary powers, or whether in virtue of the plenary authority of the Holy Apostolic See.

In consequence, we will and command that the present ordinance, serving as a foundation for the above named association, shall be preserved in the archives of the

Oratory of the Holy Face and transcribed, together with the other title deeds, in the register of the Confraternity.

Given at Tours in our Archiepiscopal Palace, under our signature, our seal and the signature of our Secretary General.

The twenty-fifth day of the month of October, being the eve of the patronage of the Most Holy Virgin, in the year of grace 1884.

✠ GUILLAUME-RENÉ, *Arch. of Tours.*

Place of the seal.

✠ By command:

J. SELLIER,

*Canon., Secretary General*

# First Brief of the Holy Father

## According Special Indulgences
## To the Confraternity of the Holy Face
(Translation)

Leo XIII Pope.

For a perpetual remembrance.

Having learnt that, in a public Oratory of the town of Tours, dedicated to the Holy Face of our Lord Jesus Christ, there exists a pious association of the faithful, legitimately established under the title of the Holy Face: In order that this association may receive great increase day by day; putting all our confidence in the mercy of Almighty God, and in the authority of His blessed apostles Peter and Paul, we grant:

I. To each and all the faithful of both sexes who shall enter into the said association, a *plenary indulgence* and the remission of all their sins on the first day of their entrance into the association, on condition that, being truly contrite and having confessed, they shall receive the most Holy Sacrament of the Eucharist.

II. To such as shall have been already inscribed, or who shall be successively inscribed in the aforesaid association, a similar *plenary indulgence* at the article of death, provided that, being truly contrite, they confess and communicate, or if unable to do so, they at least, in a contrite spirit, devoutly invoke with their lips, or if that be not possible, with their heart, the Holy Name of Jesus.

III. To all and each of the brethren and sisters who are already, or who shall henceforward become members of the said association, a *plenary indulgence* on the feast of Saint Peter, the prince of the apostles and the principal patron of the Confraternity, whether it be on the day itself of his feast, or at their pleasure on one of the seven days immediately following, provided that, being truly penitent, and having confessed and communicated, they devoutly visit the above mentioned Oratory, and that they there piously offer to God prayers for the concord of Christian princes, the extirpation of heresies, the conversion of sinners and the exaltation of Holy Mother Church.

IV. To the same persons, a similar *plenary indulgence* every year, on a day* which must be fixed by the Ordinary, provided that they visit the above named Oratory fulfilling the conditions already mentioned, from the first vespers of that day to the setting of the sun; *(\*Note: the day fixed at Tours by the Ordinary is Passion Sunday)*

In addition, we grant to the same members of the faithful, according to the usual form of the Church, an *indulgence of sixty days* for the remission of penances which have been enjoined upon them, or which they have merited on any occasion whatever:

I. Each time that, having at least a contrite heart, they shall devoutly assist at some pious exercise in the above named Oratory;

II. Each time that they shall piously kiss the sorrowful Face of Christ, the distinctive sign of their Confraternity, whether it be sculptured, or whether it be engraved or impressed upon a cross or a picture, adding this invocation: *Lord, show us Thy Face, and we shall be saved;*

III. Lastly, each time that they shall perform some other pious, or charitable act, in conformity with the object of their Confraternity.

We grant in the Lord, that all and every one of these Indulgences, remissions of sins and dispensations of penance, may be applied, by way of suffrage, to the souls of the faithful who have departed out of this world united to God through charity.

These presents have a value in perpetuity for the future.

Given at Rome, near St. Peter, under the ring of the fisherman, the 9th of December 1884, being the 7th year of our Pontificate.

Place of the seal.

✠ For Monseigneur Cardinal CHISI,
O. PRINCHIERI, *substitute.*
Examined and certified:

Tours, 16th December 1884.
DURAND, *vic. gen.*

# Second Brief of the Holy Father

(Translation)

Leo XIII Pope.

For a perpetual remembrance.

We have been informed that, by our apostolical letters, dated the 9th of December 1884, plenary and partial Indulgences were accorded to the pious Confraternity of the Holy Face, canonically established in the town of Tours. The said Confraternity has now addressed a petition to us, requesting that, for the greater spiritual good of the faithful and the salvation of souls, we would deign to enrich it still more by fresh treasures of celestial gifts. Therefore acceding to this pious request and being charged to open with tender charity the heavenly treasures of the Church, in order to promote the faith of our people and the salvation of souls;

I. We mercifully grant in the Lord, every year, on the day of the feast of the Transfiguration of our Lord Jesus Christ, or on any one of the days of the octave which may be fixed upon, a *plenary indulgence* and the remission of all their sins to the faithful who are now, or who may henceforth become members of the above named Confraternity, provided that being sincerely penitent, and having confessed and communicated, they shall devoutly visit the public Oratory dedicated to the Holy Face in the town of Tours, and that they there pray for the concord of Christian princes, the extirpation of heresies, the conversion of sinners and the exaltation of Holy Mother Church;

II. Moreover to the same faithful, who, on any day whatever of the year which they shall choose, shall make a pilgrimage to the Oratory, whether in groups or singly, and shall there devoutly visit the picture of the Holy Face, and shall receive Holy Communion and shall pray there in the manner stated above, we also grant, in the Lord, once a year, a *plenary indulgence*, and the remission of all their sins;

III. In addition, to the same associates, who, being at least of contrite heart, shall assist at the monthly meeting of the Confraternity, held either in the above mentioned Oratory, or in any church whatever, we remit in accordance with the usual form, *seven years and seven quarantines* of the penances which may have been enjoined upon them, or which are otherwise obligatory upon them, in any manner whatsoever.

IV. We also consent that all and each one of these Indulgences, remissions of sins and dispensations from penances, may be applied, by way of suffrage, to the souls of the faithful who have departed from this world, united to God, by charity.

V. Lastly, by the tenor of these presents, we give to the above mentioned associates the faculty, if the weak state of their health prevents them from visiting their Oratory, in order to gain the *plenary or partial indulgences*, the power, freely and lawfully, with the permission and according to the judgment of their confessor, to change this act of piety for some other good work.

These presents are valid for seven years only. Given at Rome, near St. Peter, under the seal of the fisherman, the 30th March 1885, being the eighth year of our Pontificate.

Place of the seal.

✠ Cardinal LEDOCHOWSKI.
Examined and permitted to be executed:
Tours, 22nd April 1885.
J. BUISSON, *vic. gen.*

# Petition Addressed to the Holy Father to Entreat of Him that the Confraternity of the Holy Face at Tours may be Established as an Archconfraternity

(Translation)

MOST HOLY FATHER,

Pierre Janvier, priest, and the Dean of the chapter of the metropolitan church at Tours, and director of the Confraternity of the Holy Face, prostrate at your feet, humbly presents to you the following petition.

In the town of Tours, there exists a sanctuary which the deceased Archbishop, Mgr. Colet, of pious memory, on the 29th June 1876, being the feast of the apostle St. Peter, solemnly constituted to be a public chapel, in order to favor the devotion to the most Holy Face of our Lord Jesus Christ, already existing in that place. There, in fact, since the year 1851, fervent Christians, therein following the example set them by a great servant of God, Mr. Léon Dupont, offered a worship of adoration and prayer to the Face of our Lord, outraged in His Passion, before a picture of that Holy Face, being a faithful representation of the true effigy preserved at the Vatican.

This pious devotion, so conformable to what has been performed from time immemorial in the Church of Rome with regard to the veil of Veronica, has in our days, been deemed particularly suitable for exciting in our souls a more lively and more tender love to our suffering Lord, and a more ardent and efficacious zeal to repair the outrages inflicted in every place on His adorable person.

Therefore, this sacred devotion, entering as of itself, into all hearts, has by little and little, become popular. During the lapse of thirty-four years, it has extended not only throughout France, but in Belgium, in Holland, in Switzerland, in England, in Canada, in the United States of America, in Spain, in Italy, in Germany, as far as the center of Asia (at Bagdad and Mosul), as far also as the extremities of the east (at Shanghai and at Saigon); and everywhere pious laymen, eminent priests, holy religious, pastors and theologians, bishops and archbishops, welcome it, favor and propagate it.

Now the public Oratory at Tours, commonly called "the Oratory of the Holy Face," has been and still is the starting point of this providential movement of faith and of piety towards the Divine Face of the Redeemer. Consequently, it is a center which is frequented, and already celebrated, and to which pilgrimages of penance and expiation are daily made from all parts. Many come there to pray, priests celebrate there the holy mysteries, the faithful assist at Mass and communicate there; the conversion of sinners is asked for, the cure of the sick and success in affairs; above all, efforts are made, especially on certain days, to offer to the heavenly Father, in presence of the Face of His Divine Son, a worthy homage of reparation, in order to appease His justice, irritated as it is by so many crimes, blasphemies and profanations committed in our days, and to avert the  chastisements by which we deserve to be struck.  God, it appears, looks with a favorable eye on these supplications and deigns to grant these prayers; spiritual and temporal graces of all kinds are often obtained; in proof of which the walls of the sanctuary of the Holy Face are decorated with numerous tablets of marble given as ex-votos, and the altar is surrounded with crutches and sticks left there by lame persons and by the infirm who have been cured.

So great is the influx of those who come to pray there, that for the last eight years, the Archbishop of Tours has been obliged to establish a new sacerdotal society which is designated as that of "the Priests of the Holy Face," with the special mission of serving the said Oratory, and of responding to all the needs of the faithful who frequent it. These priests are in daily communication with the pastors of parishes, the superiors of communities, the faithful of all ranks and conditions, who address themselves to them from all parts, directly or by letters, in order to solicit recommendations for prayers and to have the means of establishing or propagating, in their neighborhood, the same salutary devotion.

Since they have been set apart for this work, these priests state that, in the course of eight years, they have sent to different places more than twenty thousand engravings, being authentic facsimiles of the Veronica of the Vatican; that all these effigies have been asked for in a spirit of faith, of veneration and of love for the sorrowful Face of Our Lord; and that the greater proportion of them, exposed as they are with lamps burning before them in cathedrals and parish churches, or in the chapels of communities, have become, as is the case at Tours, the object of a similar worship and often the source of great graces.

In order to direct aright this devotion, which is daily on the increase, and in order to make it produce all the fruits to be desired from it, a pious association, regularly established in proper and due form, has been deemed necessary. For a long time the minds of many have been disposed to it and a Confraternity having its special title, its organization and its own statutes was demanded for the worship of the Holy Face. This desire was realized, most happily and to the great joy of the faithful, by our present venerable Archbishop, the Right Rev. Mgr Meignan through an ordinance dated the 25th October 1884. This archiepiscopal ordinance, with the statutes or rules which it approves and which depend upon it, has already been placed before His Holiness, who deigned, by apostolical letters of 9th of December 1884 and the 30th of March 1885, to grant to the Confraternity of the Holy Face precious plenary and partial indulgences.

The joy and pious consolation which these first favors of the Holy See have been the means of bestowing upon priests and the faithful are incredible. Several thousands of persons hastened to inscribe their names in the register of the Confraternity, and continue daily to do so. Confraternities, known by the same title, adopting the same statutes and pursuing the same object, have been canonically established. In addition, there has been formed, during several years past, in different places, analogous associations or confraternities in honor of the Holy Face, which are already more or less united with us, and will be disposed to affiliate themselves canonically to our Confraternity as to a center, if we obtain this permission.

If pastors and the faithful show so much fervor and zeal for the devotion to the Holy Face and the Confraternity consecrated to it, it is because they see the precious advantages which result from it for the glory of God, the consolation of the just, the conversion of sinners and, above all, the expiation of sacrileges, of profanations and of other crimes with which the world is at this moment inundated by hell. For the express object proposed by the associates of the Confraternity in honoring the sorrowful Face of the Savior Jesus is that of hindering, or at least of repairing the inexpressible outrages which blasphemers, free thinkers and freemasons inflict on the majesty and sovereignty of God, on the Divinity of our Lord Jesus Christ and the authority of the Church. It is evident that these most desirable effects would be obtained in a still surer and more widely diffused manner if the association at Tours, the cradle and center of an ancient devotion and one ardently embraced now as a means of reparation in these our times, had the power of canonically aggregating and attaching to itself, by still closer and more sacred links, the multitude of associates spread over all parts of the universe. There would result from it, in all probability, under the banner of the sorrowful Face of the Redeemer, a great and strong unity of minds and hearts, which would favor the need so keenly felt of prayer and expiation, and which would advantageously fight against the demon of impiety and his members, united together by the hatred of all that is good.

These then are the reasons, most Holy Father, why we petition Your Holiness to deign to grant to this association of the Holy Face, established at Tours, the title and the privileges of an Archconfraternity, in such a manner that it may possess the power of aggregating to itself all other associations of the same title, already established, or which shall hereafter be established, and to communicate to them all the indulgences, with which it has been or shall be itself enriched by the Holy Apostolic See.


P. JANVIER

Tours, 1st September 1885.

We earnestly recommend this petition to Your Holiness; we consider it to be entirely worthy of your paternal benevolence, and we are persuaded that the favor demanded responds to numerous and deep seated needs and that if you deign to grant it according to your wonted goodness, it will contribute in an admirable and powerful manner to augment the knowledge and love of our Divine Redeemer in the souls of men; devotion to the interests of His worship and His honor, and above all zeal for the reparation of the crimes which so grievously outrage the dignity of His adorable Person and the authority of His Holy Church.

GUILLAUME-RENÉ,

*Archbishop of Tours.*

To this petition, thus recommended by the Archbishop of Tours, were attached a series of special recommendations inscribed in the following order:

## FRANCE

His Em. Cardinal Guibert, Archbishop of Paris.
His Em. Cardinal Caverot, Archbishop of Lyon.
His Em. Cardinal Desprez, Archbishop of Toulouse. Mgr Place, Archbishop of Rennes.
Mgr Fonteneau, Archbishop of Albi.
Mgr Le Coq, Bishop of Nantes.
Mgr Catteau, Bishop of Luçon.
Mgr Dabert, Bishop of Périgueux.
Mgr Marpot, Bishop of Saint-Claude.
Mgr Caraguel, Bishop of Perpignan.
Mgr Sourrieu, Bishop of Châlons.
Mgr Bourret, Bishop of Rodez.
Mgr Besson, Bishop of Nîmes.
Mgr Becel, Bishop of Vannes.
Mgr Laborde, Bishop of Blois.
Mgr Le Hardy du Marais, Bishop of Laval.
Mgr Bellot des Minières, Bishop of Poitiers.
Mgr de Dreux-Brézé, Bishop of Moulins.
Mgr Denéchau, Bishop of Tulle.
Mgr Fava, Bishop of Grenoble.
Mgr Dennel, Bishop of Arras.
Mgr Lebreton, Bishop of Le Puy.
Mgr Gay, Bishop of Anthédon.
The abbots of La Trappe, assembled in chapter.

Dom Couturier, abbot of Solesmes.
The Superior General of the Lazarists.
The Provincial of the Capuchins.
The Provincial of the Dominicans.
The Superior of the great Seminary at Versailles.

## BELGIUM

Mgr Bracq, Bishop of Ghent.
Mgr Doutreloux, Bishop of Liege.
Mgr Bélin, Bishop of Namur.

## ITALY

Mgr Salvaj, Bishop of Alexandria.
Mgr the Bishop of Teano.
Mgr the Bishop of Muro.
Mrg the Bishop of Acireale.
The Superior General of the Redemptorists.

## SPAIN

Mgr the Bishop of Calahorra.
The Provincial of the Carmelites.

## SWITZERLAND

Mgr Mermillod, Bishop of Lausanne and Geneva.

## AUSTRIA

Mgr Strossmayer, Bishop of Agram.
The Superior of the Seminary of Gran.
The Reverend the Father Abbot of Beuron.

## ENGLAND

His Eminence Cardinal Manning, Archbishop of Westminster.
Mgr Bagshaw, Bishop of Nottingham.

## IRELAND

Mgr Duggan, Bishop of Clonfert.

## UNITED STATES OF AMERICA

His Eminence Cardinal Mc Closkey, Archbishop of New York.

Mgr Gibbons, Archbishop of Baltimore.
Mgr Elder, Archbishop of Cincinnati.
Mgr Keane, Bishop of Richmond.
Mgr Neraz, Bishop of San Antonio (Texas).
Mgr Jansens, Bishop of Natchez.
The Fathers of the Sacred Heart at Watertown.

## CANADA

Mgr Tashereau, Archbishop of Quebec.
Mgr Colin, the superior of the seminary of Saint Sulpice at Montreal.

## COLONIES

Mgr Colombert, Bishop of Samosate, vicar apostolic of French Cochin-China.
Mgr Gouin, Archbishop of Port of Spain at Trinidad (West Indies).

# Brief of His Holiness Pope Leo XIII Establishing the Archconfraternity of the Holy Face

(Translation)

Leo XIII Pope.

For a perpetual remembrance.

According to the usages of Roman Pontiffs, our predecessors, we are accustomed to decorate and enrich with special honors and privileges the pious associations instituted for the practice of works of piety and charity. Our well beloved sons, the directors and associates of the pious Confraternity known as that of the Holy Face, canonically established in the sanctuary of the same name, in the town of Tours, and enriched by us and the Holy See with numerous privileges, have expressed to us the desire, that making use of the plentitude of our apostolic power, we should honor his association with the title of Archconfraternity and with the preeminence which is its due.

Desirous of giving to each and all of those in whose favor these letters are delivered a special mark of our benevolence, and only as regards the present case, considering them as absolved, and to be absolved from all sentences of excommunication and interdict, and from all the censures and ecclesiastical penalties which they may have incurred and which may have been inflicted on them in any manner or for any cause whatsoever, we, by our apostolical authority, in virtue of these presents, establish and constitute as a perpetual Archconfraternity, with the accustomed privileges, the so called Confraternity of the Holy Face, established in the town of Tours. And by the same our authority, in virtue of these letters, we concede and grant in perpetuity, to the directors and colleagues present and future of the Archconfraternity, the power, validly and lawfully, to aggregate to itself, throughout the whole world, excepting in our glorious city, all the other Confraternities existing in the same name and having the same object, observing always the form prescribed by the Constitution of Pope Clement VIII, our predecessor of happy memory, and the other apostolical ordinances drawn up on this subject, as well as to communicate to all and each the Indulgences, remissions of sins and dispensations of penance, which have been granted by the Holy Apostolic See to the association so erected by us into an Archconfraternity, and which are susceptible of being communicated to others.

We decree that our present letters shall be, for the present and the future, fixed, valid and efficacious; that they shall obtain and possess their full and entire effects, that they shall fully favor all and for all, whom they concern and shall concern hereafter in accordance with what has been previously enumerated, and shall be judged and defined by ordinary judges and delegates, whoever they may be, even the auditors of the suits of the Apostolic Palace, the Nuncios of the Holy See, the Cardinals of the Holy Roman Church, even legates *a latere* and all other personages, whatever their dignity and their power may be; entire power and authority to judge and interpret otherwise being withdrawn from them in general and in particular, so that if any one, whatever be the authority with which he is invested, attacks any of these clauses knowingly or through ignorance, his act shall be null and void.

And this notwithstanding the Constitutions and Apostolic ordinances, and, in as far as is necessary, the statutes, customs, and uses contrary to the above named Confraternity and all others, even when they have been confirmed by apostolic oath or any other decision whatever.

Given at Rome, near St Peter, under the ring of the fisherman, the 1st day of October 1885, being the eighth year of our Pontificate.

Place of the seal.

✠ Cardinal LEDOCHOWSKI

Examined,
We command its execution and its use.

GUILLAUME-RENÉ,
*Archbishop of Tours.*

✠　Place of the seal.

# Pastoral Letter of Monseigneur the Archbishop of Tours

### To the Clergy and the Faithful of His Diocese Announcing the Establishment of the Archconfraternity of the Holy Face in the Town of Tours

VERY DEAR BRETHREN,

We desire to make you acquainted with the very distinguished favor which the Holy Father has just bestowed upon one of our most cherished and interesting associations; namely, the Confraternity of the Holy Face. By a brief dated the 1st October 1885, Leo XIII, at our request, has deigned to raise to the dignity of an

Archconfraternity, throughout the whole Church, the diocesan association known under the name of the Confraternity of the Holy Face. You will at once understand the high importance of this solemn act and the great development which it will obtain in the future for our association, now that it has been thus blest and glorified. Our first duty is that of gratitude towards God and the successor of Saint Peter. We eagerly seize upon this opportunity in order to recall to your remembrance the spirit and the excellence of the devotion to the Holy Face of which Tours is henceforth, after Rome, the principal seat.

I. This form of worship rendered to Jesus Christ, you know, very dear brethren, is not new in the Church. It is attached to the dogma of the Incarnation, it dates back to the advent of the Son of God in the world. The first persons who contemplated and adored the Divine Face of Jesus were Mary, Joseph, the shepherds, the Magi, the disciples, and the apostles. When the people, suspended from the lips of the Man-God, admired the wisdom of His doctrine and said: "How came this man by all these things?" (Mark, vi, 2.) they were, at the same time, impressed by the incomparable charms of His eloquence, the grace of His teaching, the accent of His voice, and above all, by the aspect of His adorable Face, "upon which," says St Jerome, "shine the rays of Divine Majesty." (*Divinatis majestas lucebat in facie.*) (S. Hieron. in Math., III, 106.) For this Face, according to the learned and pious Origen, being turn by turn sweet and severe, merciful and terrible, assumed different aspects according to the interior dispositions of those who were in Its presence; It wore an expression of benignity and tenderness towards the little children, but It terrified the sellers in the Temple. The glories of Tabor, the dolors of the Passion, reflected upon the Divine Face, have been at all times the ravishing object and the subject of contemplation of noble hearts and of elect souls, such as the Augustines and the Bernards, the Gertrudes and the Mechtildes. The sublime act of a holy woman, wiping with her veil the Holy Face of Jesus, bowed beneath the weight of His cross on the path of Calvary, has always been famous; it has inspired painters and artists, and it forms the subject of the 6th station of the Way of the Cross, reproduced under so many touching forms.

It would take too long to enumerate the riches of science and of piety which the Scriptures, the Fathers, tradition, theology and history, offer to us in favor of the worship so legitimately due to the Face of our beloved Redeemer. Let it suffice us to remark that this sacred worship is preserved by an uninterrupted tradition, and from time immemorial has been practiced publicly in the basilica of Saint Peter at the Vatican; it is also well known with what jealous care, the Pontiffs, from age to age, have watchfully guarded the veil of Veronica, which the Eternal City still esteems as one of its most precious treasures.

II.　　Struck by these considerations, a pious Christian, belonging to our city of Tours, conceived, in 1851, the idea into which enlightened priests and many fervent souls soon entered, of applying the worship of the sorrowful Face of Jesus Christ to the reparation of blasphemies, of infidelity and of other forms of impiety which are the grief and dishonor of the age in which we live. The ever increasing progress of skepticism, the ravages occasioned by evil doctrines, the destructive projects of secret societies have contributed to revive and to extend more and more amongst us the sense and the need of expiation, and consequently the salutary worship in question.

Let the world but turn towards the Face of the Christ, let it but read therein the Divine teachings It gives us, let it meditate upon the lessons It presents to us, and it will quickly acquire the knowledge of its errors, it will repent on discovering in the features of the suffering Jesus, in the wounded and outraged Face of the Savior, at once His love and the precursory signs of His justice. The Holy Face, which will render it sensible of the wrong it has done and which will make it understand its offenses, will inspire it with compunction of heart. The faithful will then offer to God the homage of their faith and the tribute of their reparations.

At the present day, God is everywhere forgotten; He is often denied and blasphemed. By how many crimes is not His anger provoked! His sovereignty, His authority over families and over nations, His providence, each one of His essential perfections is misunderstood and shamefully trodden under foot by an impious sect which desires to annihilate His very name, which it no longer pronounces and which it banishes even from the lips of little children. The person of Jesus Christ, His life, the ineffable Countenance of the Incarnate Word, our Deliverer and our Savior, the ever living summary of the Redemption, the mirror which reflects It in all Its entirety, what is It for the majority of men? A cold historical souvenir, sometimes a myth, always a troublesome reproach. Hence it arises that Christ is insulted, that He is outraged, that His Name is shamefully scoffed at as in the days of those who crucified Him. When the crucifix and the pictures of saints are removed from schools, is it not because of a desire to efface the celestial impression of the adorable Face of Jesus, engraved by Christian mothers in the hearts of their children?

What remedy can be applied to so great an evil? How can the battle best be fought, at one time against such ignorance, at another against such forgetfulness, at yet another against such outrages? From the very beginning of Christianity the great apostle who made the light of the gospel to shine forth in the midst of the darkness of paganism pointed out the remedy. The goodness and kindness of God our Savior has appeared he exclaimed: *Benignitas et humanitas apparuit salvatoris nostri Dei* (Tit. III, 4.). At the present day, in these our wretched times, in which a species of paganism, worse than the ancient, has shown itself, behold this luminous Face, at once Divine and human, of our God Savior is presented to us. Already It has suffered for love of us the ignominies and the wounds of the Passion; now, a powerful advocate in heaven, It pleads our cause before Its Father; at the altar, in the sacrament of the Eucharist, although hidden and invisible, It is really present, looks at us, smiles at us, blesses us and protects us. Let us turn towards It with confidence; let us picture It to ourselves, let us question Its Divine physiognomy; let us show It under all Its different aspects to the Heavenly Father, irritated by our offenses. "O God! Look on the Face of Thy Christ...Father, forgive": *Respice in Faciem Christi tui (Ps. LXXXIII, 10). ... Pater, dimmite* (Luc, XXIII, 34.). Let us present It to men, to sinners, to those who curse and outrage It; Its tears, Its sweat, Its unalterable patience, Its invincible love, possess the power of disarming the most rebellious and touching the most hardened; in Its presence, we trust they will fall on their knees, and will strike their breasts, and will return to the knowledge and the love of their God.

Such is, in fact, the aim of the devotion to the Holy Face: to touch the heart of man, to arrest the arm of God. And what efficacy must It not possess in order to attain this twofold and so desirable object? It renders sensible to us all that is most touching and most penetrating in the adorable person of the Incarnate Word; of Him whom the prophets styled at once "the man of sorrows," and "the most beautiful among the children of men." It shows Him to us under the most merciful and the most amiable of His aspects. *It is by the countenance,* says the Scriptures, *that man is discerned and makes himself known* (*Ex visu cognoscitur vir.* (Eccle., XIX, 26.)). In Our Lord, who possessed our human nature in all its perfection, His Holy Face was the most pure mirror of His Soul, the vivid and sweet expansion of His Heart, the visible expression of His intimate thoughts and of His most tender affections. Thus, the worship of His Divine Face, although it is distinct and special, is intimately attached to the devotion to the Eucharist, and to that of the Passion. Without being confounded with these great devotions, which are so eminently Catholic and so strongly recommended, it lends them a useful aid; it completes them, illuminates them, tends to render them, at least in the case of many souls, more sensible, more attractive and more fruitful; by them, and in union with them, it helps fervent souls to enter more easily into meditation on the mysteries and the love of our Lord; it thus disposes the faithful to the most generous and the most heroic acts of penitence and reparation.

III.   These considerations, which we have only lightly touched upon and which it is not necessary to enter into more deeply, had struck us for a long time past, my very dear brethren; and they determined us to establish in the chapel of the Holy Face a special Confraternity, distinct from all those already existing, and having statutes of its own. Making use of our power as Ordinary, we realized this our idea by means of an ordinance dated the 25th of October 1884, and we canonically established in our archiepiscopal city a Confraternity of the Holy Face, properly so called.

On two different occasions the new Confraternity presented itself at Rome before the Holy Father, in order that he might condescend to bless it, to approve it and to enrich it with indulgences. His Holiness deigned to do so: the first time, by a Brief dated the 9th of December 1884, and a second time, by another Brief dated the 30th March 1885. Lastly, quite recently, by a third Brief dated the 1st October of the present year, crowning all his previous favors, acquiescing with singular benevolence in the humble request which had been addressed to him on the subject, our Holy Father, Pope Leo XIII, declared that he had raised the Confraternity of the Holy Face to the rank of an Archconfraternity, and together with this title had conferred upon it the preeminence, the rights and all the privileges attached to the title. The intention of His Holiness is that there should be no restriction and no limit assigned to it; it is in perpetuity and for all the countries of the world, wherever they may be, *ubique terrarum*, he also grants to the said Archconfraternity, the power of aggregating to itself other associations of the same kind and of communicating to them the privileges it enjoys itself, as well as the indulgences and other spiritual favors with which it has already been, or may hereafter be enriched. This concession is the largest of any which, in similar matters, it is possible to obtain from the Holy See.

We confess, very dear brethren, that we most certainly neglected nothing in order to sustain and strengthen the petition presented to the Holy Father. Nevertheless a success so prompt and so complete has overpassed all that we expected; it can only be explained, so we are told from Rome, by an unexpected intervention of Divine Providence, and by the express will of Leo XIII, arising from his desire to obtain a compensation for the trials he has suffered and which have touched him deeply.

Our gratitude is therefore equal to our admiration and our joy. You will partake it, very dear brethren; in the presence of God, you will share in the sentiments with which we are filled towards the august and well beloved Pontiff who has given us a new and touching mark of the paternal interest he takes in our metropolitan church. For you understand that the honor done to the Oratory of the Holy Face is reflected upon our archiepiscopal city and upon the whole of our diocese. We have now, in our midst, at a few steps from the ancient tomb of our great miracle worker, a new center of Divine love, a center of adoration and of acts of reparation, recognized and authorized by the Vicar of Jesus Christ, enriched by him with exceptional distinctions and precious indulgences. The modest sanctuary, in which during twenty-five years he prayed, whom the popular voiced styled the holy man of Tours, had already attracted the attention of France and of the most distant countries; pilgrims continually flocked thither, singly or in groups, from different countries. At the present day, the finger of the Sovereign Pontiff itself points out this holy place to the whole Church and assigns it, during all coming centuries, a place apart amongst those which are the most favored of such resorts. Towards this spot will henceforth turn in full assurance, from all parts of the world, the eyes and hearts of those who desire to venerate the sorrowful Face of Christ, and in it to find a means of preservation and salvation. *Show us Thy Face, O Lord, and we shall be saved (Domine ostende Faciem tuam, et salvi erimus)* (Ps. LXXIX, 4.). The Holy Father grants sixty days of indulgence to those who recite these words and devoutly kiss a picture of the Holy Face. This suppliant cry of the Prophet King, issuing from the Oratory where Mr. Dupont so often uttered it, in the recollection and the fervor of prayer, will be reechoed from the farthest extremities of the universe, the benign words of the Sovereign Pontiff will accompany it, and guarantee its salutary effect.

IV. We are touched, very dear brethren, we thrill with joy at this thought; salvation may come, or at least it may be powerfully helped on by the Holy Face! And It is in our midst that the worship of It has been specially blessed by Leo XIII! How would it be possible for our heart not to be filled with consolation and hope? How, in this characteristic of an amiable Providence, would it be possible for us not to see a great blessing granted to our episcopate? The association which was necessarily endued with an isolated and restricted character finds itself aggrandized and confirmed by a memorable act of the Sovereign Pontiff. By decorating it with the title and the honor of an Archconfraternity, possessing the power of affiliation throughout the whole world, Leo XIII gives to the devotion of the Holy Face a principle of vitality and expansion, which it did not hitherto enjoy; a kind of apostolic sanction which renders it worthy of being recommended to the pastors and he faithful of the universal Church.

For the sake of these motives, very dear brethren, we exhort you to enter, as far as shall be possible to you, into so generous and opportune inventions. Let us honor, let us more than ever love the Holy Face of our Lord; let us offer It a frequent homage of praise and reparation. Hasten to solicit your admission amongst the associates of the Archconfraternity; it is for us to be the first to give an example of eagerness and zeal; to profit by the graces of which we here possess the center and the source. Those amongst the clergy who may judge it expedient to establish the association in their parish churches will readily obtain from us all the necessary authorizations. At their request we will deliver to them an ordinance of establishment which will permit them to receive, from the director of the Archconfraternity, a diploma of aggregation, giving a right to the indulgences and other spiritual favors.

We leave to the director of the Holy Face the duty of notifying the series of indulgences, plenary and partial, imprinted upon leaflets, which we authorize him to diffuse, together with the Rule approved by us, and the last most important Brief received from the Holy Father.

We have reason to hope that our venerable colleagues of the episcopate in France will have it at heart to favor, to the utmost of their power, in their respective dioceses, the establishment and diffusion of the new Archconfraternity, which we know a great number of them have already done with the happiest results and with abundant and consoling fruit for souls.

Our desires and our hopes go further still. Thanks to the pontifical munificence and to the extension of the powers granted to the director of the Archconfraternity, the devotion to the Holy Face will, we have no doubt, be propagated more and more amongst the most distant foreign nations, and as the religious needs of the present day are nearly everywhere the same, we believe our dear Archconfraternity called upon to produce in every place, a holy emulation of zeal for the honor of Jesus Christ, and the triumph of His Church, a vast and unanimous concert of fervent reparatory prayers, which will embrace the whole world, and which God will deign to recompense by the results which are the most conformable to the desires of His Vicar upon earth.

The present pastoral letter shall be read from the pulpit on the Sunday following its reception.

Given at Tours, in our archiepiscopal palace, on the 15th October 1885, the day of the feast of St. Theresa.

✠ GUILLAUME-RENÉ,
*Archbishop of Tours.*

# Diploma or Letters of Aggregation

(Translation)

*This diploma of aggregation, being destined for Confraternities which may be established in all the countries of the world, it was necessary that it should be drawn up in the language of the Church. We give the translation of it here for the use of the faithful and in order that our readers may have an exact knowledge of so important a document.*

## Letters of Aggregation to the Archconfraternity of the Holy Face of Our Lord Jesus Christ Canonically Established in the Sanctuary of the Same Name in the City of Tours

The admirable Providence of God has permitted that, in these our times, the ancient devotion towards the most Holy Face of our Lord Jesus Christ, which has never ceased in the Church, and which has been from time immemorial especially celebrated in the basilica of Saint Peter at the Vatican, should have been considered as a very suitable means for reviving the languishing charity of the faithful, and of repairing the offenses and the injuries of all kinds inflicted in diverse places on the Divine Majesty. Having maturely considered these things and being, moreover, urged by a desire to promote, by means of this salutary worship, the glory of God, the knowledge and the love of Jesus Christ, the spiritual consolation of the just, the conversion of sinners, and above all, an indefatigable zeal for expiating sacrileges, blasphemies and other crimes which, at the present day, cover the earth, the illustrious and most Reverend the Archbishop of Tours, Mgr Guillaume Meignan, in a chapel in his archiepiscopal city, commonly called "the Oratory of the Holy Face," where this devotion commenced to flourish in an admirable manner, instituted and canonically established a pious Confraternity under the title and invocation of the Holy Face, appropriating to it those two texts of Scripture: "Lord, show us Thy Face, and we shall be saved" and

"Behhold, O God, our Protector, and look upon the Face of Thy Christ."

The Sovereign Pontiff Leo XIII has not only willed to enrich this Confraternity with spiritual favors and indulgences, but in addition, desiring to increase its dignity and reputation, has deigned by apostolical letters, under the form of a Brief, dated the 1st of October 1885, to establish and constitute it, in perpetuity, as an Archcon-fraternity with all the singular rights, preeminence, and accustomed privileges, granting, at the same time, the power, provided that the forms of the constitution of Clement VIII of happy memory, and the other Apostolical Ordinances drawn up on this subject be observed, of aggregating to the said Archconfraternity the Confratern-ities of the same name and of the same statutes already established, or to be established hereafter throughout the whole world, as also to communicate to them freely and lawfully all the graces and indulgences granted to the above named Archconfraternity, and which are suscepti-ble of being communicated; to this end, that the faithful and the shepherds of souls, in honoring the most Holy Face of our Lord Jesus Christ laden in the Passion with so many outrages and sufferings, should endeavor, in concert and with great zeal, to prevent, or at least to repair and expiate the horrible and ceaselessly recurring injuries which blasphemers of the Divine Name, freethinkers and impious sectarians everywhere inflict, in these days, on our most amiable Redeemer, on His Vicar upon earth and on the Church, His Spouse.

As we have been informed that in the church of (N. N.) a pious Confraternity has been established under the title and invocation of the Holy Face of Our Lord Jesus Christ, canonically established by the illustrious and Right Rev. Bishop of (N. N.), his Lordship (N. N.), and that, at the same time, earnest supplications have been made that we would unite and aggregate the above named Confraternity to our primary Archconfraternity, established in the sanctuary at Tours, in conformity with the constitution *Quæcumque* of Clement VIII of happy memory dated the 7th of December 1604 and, having in view aggregations of this kind and the communications of indulgences, as well as the modifications approved by the Sovereign Pontiff Pius IX, in a decree of the Sacred Congregation of Indulgences dated the 8th of January 1861 (we give the principal heads of this Constitution as well as the above named modifications in a sheet annexed to these letters according to the tenor of a decree of the same Sacred Congregation, dated the 19th of October 1866); taking into consideration the consent and the testimonial letter of the illustrious and Right Reverend Bishop of (N.N.), his Lordship (N. N.); in virtue of the power granted to us by the Apostolical See, we unite and aggregate the above named pious Confraternity to our Archconfraternity, and by these letters patent, we will and declare it to be so united and aggregated. We also grant and communicate to the above named Confraternity and to its associates present and future, brethren and sisters, through the authority which we have received from the Sovereign Pontiff Leo XIII, all the indulgences and the spiritual favors conceded to our Archconfraternity.

We humbly entreat of the most Holy and benign Face of Our Lord Jesus that, through the intervention of the most blessed Peter, Prince of the Apostles, principal patron of the Archconfraternity, It would graciously ratify and confirm in heaven, our present act of concession and aggregation, that It would give to all the associates united with us, grace and help in this life, and that at last after this their exile It would deign to show Itself eternally to them resplendent in glory.

Given in Tours, at the Oratory of the Holy Face, under the signature of the Director of the Archconfraternity, the … of the month of … in the year of our Lord …

Place of the Signature.

✠   Place of the seal.

## Decree Annexed to the Diploma

*By a decree Urbis et Orbis of the Sacred Congregation of Indulgences dated 8th of January 1861, confirming and renewing the Constitution of Clement VIII, upon the establishment, or the aggregation of Confraternities, it is laid down that, in the formula of the aggregations which ought to be, at least in substance, conformable to that prescribed by Clement VIII, there must be inserted, at any rate, the principle points of the said Constitution together with the modifications approved by Pius IX.*

Nevertheless, at the request of some heads of orders and of Directors of Archconfraternities, in order to facilitate the printing and expedition of the Diplomas, His Holiness Pope Pius IX, in an audience of the 19th October 1886, deigned to grant that, in future, the above named points of the Constitution may be written down upon a separate sheet, but in such a manner that the communication of the sheet shall be rigorously annexed to the Diplomas and also expressed in the formula of aggregation.

Given at Rome at the Office of the Holy Congregation of Indulgences and of Holy Relics, the 19th of Oct. 1886.

Ant. M. Cardin. PANEBIANCA, Pref.
Phil. Can. COSSA, substitute.

# Principal Points of the Constitution of Pope Clement VIII

1. It is not permitted to establish and aggregate in Churches, whether belonging to Seculars or Regulars, more than one sole Confraternity of the same institution and of the same kind.
2. It is done by the consent of the Ordinary and by Testimonial Letters from him.
3. The mother Archconfraternity expressly communicates to local Confraternities the favors and indulgences which have been specially granted to itself, but not those which it enjoys by privilege of communication.
4. The statutes of the Confraternities are examined and approved by the Ordinary of the place, who may even correct them.
5. The favors and indulgences communicated to the Confraternities cannot be promulgated until they have been recognized by the Ordinary.
6. The Confraternity may receive alms, and employ them according to the manner prescribed by the Ordinary.
7. The letters of establishment and of aggregation may be expedited and accorded gratuitously, without any recompense whatever being attached to them, even if offered spontaneously and received under the pretext of a simple alms; and it is only permitted for each aggregation, establishment or confirmation, to receive a sum which in Italy shall not exceed six crowns of Roman money, and out of

Italy thirty francs of ordinary money, by way of compensation for the outlay in paper, writings, office charges, carriage and other expenses.

8. These divers prescriptions must be faithfully observed in all their particulars, otherwise the establishment, or aggregations, and the communications of favors and indulgences will be of no efficacy and of no value, and the superiors and officials will thereby, incur the deprivation of the offices which they possess, and the inability to obtain any others, a penalty which can only be remitted by the Sovereign Pontiff himself.

# Statutes and Rules of the Archconfraternity of the Holy Face

In virtue of the Apostolic Briefs of December 9th 1884, March 30th and October 1st 1885:

I. The Archconfraternity of the Holy Face has, with the authority of the Holy See, been established at Tours in the chapel of the same name, where, since the year 1852, an authentic copy of Saint Veronica's veil (preserved at Saint Peter's at Rome) has been specially venerated.

II. The chief object of this Archconfraternity is:

1. To offer to the adorable and suffering Face of our Lord Jesus Christ, imprinted on Saint Veronica's veil, the homage of worship and love which is Its due;
2. To induce members, by honoring this Holy and venerable effigy, to perform acts of faith, piety, zeal

and penance, in order to make reparation for the terrible outrages which, in these days of impiety, are constantly committed against the Majesty of God, the Divinity of our Lord and the authority of the Church.

III. Members undertake the following obligations:

1. To recite every day, for the intentions of the Archconfraternity, either in Latin or English one *Pater, Ave, Gloria* and the invocation: *Domine, ostende Faciem tuam, et salvi erimus:* "Lord, show us Thy Face, and we shall be saved";
2. To wear an effigy of the Holy Face, either on a cross, medal, or scapular;
3. To attend as often as possible the monthly meetings held in the chapel where the association is established;
4. To extend as much as they can the devotion to the suffering Face of our Savior;
5. To have their names entered on the register of the association.

IV. The faithful of any age, or of either sex, may belong to the association. When a person becomes a member, their name is entered on the register, and with their certificate of admission, they are also given a copy of the Statutes and Rules.

V. The principal Feast of the Archconfraternity is that of Saint Peter, in whose Church at Rome the veil of Saint Veronica is preserved, while its lesser feasts are those of the Crown of Thorns and the Transfiguration. Moreover, special homage is paid to the Holy Face on Good Friday, when the Church commemorates the insults our Blessed

Lord endured for us and especially the outrages offered to His Sacred Face, and also on Easter Sunday when the veil of Saint Veronica is publicly exhibited at Rome in presence of the Sovereign Pontiff.

VI.  The members meet once a month, the day and time, together with the prayers and ceremonies being fixed by the director, with the approbation of the Ordinary.

VII. The director is appointed by the Ordinary, and either he, or his deputy, has power to enroll members and to sign their certificates of admission.

Examined and approved:

On the vigil of the Feast of the Patronage of the Blessed Virgin.

Tours, October 26<sup>th</sup> 1885.

✠  GUILLAUME-RENÉ,
*Archbishop of Tours.*

# Indulgences Granted by
# Pope Leo XIII

(Applicable to the souls in purgatory)

Plenary Indulgences:
1.  On the day of admission (In order that the associate may more easily gain this plenary indulgence, unless advised to the contrary, the Director will name, for the day of his admission, a Sunday or Festival).

2. At the hour of death;
3. For every yearly pilgrimage made to the Oratory of the Holy Face;
4. On the feast of Saint Peter, or on a day during the Octave;
5. On the feast of the Transfiguration, or a day during the octave;
6. On Passion Sunday, or any other day fixed by the Ordinary.

In order to gain these last three indulgences, it is necessary to visit the seat of the Confraternity.

Partial Indulgences:

*Seven years and seven quarantines*: for each assistance at the monthly reunions.

*Sixty days:*
1. For each pious exercise performed at the seat of the Confraternity;
2. For any other work of piety offered in union with the object of the association;
3. Each time a member devoutly kisses the effigy of the Holy Face repeating the invocation: *Lord, show us Thy Face, and we shall be saved.*

*Hundred days*: for every prayer said before an effigy of the Holy Face. (*Pius IX. December 11th 1876.*)

*Forty days*: each time a member assists at any of the daily morning or evening exercises in the chapel of the Holy Face at Tours. (*The Archbishop of Tours, November 15th 1876.*)

The above indulgences which require that a visit should be made to the church, may be gained by sick persons by virtue of some other act prescribed by the confessor. (*Brief of the 30th March 1885.*)

*N. B.* The associates will endeavor to be faithful to their pious engagements, although these engagements, as they all know, do not impose an obligation of conscience, that is to say, do not oblige under penalty of sin.

## Advice to the Associates

I. To wear on their persons a picture of the Holy Face, to kiss it devoutly the first thing in the morning on awaking and at night before going to sleep, to consecrate their actions during the day to the Divine Face, to resolve to perform them in Its presence and before Its eyes.

II. At the commencement of their prayers, or of any exercise of piety, as an easy means of placing themselves in the presence of God, and of combating distractions, to think of the Holy Face whose eyes are open and fixed upon us, to adore It with faith, to look at It with love.

III. In presence of the Blessed Sacrament, to recall to our remembrance the fact that the Face of the Savior is present there in the Sacred Host; that It sees us, listens to us, blesses us, speaks to us interiorly.

IV. To endeavor in their conduct to imitate the virtues of patience, of gentleness, of serenity, of modesty, which shine in the Holy Face. Listen to the Divine Master who said *learn of Me, in seeing Me, that I am meek in face and humble of heart:* knowing that, in fact the gentleness and humility of the heart of Jesus are, as in a very clear mirror, admirably reflected on the Face of the Man-God.

V. In trials, sicknesses, accidents, temptations, to prostrate themselves before the picture of the Holy Face whether in their private Oratory, or above all, in the church of the Confraternity where it is specially exposed.

VI. To have in their houses a picture of the Holy Face which they shall honor as the protector of the family and the guardian of the domestic hearth; to recite before it the prayers which are habitually said in common by the household.

VII. When they shall hear any blasphemies pronounced, or shall see an act of impious sacrilege which they cannot prevent, to recollect themselves and to pronounce with their hearts, if they cannot with their lips, the words: "Behold, O God, our Protector, and look upon the Face of Thy Christ," or: "may the Name of the Lord be blessed!" *Sit Nomen Domini benedictum!*

VIII. To propagate the worship of the Holy Face in their locality, amongst their friends and acquaintances, and to make use of it in order to combat, in every possible manner, the terrible effects of indifference and irreligion.

## Formalities for the Aggregation to the Archconfraternity

The diplomas of aggregation to the Archconfraternity of the Holy Face are delivered to the local Confraternities which, being canonically established, desire to participate in the Indulgences and other spiritual favors granted to our work.

It is the Ordinary, otherwise styled the Bishop of the diocese, who alone has the power of establishing the Confraternity, of approving its statutes and its rule, and of authorizing its aggregation to the Archconfraternity of Tours.

Hence the three following documents required by the Roman congregations:

I. An episcopal ordinance, whereby the Ordinary establishes the Confraternity canonically;

II.   A copy of the statutes and rules, bearing the approbation and the signature of the Bishop, with the accessory modifications, appropriate to the needs of the locality and deemed to be suitable;

III.   A testimonial letter, signed by the Bishop and having his seal attached to it, by which he authorizes the Confraternity, established by him, to be aggregated to the Archconfraternity at Tours.

This last document, as well as the copy of the statutes, should be sent to the director of the Archconfraternity in order to be deposited in its archives. The ordinance of establishment must remain in the archives of the local Confraternity.


NOTA:

1.   We hold at the disposition of our colleagues two formulas drawn up in Latin, *Decretum erectionis,* and *Litteræ testimoniales,* being a copy of the formulas of the Sacred Congregation of Rites, which it will suffice to fill up and to sign. We will send them to any persons requesting to have them, and they can then submit them to the ecclesiastical authority, by way of abridging the labors of the secretaries.

2.   The accessory modifications of which our Statutes are susceptible, may be applied to article I, which it would be well to appropriate to the name of the place; to article VI, on fixing the date of the monthly meeting and, when necessary, the details of the ceremonies; to article VII, where the name of the director must be given. There may also be added at the end of Article II, the designation of certain vices proper to the locality, and which it is more particularly necessary to combat or to repair; for example, blasphemy, drunkenness, the profanation of Sunday, etc. According to canonical rules, it is permitted to add, but not to suppress anything.

These formalities being complied with, we will deliver to the director of the local Confraternity a Diploma of aggregation, drawn up in accordance with the prescriptions of the Sacred Congregations, and giving a right to the Indulgences and favors of the Archconfraternity. We will at the same time send to him a separate sheet containing on one side the principal points of the Constitution of Clement VIII, and on the other side, the table of Indulgences. These documents must be preserved in the Archives of the local Confraternity; it will even be well to have the Diploma framed.

Thenceforth, it will be no longer necessary to transmit to us the names of the associates. Each Confraternity thus aggregated has its own proper register, its special meetings and its own organization. The director may continue to address himself to us for tickets of admission, but he signs them with his own name, by the side of ours; or he may make other tickets of a different kind.

Every year, during the course of the month of July, he must make known to us the number of admissions and the state of the Confraternity directed by him. From time to time, when an opportunity occurs, he must send to us an account of the most striking ceremonies which have been performed, and of graces which have been obtained, etc. It is necessary, for the sake of the object indicated in our Statutes, and as an external sign of the work, that there should be in the place which is the center of the Confraternity an effigy of the Holy Face, similar to that in the Oratory of Tours, namely a facsimile of the veil of Veronica. It must be publicly exposed to view in a suitable place, and decorated in the manner which shall appear to be the most suitable for exciting the piety of the faithful; and, in as far as possible, it must have a lamp burning before it day and night, as a sign of honor and reparation. It is even in accordance with the spirit of the Church, that there should be given up to the Confraternity a chapel or an altar proper to it, and that it should then be called the chapel, or the altar of the Holy Face. The picture would of course naturally be placed there.

*N.B.* This information will be useful to ecclesiastics and even to laymen, who in concert with their priests, are occupied in establishing, or aggregating a Confraternity. The two formulas, the *Ordinance of establishment,* and the *Testimonial Letter,* printed in accordance with the instructions from Rome, can be sent to them in order that they may submit them to the Bishop's secretary, who will have nothing more to do except to fill them up.

*Price of each sheet:* $2^d\frac{1}{2}$. *Price of the Diploma and of the annexed sheet:* $1^s8^d$. *Voluntary offering, which, including the expenses, must not in accordance with the Constitution of Clement VIII exceed* L. 1. 5. 0.

Diploma of Union, under the title of: "Diploma of union, of prayers and of merits," Letters of affiliation may be granted to parishes, to communities, to associations and to other pious associations which, not having the Confraternity established among them, desire to be united to us by a special tie, and to cooperate in the reparatory work of the Holy Face. This Diploma of union, differing from that of the Diploma of aggregation, does not give a right to indulgences, but it confers an entire participation in the prayers, adorations, merits, and good works of the Archconfraternity.

As an exception and as a very distinguished favor, the Diploma of union may be granted to certain zelators or benefactors who have rendered signal services to the work of the Holy Face. In these cases no canonical formality is required in order for such persons to be received. In certain places where the Confraternity of the Holy Face is established, an excellent custom has been introduced which we willingly recommend. Besides the director appointed to that office by the Bishop, there is a lady president of the work, assisted by one or more counselors, and a few zelatrices; they form a little council under the authority of an ecclesiastical director, and may be of great assistance to him in all questions of detail relative to the association. This means, which is quite optional, evidently possesses precious advantages. It is for the director himself to decide whether it will be well to employ it, and thereby turn to profit the zeal and devotion of the generous souls whom Providence nearly always places at his disposal.

# General Observations upon the Worship Rendered to the Holy Face in the Archconfraternity

## I. Object of the Worship

The Archconfraternity of the Holy Face professes specially to worship the Holy Face of our Lord, outraged and disfigured in His Passion. Religion has no object more touching and more worthy of our homage.

In the Old Testament mention is often made of the Face of God. In heaven, Angels and Cherubim adore It; upon earth, under whatever visible form It may appear, patriarchs, prophets and the just of all ages contemplate It with profound veneration and religious awe. But when the Son of God is incarnated, when the Word assumes the figure and the resemblance of man, the Divine Face, in the person of Jesus, becomes an object of admiration, of respect and of love; first to Mary and Joseph, then to the disciples and to all who behold It and who appreciate Its ravishing features and Its ineffable beauty. At Bethlehem,

Nazareth, on Tabor, in the different states through which It passed, this august Face, the mirror of the holiest of souls and of the most tender of hearts, merits to be contemplated and adored.

It above all deserves to be so in the humiliating and sorrowful state to which It was subjected during the Passion. Our Lord, in no other portion of His Holy Humanity, suffered so much as He did in His amiable Face. From the Garden of Olives, where the adorable Face was covered with a sweat of blood and defiled by the traitorous kiss of Judas, to the last sigh which It exhaled at the moment of death, when It was bowed down upon the Cross, there was no species of abasement, ignominy and suffering to which Jesus did not voluntarily submit It. His head and His forehead were crowned with thorns, His eyes bathed with bitter tears, His lips steeped in gall and vinegar; blows, spittle, the most savage outrages were inflicted upon Him. "We have seen Him," says the prophet, "and there was no beauty in Him that we should desire Him, He was despised and rejected of men." The evangelists expressly say that impious spit in His Face and buffeted Him and struck His Face with the palms of their hands, saying: "Prophesy unto us, O Christ, who is he that struck Thee?" and, again spitting upon Him, they took the reed and struck His head. These minute details, at once so expressive and affecting, were not written and consigned to the Holy Scriptures without a particular design of God. They eloquently exhort us to give, whilst meditating on the different mysteries of the Passion of the Savior, a special attention to the aspect and the worship of His sorrowful Face.

## II. Practical Object

The homage which we render to the suffering Face of the Redeemer has an eminently practical object and a very real one. It is that of offering to the Divine Majesty, which has been offended, a just reparation for the inexpressible outrages which the impiety of the present times is not afraid, whether in secret or in public, of inflicting upon the sovereignty of God, on the Divinity of Jesus Christ, on all that is religious and sacred. Amongst the special crimes belonging to the time in which we live, we must include blasphemy and the profanation of Sunday.

In our days blasphemy is committed with unheard of audacity. Not content with outraging the most adorable and thrice Holy Name of God, the modern blasphemer attacks God personally; he combats Christ in the truth of His doctrine, in the morals of His Gospel, in the practice of His Sacraments, in the rights and even in the very existence of His Church. Not to speak of gross blasphemy, properly so called, which we so often hear resounding in our ears and which seems to be vomited from out the mouth of hell, but blasphemy which assumes to be doctrinal and scientific, is uttered privately in the secret societies or pompously in public discourses; it is printed and displays itself in the light of day, in newspapers, pamphlets and books; it poisons and perverts all conditions and all ages.

The violation of Sunday does not show a less undisguised contempt for the law of God and His sovereign authority. The sanctification and repose of the seventh day are no longer observed except by a small number of Christians worthy of the name. Holy days are profaned with a kind of indifference, deliberately and without remorse, in the workshop of the artisan and the counting house of the merchant, in the interior of families and in public places, in populous cities and in the smallest hamlets.

The infraction of these Divine commandments has risen to a state of social crime. It took place formerly, it is true, but never was it committed in so general a manner as at the present day. Evidently, such a state of things, so contrary to the fundamental economy of religion, over-throws at once the moral order of society, ruins the family to its foundations, and provokes the vengeance of Heaven. Such crimes cannot remain unpunished here below; they must be expiated, either by the scourge of Divine Justice or by voluntary reparation.

This reparation is an absolute and urgent necessity. At the present moment, there is not a single Catholic who does not loudly proclaim it to be so. The prosperity and peace of nations are obtainable only at this price.

What then must we do? The example given us by our enemies may serve as a lesson to us. We see them taking counsel with each other and concerting together; in freemasonry and the secret societies, men, blaspheming and profaning all that is most sacred, give each other the pass word, and link themselves together by an infernal compact; they have already reached the point of no longer dissimulating their projects; they form in the face of day frightful plots against the Lord and His Christ. Is not this then the moment for the children of God, for whoever has at heart the salvation of his brethren and the regeneration of society, to unite in the Name, and under the auspices of the august Face, so shamefully outraged, in order to erect a rampart against the torrents of Divine anger which ceaselessly accumulate against us and threaten to overwhelm us? Was ever a society of reparation more necessary? Could Providence offer us a more opportune aid, and one in closer connection with our pressing needs?

### III. The Means of Reparation

The means of making effectual reparation for the crimes of which we have just spoken is to be found in a manner equally touching and admirable in the worship of the Holy Face, as understood and practiced in our Archconfraternity.

At all times there have been in the Church chosen souls, like Saint Augustine and Saint Gertrude, who have been animated by a special veneration for the Divine Face of the Redeemer. There have even existed, at certain epochs, Confraternities having for their object Its glorification and the rendering of public homage to It. But to attach to so consoling a devotion an idea of reparation, of establishing a direct relation between the species of crime which most outrages the sovereign Majesty of God and the kind of insult which has the most ignominiously disfigured the Face of Jesus Christ, is a conception which belongs to our own times and which characterizes our new Archconfraternity! It was necessary that blasphemy and the profanation of holy things should rise to a degree of scandal and of perversity unknown until now in order to enable Christian piety to look at the Face of Jesus under a fresh aspect, and thereby to open up a new means of reparation. Hitherto the salutary means contained in the devotion to the Holy Face had not been observed and turned to account. Perhaps It would not have been remarked, even now, had it not been for a special illumination communicated to a fervent Religious of the Carmel at Tours, Sister Marie de Saint-Pierre, and without the zeal of a great servant of God and St. Martin, Mr. Dupont, who, during twenty-five years of his life, practiced acts of reparation before the Face of Jesus Christ. It was given to these two holy souls, vividly to see and feel all the power and reality existing in this means of reparation; they practiced it themselves and transmitted it to others.

It was felt that fresh needs require new remedies. Therefore, the devotion to the Holy Face enters naturally, as it were, into the souls of men and is everywhere received with eagerness and confidence. Accepting its reparatory character, the Archconfraternity of the Holy Face presents to the Heavenly Father the adorable Face of our Lord, such as It was in the days of Its Passion, wounded, spit upon, covered with sweat and with blood. "O Father, It exclaims, look on the Face of Thy only and well beloved Son; of Him who is the 'image of Thy greatness,' and the splendor of Thy glory. He has suffered for us, He has expiated our ingratitude and our crimes, look on Him and forgive us. *Respice in Faciem Christi tui.* And Thou, merciful Face of Jesus, show us what Thou art, and we shall be saved. *Ostende Faciem tuam, et salvi erimus.*"

These beautiful invocations which the Church utters so often in her Psalms, have become the watchword and the motto of our Archconfraternity. They express all that this means of reparation, placed at our disposition, contains of consolation and of hope. The scars imprinted on the disfigured Face of the Redeemer, the tears, the sweat and the blood which flow from His loving and compassionate Face, offer to the associates a rich treasure, an inexhaustible mine of merits and of satisfactions wherewith to pay their debts to Divine Justice. Let us then approach It with confidence, let us render It our homage; let us make use of this powerful advocate in order to plead our cause; the Father will "look on the Face of His Christ, and we shall be saved."

### IV. Models of Reparation

Our Lord has Himself willed to point out to us, what is, in regard to Him, the best means of reparation, first by raising up upon the road to Calvary a pious woman who offered Him the solace of which He stood in need. Veronica perceives Him laden with His Cross, climbing the mountain of His sacrifice; His Face soiled, wounded, bleeding. Listening only to her compassion and her piety, the courageous Israelite braves the raillery of her fellow citizens, and the brutality of the executioners, and, making her way through the crowd, draws nigh to Him; she detaches the veil of fine Egyptian linen which covers her head, spreads it over the wounded Face of the Savior, gently wipes with it His adorable Face, solacing, comforting and reanimating it. This was the first homage of reparation offered to our well beloved Redeemer on the path of sorrows; He showed His gratitude for it, and as a recompense He left on the veil of His compassionate benefactress the impression of His Holy Face in the state to which It had been reduced.

Tradition has transmitted to us this memorable fact; it is, in the exercises of the Way of the Cross, the subject of the sixth station, and the precious veil, with the miraculous image imprinted upon it, is kept, at the present day, in the Church of St. Peter at Rome, where from time immemorial, it has been an object of supreme honor. Veronica herself, according to the communications made to Sister Marie de Saint-Pierre, is given us by our Lord as the model of the reparatory souls of which our epoch stands in need upon that other Calvary which the Church is climbing in the 19th century; and her example should encourage Christians who feel themselves to be inspired with the desire to compensate the Savior for the outrages committed against His majesty. The recompense bestowed upon her is the exterior symbol of the spiritual graces which we are sure to obtain by devoting ourselves to the work of reparation.

Another model is given us in the person of the Good Thief, who from the cross as from a pulpit, spoke in defense of the cause of Christ, and confessed His Divinity at the very moment when it was blasphemed by the other thief and by the multitude of the impious. Turning a reverential and a suppliant countenance towards the sorrowful and wounded Face of Jesus: "Lord," he said, "remember me when Thou shalt come into Thy kingdom." His prayer is granted at that very moment. The Face of the

Lord inclines Itself towards him and His lips utter those ineffable words which ensure to this model of reparatory souls, as a supreme recompense, the immediate vision of His glorious Face: *"Amen, I say to thee, this day thou shalt be with Me in Paradise."*

The fathers of the Church are inexhaustible in their praise of the Good Thief. Saint John Chrysostom, when meditating upon his faith, raises it above that of Abraham, of Moses and of Isaiah. "They," he says, "saw Christ upon the throne and in the bosom of His glory and they believed; he sees Him in the midst of torments, and he adores Him as though He were in glory; he sees Him on His cross, and he prays to Him as though He were seated in the highest heavens; he sees a criminal, and he invokes a King..." According to the same father, the Good Thief became at once an "evangelist" and a "prophet"; he preaches the Divine Crucified, he announces His eternal Kingdom.

Tradition knows him under the name of Dismas. The Roman martyrology inscribes him amongst the saints of the 25th of March, and the Breviary, in the "Proper particular to some places," assigns him an office and indicates his feast as that of a double on the 24th of April. This prayer contains a significant expression; the Church asks: "God, who justifies sinners, to provoke us to repentance by means *of the compassionate aspect of His only Son which attracted the blessed thief*, and to grant us the same eternal glory." It would be impossible to offer to the Catholics of our days, to the zelators and apostles of the Reparation, a more worthy and better authorized model.

## V. Picture Adopted by the Archconfraternity

The picture adopted as a type by the Archconfraternity is the representation of the august Face of the Savior, as it was visibly impressed upon the veil of Saint Veronica. This picture is venerated at Rome, in equal degree with the wood of the true Cross and the iron of the holy spear; it ranks amongst the great relics which are exhibited on certain days with great solemnity in the Vatican basilica. The copies which are painted on linen or silk, if they are furnished with a seal of authentication, enjoy the same privileges as the miraculous picture itself, and according to the rules of the liturgy, ought to be equally honored; therefore it is not proper to expose them to public veneration unless a lamp or a taper be kept constantly burning before them.

Since the exile of Pius IX at Gaeta in 1848, in consequence of circumstances connected with the misfortunes of those days, these venerable copies of the Vatican picture have been diffused in great numbers amongst the faithful and above all in France (see, on this subject, the *Life of Mr. Dupont*).

One of the first sent from Rome providentially fell into the hands of Mr. Dupont in the year 1851. That great servant of God and fervent apostle of the reparation placed It in a position where It could be plainly seen in his drawing room; then he lighted a lamp before It, which he kept burning day and night, and during twenty-five years he never ceased to honor It and obtain by Its means graces and favors of all kinds.

Christian art, it is well known, takes pleasure in representing the Divine Face of the Savior under several different aspects; sometimes it is the Face of the *Ecce Homo*, otherwise called the "Christ of the Reed" wearing on his brow the crown of thorns, and sometimes the veil with which the soldiers blindfolded Him; sometimes it is the Face of the *Orante*, or the Savior in the attitude of prayer, as it is seen in the catacombs; at other times, it is the head of Christ on the Cross, or yet again, the Face of the Man God radiant with glory and majesty as on Tabor, or lastly the Face of the Infant Jesus in His cradle, or in the arms of His mother. Expressive and touching as are these different representation, the Archconfraternity, in view of the object which it proposes to itself, prefers to them the *facsimile* of the veil of Veronica (Note: It has been asked why the veil of Veronica does not wear the crown of thorns. We can give no other explanation than the following: the veil of Veronica only bore the impress of that portion of the Divine Face upon which it had been spread and which was below the crown. In representing this portion of the Face of our Lord, it was necessary, in order not to leave It incomplete, to add the upper part of the forehead, but without the crown, and this is one of the characteristics which distinguishes the veil of Veronica from the Ecce Homo).

If in fact, we look at this holy picture with the eyes of faith, we shall recognize, even from the point of view of art and without speaking of its antiquity and its miraculous origin, that it is very touching in its aspect, and well calculated to induce souls to perform acts of reparation; it is impossible to consider, without a profound feeling of compunction, the bleeding forehead of the Savior, the swollen and half closed eyes, the livid and darkened countenance. On the right cheek, in addition to the wounds, may be clearly distinguished the impress of the gauntlet of iron worn on the hand which struck Him so cruelly in the house of Annas, and on the other cheek traces of spittle. The nose is wounded and bleeding, the mouth open and filled with blood; the teeth are broken, the head and the hair torn out in different places. Thus changed and disfigured, the most Holy Face of Jesus does none the less present to us, in Its whole aspect, an ineffable mixture of greatness, of compassion, of love and of sorrow, which touches the hearts of all who look upon It. Beneath those bleeding wounds and that ignoble spittle, the Christian soul recognizes the majesty of its God, and touched with repentance at the sight of so striking an expiation of its ingratitude, it abandons itself without reserve, to a sweet confidence and an ardent love for its Redeemer.

## VI. Cross of the Archconfraternity

The Archconfraternity, having its center in the archiepiscopal city of Tours where it had its origin, adopts as a principal sign of decoration for its members a cross with two arms arranged in the manner shown in the engraving given below; on the center of one of its sides is inscribed the monogram of Christ surrounded with the words: *Reparation Pie IX* 1847, and upon the arms of the cross: *Sit nomen Domini benedictum*; on the obverse is seen engraved, on the center, the Holy Face, above which is the inscription of the Cross: *INRI*, and beneath: *Vade retro, Satana*. The associates are advised habitually to wear this cross as a safeguard; during pilgrimages and at public ceremonies, it is well to have it placed where it can be seen on the breast. The Archconfraternity is an army; the cross, such as it has been described, is its standard; let us wear it with confidence; it will help us to conquer our enemies and to repair our losses. But it is not absolutely necessary that the cross should be worn; according to the rule, it may be replaced by a medal or a scapular of the Holy Face.

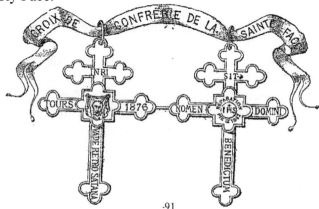

## VII. Advantages of the Archconfraternity

To honor the august Face of the Redeemer by performing at the present day the same office in regard to It which the pious Veronica fulfilled on Calvary, to render ourselves useful to the Church, to society and to souls, by endeavoring to repair the crimes which do the greatest amount of evil to our contemporaries; these two acts, so noble and meritorious in themselves, become a source of graces and benedictions for fervent souls who devote themselves to the work. To these advantages may be added the numerous indulgences whether partial or plenary which the Church grants to the associates; and the participation in the ineffable promises made by our Lord to all those who honor His most Holy Face.

## VIII. Engraving of the Holy Face

The engravings of the Holy Face are the reproduction of the veil of Veronica at the Vatican. No one is ignorant of the respect paid by the Church to the relic. Every year two Cardinals, delegated for that purpose, give the same benediction with it to the kneeling people, as that given with the Blessed Sacrament, and with the sacred wood of the true Cross. An authentic attestation of the Divinity of Jesus Christ, this blessed veil has been left to the Church, to be as it were, a precious coin, marked with the effigy of the King of kings, intended to call down upon the world which is ceaselessly impending towards its ruin, the mercies of the Lord.

Earthly coins have engraved upon them the effigy of their princes, in order to enable the kingdoms of the world freely to exchange their different products. Wherefore then, should not the kingdom of heaven also have, like the kingdoms of the earth, a coin by means of which everlasting goods may be purchased? *O God! Our Protector, look upon us, and cast Thine eyes upon the Face of Thy Christ*, ought to be our frequent cry.

Every soul attached to Holy Church, and with it to the dogma of the Divinity of our Lord, ought to make it a law of love, to have in its own little oratory a picture of the *Holy Face*. Ah! If this devotion did but reign in all hearts, we should soon see the last remnants disappear of the odious blasphemy which has come down even to our own days: the denial namely of the Divinity of Jesus! The devotion to the Holy Face is a sign of predestination, for what soul is there which after having loved and venerated this *august Face* on earth may not rest assured of one day venerating It amidst the triumphs of Its glory? (*Letter of Mr. Dupont.*)

*N.B.* These engravings come from Rome, where they are engraved under the guarantee of the proper authority. Moreover they have attached to them an authentication bearing the signature and the seal of a Cardinal, attesting that they have touched the veil of Veronica, the wood of the true Cross and the iron of the spear which transfixed our Lord. This authentication ought to be carefully preserved. The word *gratis*, painted on them in large characters, is to show that the favor of touching these holy relics is gratuitously bestowed, and that the blessing attached thereto is not sold; but it does not mean to imply that the engravings themselves are not to be sold at a proper price, calculated to cover the expenses of the paper, linen or silk of the engraving, of the carriage, etc.; these prices are, moreover, made as low as possible and ought never to be an object of speculation.

Since the earlier pages of this Manual were printed, we have asked His Holiness Pope Leo XIII to grant additional favors to the associates of the Archconfraternity of the Holy Face.

The Holy Father, by a Brief dated the 15th of January 1887, has deigned to grant to the associates a plenary special indulgence for the monthly meetings of the Archconfraternity, which may be gained four times a year, on such days of the meetings as shall be fixed upon by the Bishop of the place.

The Archbishop of Tours has fixed for his diocese, the meetings taking place in the months of January, April, June and October.

––––––––––

### Notices

*\*Note: The following information is for historical context. It shows the daily and weekly Mass and prayer schedule as it existed when the Manual of the Archconfraternity was originally published.*

*The Holy Sacrifice of the Mass:* Daily at 6, 7 and 8 o'clock.

*Recitation of the Litany of the Holy Face with Recommendations and Prayers:* Daily, in the morning after 7 o'clock Mass, and in the evening at 5 o'clock.

*Monthly meeting of the Archconfraternity of the Holy Face:* On the last Sunday of the month, at 5 o'clock in the evening; instruction and Benediction.

*The Way of the Cross:* On the second Friday of the month, at 5 o'clock in the evening.

*Nocturnal Adoration:* Every Tuesday evening, from 9:30 to 5 o'clock on Wednesday morning.

*Diurnal Adoration:* Every Wednesday, from 5 o'clock in the morning to 5 o'clock in the evening, concluding with instruction and Benediction.

*Pilgrimages of Reparation:* Every year, from Palm Sunday to Good Friday.

*Mr. Dupont's room:* May be visited at every hour in the day.

*Offering of candles:* From 25 centimes to 1 franc. *Lighted Lamp:* For a novena, 3 francs; for a month 10 francs, and for a year, 60 francs.

*Oil Holy:* Sent in a box by post. — Price: 1 fr. 50 centimes.

*Intentions for Masses:* In consequence of the expense of the work, the offering for each Mass required at the Oratory is 2 francs, of which 50 centimes is appropriated to the Work.

The chaplets, medals of Saint Benedict and others which are forwarded from the Oratory, receive the blessings and Indulgences suitable to them, and do not lose them by being gratuitously distributed.

*Correspondence:* Letters to be prepaid, and postage stamp enclosed, if an answer be required. Address to be legibly written and the railway station specified to which articles are to be sent. Address: *M. le Chanoine Pierre Janvier, Directeur des Prêtres de la Sainte-Face; rue Bernard-Palissy; 8 (formerly rue Saint-Étienne), Tours (Indre-et-Loire).*

The Oratory is open to foreign pilgrims every day, from 5:30 in the morning to 6:30 in the evening. Two confessionals are placed at their disposal.

Recommendations may be sent by post, or entered in a book kept for the purpose in the vestibule of the Oratory.

Persons are earnestly requested to notify in writing any graces received, and also to have *ex-voto* put up in token of thankfulness.

# Second Part
# OBSERVATIONS

✠

# Exhortation to the Worship
# of the Holy Face

The devotion of the Holy Face has, for its principal object, the rendering to the adorable Face of Jesus Christ, disfigured in the Passion, a special homage of respect and love; of repairing the blasphemies and the violation of Sunday which outrages It afresh, and lastly, the obtaining from God the conversion of blasphemers and of those who profane His holy day.

This touching devotion, which our Lord seems Himself to have instituted on the day of His death, by miraculously impressing His bleeding countenance upon the veil of Veronica, has been always known and practiced in the Church. The holy veil piously preserved at Rome in the Vatican basilica is honored and surrounded with signs of confidence. Several times in the year it is exposed and venerated by the faithful. The sovereign Pontiffs have granted numerous indulgences to those who piously visit the sacred relic.

Many saints have been distinguished by their piety towards the Holy Face and have derived from it all kinds of graces and fruits of salvation; we may cite amongst others: the holy king David, Saint Augustine, Saint Bernard, Saint Gertrude, Saint Mechtilde, and in our own days, Sister Marie de Saint-Pierre, the Carmelite of Tours, and the venerable Mr. Dupont, the indefatigable propagator of the devotion of the Holy Face. This devotion has recently grown. It is an inspiration of the Holy Ghost passing through the Catholic world. It is a providential remedy offered to the world to combat the ravages of impiety and to be a shield against the scourges of Divine Justice.

The magnificent and consoling promises of our Lord, confirmed by a happy experience, show how pleasing the devotion of the Holy Face is to God, and how useful to Christians. How many special graces, what unhoped-for conversions, what success in business, what supernatural lights, have been obtained by this means! Above all, what a number of miraculous cures have been obtained by the virtue of the oil which burns constantly before the venerated picture at Tours!

It is remarkable that in no other part of His adorable Body did our Lord suffer such outrages, such ignominies and insults, as in His amiable Face. No other circumstance of the Passion was so clearly announced by the Prophets, or so minutely related by the Evangelists. All these details were not preserved in the Scriptures without a particular design of God. They exhort us eloquently to give a place among the mysteries of the sorrowful Passion of the Redeemer, to the humiliations and sufferings of His most Holy Face. Christians, who have at heart the glory of God and the salvation of your neighbor, honor with profound veneration the blood-stained and humiliated Face of our Savior, and pray to It with absolute confidence. In reparation of the impiety of the world, offer to the eternal Father this adorable Face, with Its sadness, Its ignominy, Its blood, Its tears, Its bruises, and Its wounds. By so doing, you will appease the anger of God, obtain the conversion of your erring brethren, contribute powerfully to the triumph of the Church, and participate in the glorious rewards promised by our Lord.

# Promises of Our Lord Jesus Christ in Favor of All Who Honor His Holy Face

1. They shall receive in themselves, by the impression of My Humanity, a bright irradiation from My Divinity, and shall be so illuminated by it in their inmost souls that by their likeness to My Face they shall shine with a brightness surpassing that of many others in eternal life. (St. Gertrude, *Insinuations*, book IV, ch. VII)

2. St. Mechtilde having asked our Lord that those who celebrate the memory of His sweet Face should never be deprived of His amiable company, He replied: "Not one of them shall be separated from Me." (St. Mechtilde, *De la Grace Spirituelle (Of Spiritual Grace),* book I, ch. XIII)

3. "Our Lord," said Sister Saint-Pierre, "has promised me that He will imprint His Divine likeness on the souls of those who honor His most Holy Countenance." (January 21, 1847) "This adorable Face is, as it were, the seal of the Divinity, which has the virtue of reproducing the likeness of God in the souls that are applied to It." (November 6, 1845)

4. "By My Holy Face you shall work miracles." (October 27, 1845. Our Lord to Sister Marie de Saint-Pierre)

5. "By My Holy Face you will obtain the conversion of many sinners. Nothing that you ask in making this offering will be refused to you. No one can know how pleasing the sight of My Face is to My Father!" (November 22, 1846)

6. "As in a kingdom you can procure all you wish for with a coin marked with the prince's effigy, so in the Kingdom of Heaven you will obtain all you desire with the precious coin of My Holy Humanity, which is My adorable Countenance." (October 29, 1845)

7. "All those who honor My Holy Face in a spirit of reparation will by so doing perform the office of the pious Veronica." (October 27, 1845)

8. "According to the care you take in making reparation to My Face, disfigured by blasphemies, so will I take care of your soul, which has been disfigured by sin. I will reprint My image and render it as beautiful as it was on leaving the baptismal font." (Our Lord to Sister Marie de Saint-Pierre, November 3, 1845)

9. "Our Lord has promised me," said again Sister Saint-Pierre, "for all those who defend His cause in this Work of Reparation, by words, by prayers, or in writing, that He will defend them before His Father; at their death He will purify their souls by effacing all the blots of sin and will restore to them their primitive beauty." (March 12, 1846)

---

## Devotion of Saint Gertrude Towards the Holy Face

The following revelation was one day made to Saint Gertrude. Our Lord showed Himself to her in the state in which He was when He had been bound and tied to a pillar between two executioners, one of whom lacerated His flesh with thorns, whilst the other lashed Him with scourges, both of them struck Him on the Face, and It appeared to Saint Gertrude in so disfigured a state, that she was penetrated with grief; nor could she retain her tears every time the thought of the vision recurred to her mind.

It seemed to her as though Jesus Christ turned His Face from one side to the other, but that each time that He turned It away from one of the executioners, the other struck It more cruelly, and then turning Himself towards her, He said: *"Have you not read what is written of Me: Vidimus eum tanquam leprosum?* (Is. 53) *We have seen Him in a state as pitiable as that of a leper."* Then Saint Gertrude answered: "Alas! Lord, what remedy can now be found which would be capable of softening the sharp sufferings of Thy Divine Face?" And the Savior said to her: *"If anyone meditated upon and considered My sufferings with tenderness and compassion, and charitably prayed for sinners, his heart would be to Me as a salutary balm and it would assuage My sufferings."*

Let us profit by these Divine words, and let us not oblige our tender Master to address to us the reproach: *"I have waited, and no one has come to console Me."* Let us offer to Him the sentiments of a heart which compassionates Him for the outrages inflicted on Him; let us present to Him our homage and our adoration, and as He will not allow Himself to be vanquished in generosity, He will, by the virtue of His adorable Face, engrave in us His portrait, He will impress in our souls the features of the Divine resemblance of Him which has been effaced by our sins.

Another fact related in the life of the same Saint is as follows: She was preparing herself, on a certain occasion, by a humble remembrance of her sins, to venerate the picture of the Holy Face, as is the custom of all the faithful at Rome. She pictured to herself our Savior all disfigured by the sins which she had committed, and penetrated with grief, she cast herself at His feet, in order to beg forgiveness from Him. Then the Savior, raising His hand, blessed her, saying: *"By the bowels of My mercy, I remit all your sins, and in order,"* He added, *"that a real amendment should take place in you, I order you, for the satisfaction of all these your sins, to do something every*

103

*day, during a year, in memory of the indulgence I have just granted you."* Our Lord then made her the promise already cited: *"All those,"* He said, *"who, in order to testify to their love for Me, shall often recall to mind the picture which represents My Divine Face, shall receive in themselves, through the impression of My humanity, a shining ray of My Divinity, and by means of the resemblance to My Face, wherewith they shall be impressed, they shall shine more than many others in the life eternal."*

What a precious promise! Is it not a truth, capable of reanimating our piety towards the adorable Face of the Divine Savior? And if we cannot journey as far as the city which is the center of Christianity, in order to enjoy the consolation of venerating the celebrated picture which is there exposed solemnly to the faithful, we may at least delight to possess a copy of it, to which we may pay the just tribute of our respect and love.

---

# Pious Reflections upon the Holy Face
(From the works of Sister Saint-Pierre)

### 1. *The Holy Face and the Holy Name of Jesus*

A comparison, as simple as it is just, will show us how the impious by their blasphemy outrage the adorable Face of our Lord, and how faithful souls glorify It by the praises they render to His Name and Person.

Merit belongs to people, and the honor which they have is due to their name. When pronounced it carries with it merit or demerit, as it is deserved. The Holy Name of Jesus testifies to the glorious victory He has achieved over hell, and expresses the adorable merits of His Person.

The Holy Name of God testifies to His Divinity, and contains within itself all the perfections of the Creator; it follows, therefore, that those who blaspheme these sacred Names directly attack God Himself. Let us here recall those words of Jesus: *"I belong to My Father, and My Father belongs to Me."* Jesus became passive through the Incarnation; it is He who suffers in His adorable Face the outrages to the Name of God by blasphemy. There is a look of pain upon the face of a man that is despised; his name and his face seem to bear an analogy one to the other. Behold a man, equally distinguished for his name and good qualities, in the presence of his enemies. They do not lift their hands to strike him, but they overwhelm him with abuse; they add derisive epithets to his name in place of the honorable titles which are his due. Observe again, the look that passes over this man's face. Would you not think that all the abuse from the lips of his enemies is centered here, causing him to endure poignant anguish? The face is suffused with shame and vexation; the opprobrium and ignominy he suffers are harder to bear than real pain in other parts of his body. This then, is a feeble explanation of our Lord's Face outraged by the blasphemy of the impious.

Imagine this same man in the presence of his friends, who hearing of the insults heaped upon him by his enemies, make haste to console him. They respect his dignity, do homage to his high name, by giving him all the titles that belong to him. Do you not observe how this man's face changes under the sweet influence of this praise? There is a halo on his brow, which, spreading over the face, causes it to beam brightly; joy sparkles in his eye; there is a smile upon his lips — in a word, his faithful friends have healed the agonizing wounds of that face outraged by enemies; honor has superseded opprobrium. This is done by the friends of Jesus in the Work of Reparation; the glory with which they surround His Name beams upon His august brow and causes His Holy Face to rejoice.

## 2. *Double Motive for the Work of Reparation through the Holy Face*

This work has two ends, the reparation of blasphemy and the reparation of the profanation of Holy Days; it therefore encompasses all outrages to God, and to His Holy Name. Should the devotion of the Holy Face be united to this work? Yes, it forms part of its riches, and is its most precious ornament, since our Lord has made an offering of His Holy Face as an object of devotion to the members. They are all powerful with God because of the offering they make Him of that august and Divine Face, whose sight is so pleasing to Him that it invariably softens His anger and obtains for poor sinners His infinite mercy. Yes, when the Eternal Father contemplates the Face of His well beloved Son, which has been buffeted, bruised, and covered with ignominy, the sight moves the bowels of His mercy. Let us endeavor to profit by this precious gift, and let us beg this Divine Savior to teach us the patience of His Face during these evil days.

## 3. *Why the Holy Face is the Visible Sign of Reparation*

This August Face offered for our devotion is the ineffable mirror of the Divine Perfection contained and expressed in the Holy Name of God. As the Sacred Heart of Jesus is the visible sign offered for our devotion to typify the immensity of His love in the Sacrament of the altar; in like manner the adorable Face of our Lord is the visible sign offered for our devotion to repair the outrages committed by blasphemers towards the Majesty and Sovereignty of God, of which the Holy Face is the form, the mirror or expression. Thus, by virtue of this Holy Face offered to the Eternal Father, we may appease His anger and obtain the conversion of the impious and blasphemous.

One may say with truth, that sectarians and blasphemers renew the opprobrium of the Passion towards the Holy Face of our Lord. The impious who utter horrible language and blaspheme against the Holy Name of God, spitting in the Face of the Savior and covering it with filth; and sectarians who attack the Church and religion renew the many blows the Face of our Lord has received, making this Divine Face sweat again with their efforts to efface His wonderful works. There is need of more Veronicas to do honor to this Divine Face that has so few to adore It. All those who dedicate themselves to the Work of Reparation fill the place of the pious Israelite, and our Lord has constituted St. Louis, King of France, as one of the protectors of this Work of Reparation, because of the zeal he showed for the glory of His Name.

## 4. *The Office of the Pious Veronica*

The pious service rendered by St. Veronica to our Lord was that of wiping His Holy Face. Yes, all blasphemies hurled by the impious against the Divinity fall like spittle on the Holy Face of our Lord, who has offered Himself up as a victim for sinners. We thus see that by giving ourselves up to the exercise of repairing blasphemy, we render our Lord the same service as that of the pious Veronica, and that He looks upon those who offer it to Him with the same beneficent eyes as those with which He looked upon that holy woman during the Passion.

## 5. *Power of the Holy Face over St. Peter*

There are men on earth who can restore the body, but our Lord alone can restore the soul to the image of God; this then, is the grace the Divine Master has promised to those who render to His adorable Face the homage and honor It merits, with the intention to repair by this homage the opprobrium It receives from blasphemers.

One sees in the Apostle St. Peter an example of the power of the Holy Face. This apostle had by his sin effaced the image of God in his soul, but Jesus turned His Holy Face towards the unfaithful apostle and he became penitent: "Jesus looked upon Peter, and Peter wept bitterly." This adorable Face is like the seal of the Divinity, with power to imprint in the souls of those who devote themselves to the image of God.

## 6. *The Holy Face represents the adorable Trinity*

Remember, O my soul, the Divine lesson thy Heavenly Spouse has taught thee of the adorable Face. Remember that this Divine Head represents the Eternal Father, who is not begotten; that the Mouth of this Holy Face represents the Divine Word made Flesh by the Father, and the Eyes of this Holy and Silent Face represent the reciprocal love of the Father and the Son — for His Divine Eyes have but one light, one intelligence, and produce one love, which is that of the Holy Ghost. Behold in the Hair, the diverse perfections of the Holy Trinity. Look upon the Majestic Head as a precious part of the Holy Humanity of our Lord, the image of the Unity of God; and it is this adorable and silent Face of the Savior that blasphemers overwhelm with fresh insults. Thus, they renew in some measure the sufferings of the Passion, by their blasphemy they attack the Divinity which is the image of the Holy Face.

---

# Novena to the Holy Face

(Series of Meditations)

## First Day: The Holy Face at Bethlehem

At the commencement say: Lord, I desire to seek Thy Face; do not Thou keep me from It on account of my sins; do not separate Thy Holy Spirit from me. Let the light of Thy Face shine upon me; teach me in the way of Thy commandments.

Enter into the grotto at Bethlehem, consider the new born Child, laid in the cradle, wrapped in poor swaddling clothes. Mary and Joseph stand before Him and contemplate Him. You also gaze upon His sweet and radiant Face. It is the Face of the Emmanuel, of the Son of "God with us," of the "most beautiful of the children of men." During four thousand years the patriarchs and prophets had desired to see It; they earnestly entreated for It as the "salvation" promised to the world. "Lord," they unceasingly exclaimed, "show us Thy Face, and we shall be saved." Behold It here! It shows Itself at last! See how ravishing and amiable It is; how It already hastens to give you all the most precious things that It possesses.

I. *It gives you Its first prayer*

Already in Its cradle, It turns towards heaven; towards the sovereign Father of Angels and of men; the author of all things. It adores Him in your name, It prays for you. "Behold Me," It says, "O My Father, I come to fulfill Thy will." Now, this will is to deliver you from eternal death, and to accomplish your salvation. When allowing Itself to be seen for the first time, the Face of Jesus is humble and suppliant; associate yourself with His prayer; determine to labor efficaciously for the great affair of your salvation, which is the object of His coming.

## II. *It gives you Its first tears*

Behold the innocent and delicate cheeks of the newborn infant benumbed with cold, bathed with the tears which are caused less by the sufferings of the body, than by the grief excited in His soul by the sight of the world. The sweet Face of the little Child Jesus is already the victim of reparation, of justice and of expiation; It suffers, It weeps, It satisfies for your sins. Gather up with reverence these holy tears, one alone of which possesses infinite value; offer them to the Eternal Father for the payment of your debts towards Him.

## III. *It gives you also one of Its first smiles*

It has already smiled on Mary, It has smiled on Joseph; now from out the midst of Its swaddling clothes, from out Its tears, It turns towards you, It becomes sweetly radiant whilst looking at you, It gives you Its infantine smile; a smile of peace and love, a smile of heaven, which invites you, which calls you, which seems to say to you: *"The Face which smiles on you is that of a friend, of a brother, of a Savior. Draw near, have confidence, I love you."*

### Act of love
If the Child Jesus loves you, if His Holy Face gives you the proof of it, what is it that holds you back? Render to Him love for love.

### Virtue to be practiced
Detach yourself, at least in heart, from all earthly things; let Jesus be your treasure.

### Spiritual bouquet
Dry that first tear; carry away with you that first kind smile of the Holy Face, lay it in the deepest part of your soul, as a ray of hope, as a spark of love, and say with the prophet: "The light of Thy Face has been shed upon us, O Lord; Thou hast given joy to our heart."

*Aspirations*

I have called upon Thy Face with my whole heart; have pity on me according to Thy promises. Let the light of Thy Face shine upon me. Save me in Thy mercy; Lord, I shall not be confounded because I have called upon Thee.

*Prayer*

God all powerful and merciful, grant we entreat Thee, that venerating the Face of Thy Christ, disfigured in His Passion because of our sins, we may deserve to contemplate It eternally in the splendor of the glory of heaven. Through the same Jesus Christ. Amen.

## Second Day: The Holy Face in the Midst of the People of Judea

At the commencement say: Lord, I desire to seek Thy Face; do not Thou keep me from It on account of my sins; do not separate Thy Holy Spirit from me. Let the light of Thy Face shine upon me; teach me in the way of Thy commandments.

Follow our Lord during His public life, traversing the towns and villages of Judea, announcing the good tidings of the Gospel, curing sicknesses and infirmities, doing good everywhere as He passed. Observe what part the Holy Face took in this mission of teaching and of charity. As the Son of God had really united the whole of our nature to Himself, He showed Himself to men, with a human face, having its own individual features, and a physiognomy which caused Him, at all times and everywhere to be known by the aspect of His countenance; for "man," says the prophet, "is known by the aspect of his face." The people strove with all their might to see the Face of Jesus.

Admire the three wonders of grace, which the sight of the adorable Face produced upon all those who drew nigh to It.

I. *It ravished the multitude*

When Jesus appeared in public, the people surrounded Him, eager to see and hear Him; transfixed on His Divine lips, they said: "Never has man spoken like this man!" And they were plunged into ecstasy and astonishment. The reason is that, very different from Moses, the Man-God did not cover His Face with a veil; He revealed Himself to every eye; He conversed with all indiscriminately, tempering through the sweetness and charm of His humanity, the too dazzling rays of the Divinity which dwelt corporeally in Him. His Face was really the mirror of His soul, the outward expression of His heart, the visible manifestation of His internal feelings.

Is it surprising that His aspect ravished all behold-ers? Come you also near, contemplate with avidity His Face at once human and Divine, listen with reverence to the words of His mouth; delight to listen to It, to question It, to converse with It.

II. *It attracts the Apostles*

On a certain day, the Savior passed near to a publican seated at his desk: *"Follow me,"* He said, and the man immediately arose and followed Him; he became one of His Apostles and His first evangelist. "It was," says St. Jerome, "because at the same time that Matthew heard the voice of Jesus, he saw on His Face a ray of Divine Majesty which enlightened him and stirred the very depths of his soul." On another occasion, Andrew brought Him his brother. Jesus, casting a penetrating glance upon him, said: *"Thou shalt be called Peter."* He transformed him and made of him the chief of His Apostles, the cornerstone of His Church. Walking beside the lake, He perceives two fishermen, two brothers, who were mending their nets; He stops, looks *at them; "Follow Me,"* He says. On hearing the imperative command and on beholding the splendor which illuminated the eyes and the Face of Him who called to them, they abandon their nets, their bark, their father, and immediately follow Him.

Are there not moments in which the Holy Face enlightens you, urges you and touches you? Do not make any resistance or delay when you are thus attracted by It; let It work in you the change which It desires to do.

III. *It is compassionate and merciful towards all*

Little children are the object of Its embraces and Its caresses. It gives to the prodigal son the kiss of peace and reconciliation. Inclined towards the ground in the presence of the repentant sinner, It is raised again in order to look at her and to say: *"Go in peace, and sin no more."* Attentive to the needs of the multitude in the desert, It raises Its eyes towards heaven and calls down the blessing which multiplies the bread necessary for the subsistence of the hungry people. It sheds tears over the tomb of Lazarus and communicates to the four-day corpse, a miraculous resurrection, an image of the possible conversion of the most hardened sinner. Light, grace, pardon, life, flow like rays from the adorable Face; gather them up with avidity according to the needs and the different states of your soul.

*Act of confidence*

Everywhere that It showed Itself upon earth, the Holy Face blessed, pardoned, cured, did good. I will call upon It; wherefore should I not be heard?

*Virtue to be practiced*

Be docile to the impressions of grace; a grace is a glance of the Face of Jesus which solicits and urges you. Give yourself up to Its heavenly influence.

*Spiritual bouquet*

My beloved, show me Thy Face; make Thy voice resound in my ears; Thy voice is as sweet as Thy Face is lovely; I desire at the same time to see and to hear Thee.

*Aspirations*

I have called upon Thy Face with my whole heart; have pity on me according to Thy promises. Let the light of Thy Face shine upon me. Save me in Thy mercy; Lord, I shall not be confounded because I have called upon Thee.

*Prayer*

God all powerful and merciful, grant we entreat Thee, that venerating the Face of Thy Christ, disfigured in His Passion because of our sins, we may deserve to contemplate It eternally in the splendor of the glory of heaven. Through the same Jesus Christ. Amen.

## Third Day: The Holy Face on Tabor

At the commencement say: Lord, I desire to seek Thy Face; do not Thou keep me from It on account of my sins; do not separate Thy Holy Spirit from me. Let the light of Thy Face shine upon me; teach me in the way of Thy commandments.

Ascend with Our Lord on Tabor. He climbed the mountain with three privileged disciples, Peter, James and John, and He began to pray. Whilst He prayed, His Face was transfigured before them; His Holy Face became resplendent like the sun; His vestments were white as snow. Jesus willed to give, in this manner, a free outlet to the rays of the Divinity which was hidden in Him; for the first time He revealed before mortal eyes, His adorable

Face with the splendor of the glory and the beauty which belong to It.

You will find in this mystery three subjects worthy of your attention:

I. *A spectacle to contemplate*

The Face of our Lord beaming with splendor and grace. The light which flows from His Divine Face communicates to the raiment of the Savior and to the whole of His person a virginal whiteness, incomparable in its purity. It is a light which casts its beams into the air, envelopes the whole mountain and ravishes the three disciples who are present, with admiration. They experience an ecstasy of happiness, a foretaste of the happiness of heaven, and Saint Peter exclaims: "It is good for us to be here, let us make three tabernacles!" And yet it was only a passing ray of the eternal splendor, a drop of that ocean of felicity, of that plenitude of life of which the Face of the Lord is the source. What will it be when you drink It in copious drafts and when you will have full possession and assured enjoyment of the very source Itself?

II. *A conversation to which to listen*

Listen to the conversation which Moses and Elias have with Jesus in the presence of the Holy Face thus transfigured. The subject which occupies them is the work of the Redemption of the human race, which the Son of Man has come to accomplish; they speak of His "going out of the world," that is to say, of His Passion and death. The Face of the Redeemer, at that moment so radiant and so beautiful, will soon be wounded, bleeding, spit upon, outraged in a thousand ways. Lifted up upon an infamous gibbet, It will utter in the face of heaven a cry of pardon when expiring, and It will be the consummation of our salvation, the conquering signal of peace, the warrant of an entire reconciliation between God and man. In this mysterious conversation, the Face of Jesus offers Itself to us under two very different aspects; It is at once the glorious and the sorrowful Face. Tabor and Calvary approach each other and are united together; it was meet that it should be so; it is on Calvary, upon the Cross, by the sufferings and ignominy of the Passion concentrated in the Face of our Lord, that Redemption will be accomplished and that we shall merit together with the beatific vision, the delights of Paradise. Do not separate the idea of the sacrifice from that of the recompense; if the joys of Tabor are sometimes granted you, remember that it is to give you strength the better to follow Jesus to Calvary, and to bear the Cross with Him.

### III. *An order to receive*

This order emanates from the Eternal Father, who, from the summit of the mountain, as from an awe inspiring tribune, desires to render, in the face of heaven and earth, a solemn homage to the Face of His Son. It is in fact the splendor of His glory, the figure of His substance, the most pure splendor of His eternal light, the spotless mirror of His justice and of His infinite perfections. He there enhances Its glory, by surrounding It as in a splendid frame, with a luminous cloud, which comes down from heaven, as the symbol of the Holy Ghost, from out the bosom of which issues a voice full of power and majesty: *"This is My beloved Son in whom I am well pleased, hear ye Him."* Such is the command which God gives to every creature. He glorifies the Face of His Word, He makes a solemn exposition of It on the highest mountain of the Holy Land, in order to show in It, to all people and to all centuries, the sign of salvation and the organ of truth. Look at It then, "and act according to the model which is presented to you on the mountain."

*Act of hope*
Yes, I know it; my Redeemer is living. I shall see Him one day with my eyes in His glory, myself and not another; this is the hope which is laid up in my bosom.

*Virtue to be practiced*
Fidelity in obeying the Divine commandments. "Speak, Lord, Thy servant harkens."

*Spiritual bouquet*
"It is good for us to be here." Say these words in the presence of the tabernacle, at the foot of the altar; there is your Tabor, for the immortal and glorious Face of Jesus is, through the Eucharist, present to the eyes of your faith; make It the object of your delights and your joys.

*Aspirations*
I have called upon Thy Face with my whole heart; have pity on me according to Thy promises. Let the light of Thy Face shine upon me. Save me in Thy mercy; Lord, I shall not be confounded because I have called upon Thee.

*Prayer*
God all powerful and merciful, grant we entreat Thee, that venerating the Face of Thy Christ, disfigured in His Passion because of our sins, we may deserve to contemplate It eternally in the splendor of the glory of heaven. Through the same Jesus Christ. Amen.

## Fourth Day: The Holy Face in the Garden of Olives

At the commencement say: Lord, I desire to seek Thy Face; do not Thou keep me from It on account of my sins; do not separate Thy Holy Spirit from me. Let the light of Thy Face shine upon me; teach me in the way of Thy commandments.

Follow Jesus going after the last supper to the Mount of Olives, in order to prepare Himself for His Passion. He kneels down apart in a solitary grotto; He prays for a long time, for three hours. His soul is a prey to sorrow, to fear, to the anguish of death. From time to time He interrupts His prayer in order to go to His disciples and to seek from them a little support and consolation, and He meets with neither. *"I have sought,"* He says, *"someone who would console Me, and I have found none."*

You may here observe three things:

I. *The sorrowful state of the Holy Face*

It reflects all the impressions of His soul; It is sorrowful, desolate, quivering; It sheds tears; sorrowful sighs escape from Its lips. See also how, after having prayed on His knees, the Savior, in order to give to His petitions more intensity and fervor, prostrates Himself with His Face to the ground. Contemplate His Divine Face abased to the dust, cleaving to the earth which, cursed through the sin of Adam and condemned to produce nothing but thorns, was purified by the kiss of peace, and by the tears of the Holy Face. Our earth henceforth, will witness its inhabitants produce a rich harvest of flowers and fruits of virtue; but Jesus takes the thorns for Himself and with them crowns His brow.

II. *The apparition of the angel*

At that moment, the anguish of the Man-God is redoubled; He experiences mortal anguish; a mysterious sweat, a sweat of blood, bathes His Face, runs down from His brow and falls, drop after drop, upon the ground where He is prostrated. An angel appears in order to strengthen Him; reanimated by the heavenly aid, Jesus rises, accepts the chalice offered to Him by His Father, and lovingly drinks it down to the very dregs.

Angel of consolation, you give me an example; I envy you your destiny; I desire to put myself in your place; let it be my portion to raise that suffering and languishing

Face, to compensate It by the tenderness of my love, and the generosity of my sacrifices; since it is for me that It suffers and that It is humiliated; it is for me that It resigns Itself to drink the chalice presented to It by Its Father.

III. *What you have to do*

It is to offer yourself to It and to imitate It. Adorable Face, Thou didst not refuse the help offered by another and the consolation of an angel. Permit me, in spite of my unworthiness, to draw nigh to Thee, and to render Thee the like service. Permit me to compassionate Thy sorrow, to raise Thee from the ground and to hold Thee reverently in my arms. It is for me to prostrate myself to the ground, to annihilate myself in a spirit of reparation; I associate myself with Thy humiliations and Thy sufferings; like Thee I accept the chalice of suffering, and I give myself up to the Divine will, saying: "Behold me, Lord, I come to do Thy will. Thy law shall be engraved forever in my heart. Thy will and not my own be done; not what I will, O Lord, but what Thou willest!"

*Act of abandonment*

Offer yourself wholly to God in order never to do aught save His adorable will; make the offering in union with Jesus praying in the garden.

*Virtue to be practiced*

Do penance; excite yourself to contrition for your own sins and for those of others; accept in a spirit of expiation the trials of life and the bitter sorrows it may please God to send you.

*Spiritual bouquet*

My food, that is to say, my joy and my delight, are to do the will of my Father who is in heaven.

*Aspirations*
I have called upon Thy Face with my whole heart; have pity on me according to Thy promises. Let the light of Thy Face shine upon me. Save me in Thy mercy; Lord, I shall not be confounded because I have called upon Thee.

*Prayer*
God all powerful and merciful, grant we entreat Thee, that venerating the Face of Thy Christ, disfigured in His Passion because of our sins, we may deserve to contemplate It eternally in the splendor of the glory of heaven. Through the same Jesus Christ. Amen.

## Fifth Day: The Holy Face in the House of Caiaphas

At the commencement say: Lord, I desire to seek Thy Face; do not Thou keep me from It on account of my sins; do not separate Thy Holy Spirit from me. Let the light of Thy Face shine upon me; teach me in the way of Thy commandments.

It is the night of the Passion. Jesus, after a derisive judgment, has been disdainfully sent with His hands tied to the house of Caiaphas.

I. *Outrages*
He is at the mercy of a band of servants and of soldiers, who make it a cruel sport to load Him with outrages and insults of every kind. His Holy Face is their target. The whole night, It has to suffer the most humiliating insults which can be invented by the malice of men and the rage of devils. They outrage Him by blows, they wound Him and cover Him with blood by giving Him cuffs with their hands, they soil Him with spittle, a kind of insult particularly felt by the Savior. He complains of it by the mouth of the prophet: *"They were not afraid to spit in My Face,"* and when predicting to His Apostles the Passion

which He was about to undergo at Jerusalem, He specified the spittings which would be given Him: *"The Son of man shall be spit upon."*

II. *Conversion of Saint Peter*

In the midst of this ignominious treatment, what patience on the part of the Savior! What serenity! What sweetness! He does not complain, He does not murmur; He prays, He loves, He expiates and repairs the outrages which our sins have inflicted and still inflict on the majesty of His heavenly Father. At the very culmination of His ignominies His sorrowful Face finds means to perform an act of mercy and of ineffable charity; It casts Its eyes on the Prince of the Apostles and raises him up after his fall. Peter was there, at some distance from Him, an unfaithful disciple, mingling in the crowd of the enemies of His Master, he had shamefully denied Him, no less than three times. All at once he encounters the Divine eyes fixing upon him a look of gentle reproach, of compassion and of love. It is enough. The sight of that sorrowful Face, of that ray of light which issues from those sad eyes pierces the heart of the apostle; penetrated with shame and repentance, he turns aside and weeps bitterly.

III. *Application to yourself*

O Divine Face who raisest up and transformest wandering souls, cast Thine eyes upon me, have pity on me, I have not, after having offended God, responded to the attractions of Thy grace, or if I have shed a few tears, they have only been the result of a passing feeling of humility, of a sadness in which self-love had a larger part than true repentance. Since Thou art, O adorable Face, a sun of justice, able to soften our souls and to purify our consciences, burn and consume in me all that is contrary to the purity of Thy love; may Thy heavenly rays inflame me, and make me weep secretly over my past offenses; I also am an unfaithful disciple, or rather, I have been, but will no longer be one!

Thou hast been so merciful as to forgive me my revolts and to turn away Thine eyes from my sins. No, my Jesus, whatever may happen, and whatever it may cost me, I will not renounce Thee anymore; I will, on the contrary, glorify Thee by my penitence and my good works.

### Act of contrition
Lord, turn away Thy Face from my sins, and blot out all my iniquities. I detest them and desire to make reparation for them.

### Virtue to be practiced
Have the courage of your faith, do not fear the eyes and the words of men when there is a question of a duty to be fulfilled or of a fault to be avoided.

### Spiritual bouquet
"Jesus looked at Peter, and Peter wept bitterly."

### Aspirations
I have called upon Thy Face with my whole heart; have pity on me according to Thy promises. Let the light of Thy Face shine upon me. Save me in Thy mercy; Lord, I shall not be confounded because I have called upon Thee.

### Prayer
God all powerful and merciful, grant we entreat Thee, that venerating the Face of Thy Christ, disfigured in His Passion because of our sins, we may deserve to contemplate It eternally in the splendor of the glory of heaven. Through the same Jesus Christ. Amen.

## The Sixth Day: The Holy Face at the Prætorium of Pilate

At the commencement say: Lord, I desire to seek Thy Face; do not Thou keep me from It on account of my sins; do not separate Thy Holy Spirit from me. Let the light of Thy Face shine upon me; teach me in the way of Thy commandments.

I. *The sufferings of the Holy Face*

The lashes which the executioners inflicted on Jesus did not spare His sweet and amiable Face. It is furrowed in every direction, wounded, bleeding, lacerated by scourges. Then, seeing that Jesus was condemned to death, because He had called Himself "King," the soldiers turn this title into a subject of bitter derision and of sacrilegious mockeries. They cast upon His shoulders a purple robe; instead of a scepter, they place a reed in His hand, and by an incredible refinement of malice they fashion a crown for Him out of thorns which they interlace together, and which they fasten on His brow with great blows. The long, hard, sharp thorns entering deeply into the head of the Savior caused Him dreadful suffering, and inundated His Holy Face with streams of blood.

II. *Humiliations of the Holy Face*

It was in this pitiable state Pilate presented Jesus to the people, hoping thereby to excite their compassion and to deliver Him. "Behold the Man!" he said. The sight only inflamed their fury. "Crucify him, crucify him," they exclaimed. "Shall I crucify your king?" — "We have no other king than Caesar, we will not have this man to reign over us." The enemies of the Savior triumphed. Amongst the crowd there were many whom He had overwhelmed with blessings, who perhaps, in secret, called themselves His disciples and friends; yet not one amongst them raised his voice in order to declare himself in His favor, and to defend Him; not one of them dared to recognize Him for his King and his God. This miserable, cowardly abandonment, joined to the other outrages inflicted on the Holy Face, was a sorrowful martyrdom for Jesus. *"My people, what have I done to you? Why do you outrage the Face of your Savior? Why have you surrounded It with a diadem of thorns?"*

III. *Honor due to the Holy Face*

There is a profound mystery contained in the crowning of the Divine Face; it was destined to reign. The soldiers, though unconscious of it, attest to the royalty of Jesus Christ, as well as Pilate; without being aware of it, they enter into the designs of God, Who wills that His Son should be recognized as King and under that title, should receive the homage of all creatures. Yes, O Jesus, by the diadem which crowns Thy Face, Thou hast acquired the right of reigning over my heart; Thy diadem of ignominy and of suffering is a crown of expiation and of love. Many times I have cast dishonor upon Thy royalty by despising Thy holy law and Thy Divine teachings; many times I have caused the blood to flow down Thy august Face through my reiterated sins, which have driven ever deeper into Thy flesh the thorns which transpierce Thy brow; I have run after the joys of this world, and I have crowned myself with roses; I have longed after the luxurious delights of an easy and pleasant life, not remembering that I am the subject of a King crowned with thorns.

No, adorable Face, I will not allow Thee any more to suffer the thorns of my iniquities; I desire that Thou shouldst rejoice in my homage; that Thou shouldst be crowned with flowers of my virtues, and that Thou shouldst triumph in me by a generous love worthy of Thee.

*Act of offering*
O Jesus, my King and my God, behold my mind with its thoughts, my heart with its affections, my will with its tendencies, behold my soul and my body; I put them wholly and entirely under the empire of Thy Holy Face, reign over me forevermore.

*Virtue to be practiced*
Make all the desires and ill regulated movements of your heart and mind which may offend the Holy Face and renew Its sufferings, to die in you by means of mortification.

*Spiritual bouquet*
Can a member be fastidious and sensual under a head that is crowned with thorns?

*Aspirations*
I have called upon Thy Face with my whole heart; have pity on me according to Thy promises. Let the light of Thy Face shine upon me. Save me in Thy mercy; Lord, I shall not be confounded because I have called upon Thee.

*Prayer*
God all powerful and merciful, grant we entreat Thee that venerating the Face of Thy Christ, disfigured in His Passion because of our sins, we may deserve to contemplate It eternally in the splendor of the glory of heaven. Through the same Jesus Christ. Amen.

## Seventh Day: The Holy Face on the Path to Calvary

At the commencement say: Lord, I desire to seek Thy Face; do not Thou keep me from It on account of my sins; do not separate Thy Holy Spirit from me. Let the light of Thy Face shine upon me; teach me in the way of Thy commandments.

Behold, Jesus ascending the mount of His sacrifice, laden with the weight of His Cross. After the painful and humiliating fall which He has had, His adorable Face is soiled with dust, with sweat and with blood. The spectacle excites the contempt of the crowd and the mockeries of the executioners.

I. *Reparation offered to the Holy Face*

In this state of abandonment and of opprobrium, the Savior, all at once, receives a mark of devotion and of tenderness which compensates and consoles Him. A courageous woman, Veronica, has been touched with compassion. Listening only to her faith and her love, she makes her way through the crowd, puts aside the executioners, and filled with reverence and emotion, draws near to Jesus. Then she takes the soft white veil of fine Egyptian linen which covers her head; she spreads it over and gently applies it to the bleeding and wounded Face of the Man-God! She wipes It and raises It; it is a real service which she renders to Him, and which for a moment relieves His sufferings and reanimates Him. As a recompense, Jesus immediately leaves the impression of His Holy Face upon the linen, of which, she had made use for the performance of this heroic act.

II. *Veronica our pattern*

Congratulate Veronica; look upon her as an admirable model, learn from that generous woman how to make reparation to the suffering Face of your God.

Impiety renews, in these our days, the outrages He endured on Calvary. His Holy Face is especially insulted and spit upon by all the horrible blasphemies which hell vomits forth against His Divinity. The Savior complains; He seems to say to those who know and who love Him: *"I have sought consolers around Me, and I have found none."* Let your heart answer: "Behold me Lord; I am Thine, ready to do Thy good pleasure. Must I lose my faith, my adoration, my model to hatred and contemptuous impiety? I am ready to do Thy will."

III. *A good inspiration to follow*

Divine Master, Thou hast said in Thy Gospel: *"Whoever shall glorify Me before man, I will glorify him in My turn, before My Father who is in heaven."* At the present day, perverse and sacrilegious sects outrage Thy adorable Face; I desire to glorify It by my expiations, by my praises, by all the fervor of my love. Animate me with the spirit with which Veronica was inspired upon the ascent to Calvary. What are the railleries of the world, and the rages of hell to me? I will listen to the voice of the Church, I will follow the inspirations of my heart, I will go to Thee, O sweet Face of my Savior; I will wipe away the tears with which It is inundated; I will soothe the wounds which make It suffer, I will efface the ignominious blemishes with which wicked men have attempted to soil It. In Thy turn, inspire me with the rays of Thy grace, and engrave in my heart the celestial imprint of Thy virtues.

*Act of charity*

Love the Holy Face and have compassion on the outrages It was made to suffer; love your wandering brethren, and pray to God to spare and convert them.

*Virtue to be practiced*
Let zeal for reparation inflame you; exercise it by communions, by your prayers, by your words, by your example, by all the ways the sight of evils committed ought to inspire you.

*Spiritual bouquet*
"*I want Veronicas,*" said our Lord to Marie de Saint-Pierre. "*My daughter, take My Face as a precious coin wherewith to pay My Father the debts of His justice.*"

*Aspirations*
I have called upon Thy Face with my whole heart; have pity on me according to Thy promises. Let the light of Thy Face shine upon me. Save me in Thy mercy; Lord, I shall not be confounded because I have called upon Thee.

*Prayer*
God all powerful and merciful, grant we entreat Thee, that venerating the Face of Thy Christ, disfigured in His Passion because of our sins, we may deserve to contemplate It eternally in the splendor of the glory of heaven. Through the same Jesus Christ. Amen.

## Eighth Day: The Holy Face on the Cross

At the commencement say: Lord, I desire to seek Thy Face; do not Thou keep me from It on account of my sins; do not separate Thy Holy Spirit from me. Let the light of Thy Face shine upon me; teach me in the way of Thy commandments.

Upon the Cross, where It is placed as upon an altar of propitiation between heaven and earth, the Holy Face acts as our intercessor and our mediator.

### I. *The pardon of the Holy Face*

Raising Its eyes bathed in tears towards the heavenly Father, It entreats our pardon: *Pater, dimitte illis.* O Father, remit the debt of these sinners; give back to them Thy friendship. Then turning towards us, It inclines Itself lovingly, as though to offer us the kiss of peace and of reconciliation. O how touching, at that moment, is the aspect of the sorrowful Face of the Redeemer; what sufferings upon that bed of anguish! What a prolonged agony! And what patience also! What gentleness, what an ineffable serenity in Its movements and Its words!

As often as seven times, the Divine Face, giving a respite to Its sufferings, opens Its blessed lips; each one of Its words is a lesson, a grace, and as it were, a reiterated and supreme adieu which It addresses to the world. It does not murmur; It is not irritated; It prays, It pardons, It blesses; at last It utters a loud cry and expires.

### II. *The appeal made to Divine mercy*

O God, our Creator and our Father, we dare not raise our eyes towards Thee; for we have sinned; we have abused Thy innumerable blessings; we are guilty in the highest degree, we deserve the blows of Thy Divine justice. But, Lord, behold Thy Christ on the Cross, look at His merciful and compassionate Face which implores Thee. Listen to the voice of Its prayer. Behold Its tears, the thorns of Its crown, the blood with which It is inundated. Behold It mute, inanimate, growing cold in the death agony. It is given up to death for us, O Father; It has taken our place before Thee, It has deserved to disarm Thy anger. Look, look at the Face of Thy well beloved Christ, in the state to which It has been reduced. Pardon us, O most merciful Father, and save us.

### III. *Christian pardon*

Most Holy Face of Jesus on the cross, what a lesson Thou givest to me! Thy charity has reached even to the extent of pardoning Thy executioners and praying for them. It is above all, for those who struck Thee, wounded Thee, dealt Thee blows, covered Thee with spittle, that Thou aidst: *"Forgive them, Father, they know not what they do."* When they struck Thee, Thou didst endure them, gently and in silence. Now, Thou raisest Thy voice to excuse and defend them, to obtain pardon for them; in offering for them Thy blood, Thou givest them the greatest proof of Thy love. Teach me this, Thy patience with our neighbor and this Thy generosity in pardoning even our most cruel enemies. Yes, I forgive, for love of Thee, all who have offended me. With Thee, I pray for the sinners who outrage Thee, for the wretched men who blaspheme Thee; I beg of Thee their conversion and their salvation. Let them but turn to Thee, O most Holy Face, let them invoke Thee; it is enough! Whoever looks on Thee, O Blessed Face, with faith and repentance, will escape the sting of the serpent and will find life.

*Act of generous love*
My God, I forgive the injuries which have been inflicted on me I pardon all those who have offended me in any way whatever; I love them sincerely, I pray for them, and I entreat Thee to save them.

*Virtue to be practiced*
Bear the injuries inflicted on you and the coldness shown you by your neighbor, accept all that is painful in them to your heart and mind in reparation for what the Holy Face has suffered.

*Spiritual bouquet*
God our Protector, cast Thine eyes upon the Face of Thy Christ.

*Aspirations*
I have called upon Thy Face with my whole heart; have pity on me according to Thy promises. Let the light of Thy Face shine upon me. Save me in Thy mercy; Lord, I shall not be confounded because I have called upon Thee.

*Prayer*
God all powerful and merciful, grant we entreat Thee, that venerating the Face of Thy Christ, disfigured in His Passion because of our sins, we may deserve to contemplate It eternally in the splendor of the glory of heaven. Through the same Jesus Christ. Amen.

## Ninth Day: The Holy Face on the Day of the Resurrection

At the commencement say: Lord, I desire to seek Thy Face; do not Thou keep me from It on account of my sins; do not separate Thy Holy Spirit from me. Let the light of Thy Face shine upon me; teach me in the way of Thy commandments.

On the day of His Resurrection, our Savior showed Himself several times to His holy mother, to the holy women and to His apostles. He came forth from the sepulchre, endowed with a spiritual and incorruptible life, shining with glory and immortality. In this state, that which above all attracted attention, was the beauty and triumphant splendor of His Holy Face.

I. *Glory of the Holy Face after the Resurrection*
Look at It yourself in spirit and with the eyes of faith. What celestial fire in Its eyes! What serenity on Its brow! What harmony in Its features! What a smiling and majestic countenance! During His Passion we beheld the Face of Jesus bleeding and full of grief; at this moment,

joys beam forth from It; It overflows with consolation in proportion to the sufferings and ignominies It has suffered. O adorable Face of my Savior, it is meet, that victorious now over death and sin, Thou should appear dazzling in strength and splendor. Show what Thou art; shed all around in softened majesty, the rays of honor and glory with which Thou art crowned; advance and reign over all hearts. *Prospere procede, et regna.*

## II. *Joy which It communicates*

The first time that the Apostles, when they were assembled together in the cenacle, saw the risen Face of their Divine Master, they were thrilled, says the Evangelist, with great joy; His smile, His sweet gaze, His kind and paternal words, the breath of His lips which He shed upon them, inundated them interiorly with a delicious peace which they had never before experienced.

What will be the joy of the elect, when they shall behold, in Its full splendor, without a cloud and without a shade, the glorious Face of the Incarnate Word. The sight will enable them to penetrate as through a most pure mirror, into the secrets of the Divine Essence, where they will find perfect beatitude and the sovereign good. They will see It even as It is, that most Holy Face, and they will become like to It; perfection of soul and of body will be theirs through the light of Its glory, with which they will feel themselves to be penetrated.

## III. *Its praises throughout eternity*

Lord, permit me "to behold Thee," permit me to see Thy Face in Its pure and real glory; when Thy glory shall thus appear to me, then my heart will be satiated with joy. Being then, says Saint Augustine, free and disengaged from all cares, "we shall see, we shall love, we shall praise." We shall see the Face of the Divine King so ravishing and so beautiful; we shall love the Face of the Man-God, of the Son of Mary so sweet and so amiable; we shall praise the Face of the Redeemer, so victorious and so powerful. We shall behold It forever, we shall love It without distaste; we shall praise It without weariness, with transports of ever reviving, ever renewed joy, forever and ever. Amen.

*Act of desire*
When shall I go and appear before the Face of my God? When shall I see Him face to Face?

*Virtue to be practiced*
Detach yourself, little by little, from the deceptive and passing joys of this world; seek the treasures of heaven where the risen Jesus awaits you.

*Spiritual bouquet*
May I expire thirsting with an ardent thirst to see the desirable Face of our Lord, Jesus Christ. (Last words of the Venerable Mr. Dupont.)

*Aspirations*
I have entreated Thy Face with my whole heart; have pity on me according to Thy promise. Make the light of Thy Face to shine upon me; save me in Thy mercy; Lord, I shall not be confounded, because I have called upon Thee.

*Prayer*
Almighty and merciful God, grant we beg of Thee, that whilst venerating the Face of Thy Christ, disfigured in the Passion because of our sins, we may merit to contemplate It eternally in the splendor of Its heavenly glory. Through the same Jesus Christ our Lord. Amen.

---

# Novena Prayer

O Lord Jesus Christ, in presenting ourselves before Thy adorable Face to ask of Thee the graces of which we stand most in need, we beseech Thee, above all, to give us that interior disposition of never refusing at any time to do what Thou requirest of us by Thy holy commandments and Thy Divine inspirations.

O good Jesus, who hast said: *"Ask and you shall receive, seek and you shall find, knock and it shall be opened to you,"* give us, O Lord, that faith which obtains all, or supply in us what may be deficient. Grant us, by the pure effect of Thy charity for Thy eternal glory, the graces which we need and which we look for from Thy infinite mercy, particularly (mention the favor desired). Amen.

Be merciful to us, O God, and reject not our prayers when, amid our afflictions, we call upon Thy Holy Name and seek with love and confidence Thy adorable Face. Amen.

---

# Novena to Our Lady of La Salette

O my Blessed Lady, Queen of Heaven, to thee and to thy sacred keeping, into the bosom of thy mercy, this day and every day until the hour of my death, I commend my body and soul; my every hope, joy, and sorrow, my life and the end of my life, I commend to thee, that every act may be according to thy will and that of thy Divine Son. Amen.

Nine "Hail Marys," with the following aspirations after each:

Our Lady of La Salette, refuge of sinners, our reconciler with God, pray without ceasing for your children who have recourse to thee. Amen.

Our Lady of La Salette, pray for us. Amen.

(For the connection between the devotion of the Holy Face and La Salette, see *The Life of Sister Saint-Pierre*.)

# Third Part
# LITANIES AND FORMS OF PRAYER

# Litany of the Holy Face
## Taken from the Scriptures

Kyrie, eleison.

Lord, have mercy on us.

*Christe, eleison.*

Christ, have mercy on us.

Kyrie, eleison.

Lord, have mercy on us.

Christe, audi nos.

Christ, hear us.

*Christe, exaudi nos.*

Christ, graciously hear us.

Pater de cœlis Deus, *miserere nobis.* *(This is the response until further noted.)*

God the Father, who art in heaven, *have mercy on us.* *(This is the response until further noted.)*

Fili redemptor mundi Deus,

God, the Son, Redeemer of the world,

Spiritus sancte Deus,

God, the Holy Ghost,

Sancta Trinitas unus Deus,

Holy Trinity, one God,

Jesu, in formam servi facte,

Jesus, who didst take on Thyself the form of a servant,

Jesu, cum hominibus conversate,

Jesus, who didst converse with men,

Jesu, super Jerusalem lacrymate,

Jesus, who didst weep over Jerusalem,

Jesu, cujus Facies resplenduit sicut sol,

Jesus, whose Face didst shine like the sun,

| | |
|---|---|
| Jesu, in Faciem tuam prostrate, | Jesus, who didst prostrate Thyself upon Thy Face, |
| Jesu, sanguineo sudore Faciem perfuse, | Jesus, whose Face was bathed in a bloody sweat, |
| Jesu, osculo a Juda tradite, | Jesus, betrayed by the kiss of Judas, |
| Jesu, a ministro alapa percusse, | Jesus, who didst receive a blow from the hand of a servant, |
| Jesu, Faciem velate, | Jesus, whose Face was veiled, |
| Jesu, in Faciem conspute, | Jesus, whose Face was covered in spittle, |
| Jesu, colaphis in Faciem cœse, | Jesus, whose Face was wounded with blows, |
| Jesu, spinis coronate, | Jesus, crowned with thorns, |
| Jesu, arundine caput percusse, | Jesus, whose head was struck with a reed, |
| Jesu, a Facie cujus silet omnis terra, | Jesus, whose Face commands a reverent silence over the whole earth, |
| Jesu, ostendens Faciem tuam super sanctuarium tuum, | Jesus, who dost show Thy Face above Thy sanctuary, |
| Jesu, ante cujus Faciem prosternimus preces, | Jesus, before whose Face we utter our prayers, |
| Jesu, a Facie cujus quærimus misericordiam, | Jesus, from whose Face we expect mercy, |

Jesu, a Facie cujus non sunt absconditæ viæ nostræ,

Jesus, from whose Face none of our doings are hidden,

Jesu, a Facie cujus montes defluxerunt,

Jesus, whose Face causes the mountains to melt away,

Jesu, cujus Facies non est aversa a conspuentibus,

Jesus, who didst not turn Thy Face away from spittings,

Jesu, cujus genæ vellentibus datæ,

Jesus, who didst present Thy cheeks to those who struck Thee,

Jesu, quasi leprosus reputate,

Jesus, who was looked upon as a leper,

Jesu, cujus videmus Faciem in jubilo,

Jesus, whose Face we behold with joy,

Jesu, cujus Vultus super facientes mala,

Jesus, whose eyes observe those who do evil,

Jesu, illuminans Vultum tuum super nos,

Jesus, who causest to shine upon us the light of Thy Face,

Jesu, cujus caput aurum optimum,

Jesus, whose head is of most pure gold,

Jesu, cujus labia distillant myrrham primam,

Jesus, whose lips distill an excellent myrrh,

Jesu, in cujus labiis diffusa est gratia,

Jesus, on whose lips grace is shed,

Jesu, in cujus conspectu cœli non sunt mundi,

Jesus, in whose eyes the heavens are not pure,

Jesu, ponens lacrymas nostras in conspectu tuo,

Jesus, whose eyes are witnesses of our tears,

| | |
|---|---|
| Jesu, in conspectu cujus exultant justi, | Jesus, whose Face rejoices the just, |
| Jesu, cujus oculi in pauperem respiciunt, | Jesus, whose eyes are attentive to the poor. |
| Jesu, cujus oculi super metuentes te, | Jesus, whose eyes are upon those that fear Thee, |
| Jesu, cujus oculi super justos, | Jesus, whose eyes behold the just, |
| Jesu, cujus oculi ad fideles terræ, | Jesus, whose eyes are upon the faithful on the earth, |
| Jesu, cujus oculi sicut columbæ, | Jesus, whose eyes resemble those of a dove, |
| Jesu, cujus oculi ut lampas ardens, | Jesus, whose eyes are like a burning lamp, |
| Jesu, cujus oculi tanquam flamma ignis, | Jesus, whose eyes are like a flaming fire, |
| Jesu, cujus oculi lucidiores sunt super solem, | Jesus, whose eyes are more brilliant than the sun, |
| Jesu, cujus oculi in diligentes te, | Jesus, whose eyes rest upon those that love Thee, |
| Propitius esto, parce nobis, Jesu. | Be merciful unto us, pardon us, Jesus. |
| Ab omni malo, *libera nos, Jesu. (This is the response until further noted.)* | From all evil, *deliver us, Jesus. (This is the response until further noted.)* |
| A subitanea et improvisa morte, | From sudden and unprovided death, |

|  |  |
|---|---|
| A damnatione perpetua, | From eternal damnation, |
| Per mysterium sanctæ Incarnationis tuæ, | By the mystery of Thy holy Incarnation, |
| Per gloriosam Transfigurationem tuam, | By Thy glorious Transfiguration, |
| Per lacrymas tuas, | By Thy tears, |
| Per sanguineum sudorem tuum, | By Thy bloody sweat, |
| Per alapas tuas, | By the blows Thou didst receive, |
| Per spineam coronam tuam, | By Thy crown of thorns, |
| In die judicii, | At the day of judgment, |
| Peccatores, te rogamus, audi nos. | We sinners beseech Thee, hear us. |
| Ut peccatis mortui, justitiæ vivamus, te rogamus, audi nos, | That being dead to sin, we may live to justice, we beseech Thee, hear us. |
| Ut te passo in carne eamdem cogitatione armemur, te rogamus, audi nos. | Having suffered in the flesh, arm us with the same thought, we beseech Thee, hear us. |
| Ut te crucifixum scire ante omnia studeamus, te rogamus, audi nos. | Grant that we may apply ourselves to know nothing, save Jesus crucified, we beseech Thee, hear us. |
| Ut sicut socii passionum, ita simus et consolationis, te rogamus, audi nos. | Having taken part in Thy sufferings grant us a share in Thy consolations, we beseech Thee, hear us. |

Ut te revelata Facie aliquando cerne possimus, te rogamus audi nos.

Grant us to see Thee, face to Face, in heaven, we beseech Thee, hear us.

Fili Dei, audi nos.

Son of God, hear us.

Agnus Dei, qui tollis peccata mundi, parce nobis, Jesu.

Lamb of God, who takest away the sins of the world, spare us, Jesus.

Agnus Dei, qui tollis peccata mundi, exaudi nos, Jesu.

Lamb of God, who takest away the sins of the world, graciously hear us, Jesus.

Agnus Dei, qui tollis peccata mundi, miserere nobis, Jesu.

Lamb of God who takest away the sins of the world, have mercy on us, Jesus.

## ANTIPHONA

## ANTIPHON

A Facie furoris tui, Deus, conturbata est omnis terra, sed tu, Domine Deus, miserere, et ne facias consummationem; ostende Faciem tuam, et salvi erimus.

O God, the whole earth is troubled when anger shows itself on Thy Face; but, O Lord our God, grant unto us mercy, and do not proceed to the last extreme; show us Thy Face and we shall be saved.

V. Exurgat Deus, et dissipentur inimici ejus.

V. Let God arise, and let His enemies be scattered.

R. Et fugiant omnes qui oderunt eum a Facie ejus.

R. And let all who hate Him, flee before His Face.

## OREMUS

## PRAYER

Concede, quæsumus, omnipotens et misericors Deus, ut qui Filii tui Domini nostri Jesu Christi Faciem propter peccata nostra in Passione deformatam veneramur, eamdem

Almighty and merciful God, grant, we beseech Thee, that whilst reverencing the Face of Thy Christ, disfigured in the Passion because of our sins, we

in cœlesti gloria fulgentem contemplari perpetuo mereamur. Per eumdem Dominum nostrum. Amen.

may merit to contemplate It, shining forever in celestial glory. Through the same Jesus Christ. Amen.

---

# Litany of the Holy Face

In Reparation for Blasphemies
Implored of God by the Adorable Face of His Son
For the Conversion of Blasphemers

Lord, have mercy on us.

*Christ, have mercy on us.*

Lord, have mercy on us.

Christ, hear us.

*Christ, graciously hear us.*

Holy Virgin Mary, *pray for us.*

O adorable Face, which was adorned with profound respect by Mary and Joseph when they saw Thee for the first time, *have mercy on us.*

O adorable Face, which in the Stable of Bethlehem didst ravish with joy the angels, the shepherds and the Magi, *have mercy on us.*

O adorable Face, which in the Temple didst transpierce with a dart of love the saintly old man Simeon and the prophetess Anna, *have mercy on us.*

O adorable Face, which was bathed in tears in Thy Holy Infancy, *have mercy on us.*

O adorable Face, which, when Thou didst appear in the Temple at twelve years of age, didst fill with admiration the Doctors of the law, *have mercy on us.*

O adorable Face, white with purity and ruddy with charity, *have mercy on us.*

O adorable Face, more beautiful than the sun, more lovely than the moon, more brilliant than the stars, *have mercy on us.*

O adorable Face, fresher than the roses of spring, *have mercy on us.*

O adorable Face, more precious than gold, silver, and diamonds, *have mercy on us.*

O adorable Face, whose charms are so ravishing, and whose grace is so attractive, *have mercy on us.*

O adorable Face, whose every feature is characterized by nobility, *have mercy on us.*

O adorable Face, contemplated by angels, *have mercy on us.*

O adorable Face sweet delectation of the saints, *have mercy on us.*

O adorable Face, masterpiece of the Holy Ghost, in which the Eternal Father is well pleased, *have mercy on us.*

O adorable Face delight of Mary and of Joseph, *have mercy on us.*

O adorable Face, ineffable mirror of the Divine perfections, *have mercy on us.*

O adorable Face, whose beauty is always ancient and always new, *have mercy on us.*

O adorable Face, which appeasest the wrath of God, *have mercy on us.*

O adorable Face, which makest the devils tremble, *have mercy on us.*

O adorable Face, treasure of graces and of blessings, *have mercy on us.*

O adorable Face, exposed in the desert to the inclemencies of the weather, *have mercy on us.*

O adorable Face, scorched with the heat of the sun and bathed with sweat in Thy journeys, *have mercy on us.*

O adorable Face, whose expression is all Divine, *have mercy on us.*

O adorable Face, whose modesty and sweetness attracted both the just and sinners, *have mercy on us.*

O adorable Face, which gavest a holy kiss to the little children, after having blessed them, *have mercy on us.*

O adorable Face, troubled and weeping at the tomb of Lazarus, *have mercy on us.*

O adorable Face, brilliant as the sun, and radiant with glory on Mount Tabor, *have mercy on us.*

O adorable Face, sorrowful at the sight of Jerusalem and shedding tears on that ungrateful city, *have mercy on us.*

O adorable Face, bowed to the earth, in the Garden of Olives, and covered with confusion for our sins, *have mercy on us.*

O adorable Face, bathed in a bloody sweat, *have mercy on us.*

O adorable Face, kissed by the traitor Judas, *have mercy on us.*

O adorable Face, whose sanctity and majesty smote the soldiers with fear and cast them to the ground, *have mercy on us.*

O adorable Face, struck by a vile servant, shamefully blindfolded, and profaned by the sacrilegious hands of Thine enemies, *have mercy on us.*

O adorable Face, defiled with spittle and bruised by innumerable buffets and blows, *have mercy on us.*

O adorable Face, whose Divine look wounded the heart of Peter, with a dart of sorrow and love, *have mercy on us.*

O adorable Face, humbled for us at the tribunals of Jerusalem, *have mercy on us.*

O adorable Face, which didst preserve Thy serenity when Pilate pronounced the fatal sentence, *have mercy on us.*

O adorable Face, covered with sweat and blood, and falling in the mire under the heavy weight of the Cross, *have mercy on us.*

O adorable Face, worthy of all our respect, veneration and worship, *have mercy on us.*

O adorable Face, wiped with a veil by a pious woman, on the road to Calvary, *have mercy on us.*

O adorable Face, raised on the instrument of the most shameful punishment, *have mercy on us.*

O adorable Face, whose brow was crowned with thorns, *have mercy on us.*

O adorable Face, whose eyes were filled with tears of blood, *have mercy on us.*

O adorable Face, into whose mouth was poured gall and vinegar, *have mercy on us.*

O adorable Face, whose hair and beard were plucked out by the executioners, *have mercy on us.*

O adorable Face, which was made like to that of a leper, *have mercy on us.*

O adorable Face, whose incomparable beauty was obscured under the dreadful cloud of the sins of the world, *have mercy on us.*

O adorable Face, covered with the sad shades of death, *have mercy on us.*

O adorable Face, washed and anointed by Mary and the holy women and wrapped in a shroud, *have mercy on us.*

O adorable Face, enclosed in the sepulchre, *have mercy on us.*

O adorable Face, all resplendent with glory and beauty on the day of the Resurrection, *have mercy on us.*

O adorable Face, all dazzling with light at the moment of Thy Ascension, *have mercy on us.*

O adorable Face, hidden in the Eucharist, *have mercy on us.*

O adorable Face, which will appear at the end of time in the clouds with great power and majesty, *have mercy on us.*

O adorable Face, which will cause sinners to tremble, *have mercy on us.*

O adorable Face, which will fill the just with joy for all eternity, *have mercy on us.*

Lamb of God, who takest away the sins of the world, *spare us, O Lord.*

Lamb of God, who takest away the sins of the world, *graciously hear us, O Lord.*

Lamb of God, who takest away the sins of the world, *have mercy on us, O Lord.*

---

## Litany to Obtain Humility

Lord, *have pity on me.*

O Jesus, meek and humble of Heart, *hear me.*

O Jesus, meek and humble of Heart, *graciously hear me.*

From the desire of being esteemed, *deliver me Jesus.*

From the desire of being loved, *deliver me Jesus.*

From the desire of being sought after, *deliver me Jesus.*

From the desire of being praised, *deliver me Jesus.*

From the desire of being honored, *deliver me Jesus.*

From the desire of being preferred, *deliver me Jesus.*

From the desire of being consulted, *deliver me Jesus.*

From the desire of being approved, *deliver me Jesus.*

From the desire of being humored, *deliver me Jesus.*

From the fear of being humbled, *deliver me Jesus.*

From the fear of being despised, *deliver me Jesus.*

From the fear of being rebuffed, *deliver me Jesus.*

From the fear of being calumniated, *deliver me Jesus.*

From the fear of being forgotten, *deliver me Jesus.*

From the fear of being mocked, *deliver me Jesus.*

From the fear of being scoffed at, *deliver me Jesus.*

From the fear of being insulted, *deliver me Jesus.*

O Mary, mother of the humble, *pray for me.*

Saint Joseph, protector of humble souls, *pray for me.*

Saint Michael, who was the first to tread pride under foot, *pray for me.*

All the just who are sanctified, above all, by the spirit of humility, *pray for me.*

## Invocation

O Jesus, whose first lesson was this:
*"Learn of Me, who am meek and humble of Heart,"*
teach me to become humble of heart like Thee. Amen.

———————

*By a Rescript dated 27th of January 1853, His Holiness Pope Pius IX grants to all who recite, with a contrite heart, these prayers in honor of the Holy Face of Jesus Christ an indulgence of a hundred days for each time; applicable to the souls in Purgatory.*

## Prayer I

I salute Thee, I adore Thee, and I love Thee, O Jesus, my Savior, outraged anew by blasphemers, and I offer Thee, through the heart of Thy blessed Mother, the worship of all the angels, and saints, as an incense and a perfume of sweet odor, most humbly beseeching Thee, by the virtue of Thy Sacred Face, to repair and renew in me and in all men Thy image disfigured by sin. Amen.

*Pater, Ave, Gloria*
*(Say one Our Father, one Hail Mary, one Glory Be)*

## Prayer II

I salute Thee, I adore Thee, and I love Thee, O adorable Face of Jesus, my Beloved, Noble Seal of the Divinity; with all the powers of my soul I apply myself to Thee, and most humbly pray Thee to imprint in us all the features of Thy Divine likeness. Amen.

## Prayer III

O adorable Face of my Jesus, so mercifully bowed down upon the tree of the Cross, on the day of Thy Passion for the salvation of men, now again, incline in Thy pity towards us poor sinners; cast upon us a look of compassion, and receive us to the kiss of peace. Amen.

Sacred Heart of Jesus, have mercy on us. Amen.

Sit nomen Domini benedictum! Amen.

# An Act of Honorable Amends

*To the most Holy Face of Our Lord Jesus Christ,*
*In Reparation for the Sins of Blasphemy,*
*Of the Profanation of Sundays,*
*And Other Impious Crimes against God and the Church.*
*To be Recited Publicly at the Monthly Meetings*
*Of the Archconfraternity*

Most holy and most adorable Face of the Savior, humbly prostrate in Thy presence, we present ourselves before Thee, in order, by a solemn act of faith and of piety, to render Thee the homage of veneration, praise, and love which is Thy due. We also desire to offer to Thee honorable amends and a public reparation for the sins, blasphemies, and sacrileges of which the present generation has rendered itself culpable towards the Divine Majesty, and which, in regard to Thee, O well beloved Face, renew the ignominies and the sufferings of Thy Passion.

It is with terror and profound affliction that we are witnesses of these monstrous crimes, which cannot fail to draw down upon society and upon our families, the malediction and the chastisements of Divine Justice. We see, in fact, all around us the law of the Lord and the authority of His Church despised and trodden under foot; His thrice Holy Name denied or blasphemed, the Sunday which He has reserved for His worship, publicly profaned; His altars and His offices forsaken for criminal or frivolous pleasures. Impious sectarians attack all that is sacred and religious. But it is, above all, the Divinity of Christ, the Son of the living God; it is the Incarnate Word; it is the august Face and the Crucifix which they attack with the greatest fury; the spit and the blows of the Passion are renewed by the insults and the outrages which their hatred dares, in every possible manner to inflict upon Thee, O Face full of sweetness and of love.

153

Pardon, a thousand times pardon, for all these crimes! May we make amends for them by our humble supplications and the fervor of our homage! But, guilty and sinners as we are, what can we offer the Eternal Father in order to appease His just anger, if it be not Thyself, O sorrowful Face, who has deigned to make Thyself our advocate and our victim? Supply what may be wanting in us by Thy satisfactions and Thy merits.

Heavenly Father, we entreat Thee, "Look on the Face of Thy Christ." Behold the wounds which disfigure It, the tears which escape from Its sunken eyes; the sweat with which It is bathed; the blood which flows in streams down Its profaned and wounded cheeks. Behold also Its invincible patience, Its unalterable gentleness, Its infinite tenderness and Its merciful goodness towards sinners. This Holy Face is turned towards Thee, and before exhaling Its last sigh, lovingly inclined upon the Cross, It implores Thee in favor of those who curse and outrage It. O Father, listen to that suppliant cry, permit Thyself to be touched; have pity on us and pardon us. Grant, moreover, that in the presence of this Divine Face, equally formidable and powerful, the enemies of Thy Name may take flight and disappear; that they may be converted and live!

(Aspirations and invocations which the people repeat - alternating after the celebrant)

May the most adorable Name of God be adored forever and ever!

May the Holy Day of the Lord be sanctified by all men!

May the Holy Face of Jesus be loved by every heart!

May the Holy Church, our Mother, be exalted throughout the whole earth!

May our Holy Father the Pope, Vicar of Jesus Christ, be venerated by all people!

Saint Peter, Prince of the Apostles, and Patron of the Archconfraternity, pray for us.

Lord, show us Thy Face, and we shall be saved.

Amen!

Amen!

---

## Consecration to the Holy Face

For the Use of the Members
Of the Archconfraternity

I (N. N.), in order to give still greater increase to the glory of Jesus, dying for our salvation upon the Cross; in order to correspond to the merciful love with which His Holy Face is animated towards poor sinners, and in order to repair the outrages which the frightful crimes of the present day inflict upon His august Face, the most pure mirror of the Divine Majesty, I associate myself, fully and freely, to the faithful received into this pious Archconfraternity; I desire to participate in the indulgences with which it is enriched and in the good works practiced therein, as well for the expiation of my sins as for the solace of souls suffering in Purgatory. Amiable Redeemer, most sweet Jesus, hide in the secret of Thy Face all the members of this association; may they there find shelter from the seductions of the world, and the snares of Satan; grant that, faithfully keeping all the precepts of Thy law and fulfilling the special duties of their state, they may be more and more inflamed with zeal for reparation, and with the flames of Thy Divine love.

---

# Consecration of Ourselves

To the Holy Face

O adorable Face of my Jesus, humbly prostrate in Thy Divine presence, I desire to consecrate myself wholly to Thee and henceforth to live only for Thee. Why have I not at my disposal, the hearts of all creatures, in order to offer them up as a holocaust to Thee? Alas! O well beloved Face, I have only my own, unworthy as it is of Thy attention and often rebelling against the movements of Thy grace; nevertheless, I give it to Thee, my poor heart, and I consecrate it to Thee, in order that, from this moment and during all the days of my life, it may be inflamed with the holy ardor of Thy Divine love. Purify it, warm it with the blessed rays of Thy eternal light, so that I may henceforth exclaim with the prophet king: "Lord, the light of Thy Face is engraved upon us; Thou hast caused joy to spring forth in my heart." (Ps. IV, 7.)

I offer Thee then this day, deliberately and with great joy, the sacrifice of all the delights which may be offered me on earth. Accept, O adorable Face, O Thou whom I love more than aught else in the world, accept the homage of myself, which I present to Thee at this moment. I thrill with gladness and with love, whilst thus consecrating to Thee the whole of my being. Yes, I offer and consecrate to Thee my heart, my body, my soul, my spirit, and my life; my heart, to love only Thee, O beauty ever ancient and ever new; my body, to serve as an instrument of reparation and of all that belongs to Thy glory; my soul, to reflect unceasingly the image of Thy different graces; my spirit, to think only upon Thee, and upon all that will tend to spread devotion to Thee; my life, my whole life, in order that it may be penetrated with Thy sweet memory, and filled with actions worthy of Thy Name, so that I may one day merit that life eternal, in which, according to the expression of Thy apostle, I may contemplate Thee, no longer as in an enigma and through a mirror, but face to Face, and as Thou art.

Whilst waiting until this supreme grace shall be accorded to me, O Holy Face of Jesus, make me walk here below in the light of Thy benign eyes, that when I shall appear before Thee, Thou mayest name me by my name, Thou mayest kiss me with the kiss of Thy mouth, and Thou mayest introduce me into the immortal society of the blessed who are occupied without ceasing in contemplating Thee, praising Thee, adoring Thee, and eternally singing Thy mercies. Amen.

## Act of Love to the Holy Face

Adorable Face of my Jesus, my only love, my light and my life, grant that I may see no one except Thee, that I may know no one except Thee, that I may love Thee alone, that I may live with Thee, of Thee, by Thee, and for Thee. Amen.

## Act of Reparation

O well beloved Face of Jesus! Humbly prostrate in Thy presence, we adore Thee for those who refuse to adore Thee; we love Thee and we pray to Thee, for those who refuse to love Thee and who blaspheme Thee. Unhappy madmen! If they knew Thee better, with what repentance and confusion would they turn towards Thee, how they would seek to make compensation to Thee for all which Thou hast suffered for them!

The audacity of impiety has increased, a clamor issuing from hell has been raised for the purpose of denying Thy Divinity and outraging the Church, a diabolical pact has been formed against God and against His Christ. It is for us, faithful Christians, to close our ranks under the banner of the Holy Face, to multiply our phalanx of reparation, to offer to Jesus, as did Veronica, the veil of our love and of our veneration. We need no longer, O merciful Face, envy the happiness of that heroic woman; by a redoublement of faith, of fervor and of zeal, we may, like her, wipe Thy tears away, staunch Thy blood, and solace Thy sufferings.

O Sacred Face! Permit us to weep over the crimes of our erring brethren. Enable us to repair, by our sighs and our love, the attempts made against Thy Divinity. Ah! we attest that Divinity which has its habitation in Thee, with our whole heart; and if, in order to maintain it, the sacrifice of our life were necessary, we would joyously make an offering of it to Thee.

O well beloved Face! let Thy eyes of mercy and compassion rest upon us. Pardon this deicidal century, which refuses to bend its proud head to Thy sovereign authority. Dissipate, by the light of Thy presence, the darkness which envelops us, and which, if it were not for Thee, would drag us down into the still deeper darkness of death. Convert the blasphemers, bring back to the light of faith the ignorant and incredulous, console the just, strengthen the weak, and grant that all, with one accent of faith and love, may exclaim with the Prophet: "Now, Lord, we follow Thee with our whole heart, we fear Thee and we seek after Thy adorable Face." (Dan. III, 41.)

---

# Prayer of Saint Augustine

I present myself before Thy Holy Face, O my Savior, laden with my sins and the penalties which they have brought upon me. My sufferings are far less than what I deserve, for although I am conscious of the just punishment of my sins, I do not, on that account, cease to commit fresh ones every day. I am bowed down under Thy scourges, and I do not become better; my heart is full of bitterness, and my obstinacy in doing evil, remains forever the same. My life passes away in misery, and I do not correct myself. When Thou chastisest me, I make the best promises in the world; as soon as Thou liftest up Thy hand, I forget all that I promised Thee.

I make to Thee, O God! a sincere confession of my sins; I protest in Thy presence, that if Thou do not show mercy upon me, I shall be in danger of perishing utterly. Grant me, my Savior, what I beg of Thee, although I do not deserve it, since Thou hast out of Thy goodness drawn me out of nothingness to put me into a state wherein I can pray to Thee. Amen.

---

# Act of Reparation

For all the Outrages which Jesus Christ
Has Suffered in His Holy Face

I adore Thee, and I praise Thee, O my Divine Jesus, Son of the living God, for all the outrages Thou hast endured for me, who am the most miserable of Thy creatures, in all the sacred members of Thy body, but especially in the most noble part of Thyself, that is to say, in Thy Face. I salute Thee, amiable Face, wounded with blows and scourges, soiled with spittle and disfigured by the evil treatment which the impious caused Thee to suffer. I salute Thee, O lovely eyes, all bathed in the tears shed for our salvation. I salute Thee, sacred ears, tormented by an infinity of blasphemies, injuries and shameful mockings. I salute Thee, O holy mouth, filled with grace and sweetness towards sinners, and made to drink of vinegar and gall. In reparation for all these ignominies, I offer Thee all the homage which has been rendered Thee in the holy place, where Thou hast willed to be honored by the special devotion, to which I unite myself with my whole heart. Amen.

----

## Act of Admiration
When Contemplating the Holy Face

O Lord! wherefore hast Thou given us an imprint of Thy Holy Face, in the sad and pitiful state of Thy Passion? Why didst not Thou rather portray It with those sweet traits which enrapture all hearts, or with the dazzling splendor with which It was clothed on the day of Thy glorious Transfiguration? It seems to me as though Thy admirable beauty would have caused us to feel more delight in Thee and more love for Thee, and that the majesty of Thy Face would have inspired us with more reverence! Would not Thy august brow have worn a more gracious aspect, if It had been adorned with a crown of light, or with a diadem, than with only a circlet bristling with thorns? But no, Divine Savior! Thy Face in Its dazzling glory is reserved to be forever the object of the joy of the blessed in Paradise, but Thy Face, disfigured by the ignominy of Thy Passion, ought to be the ordinary subject of our veneration here below, and the model for our imitation. We shall every day understand that nothing is is more efficacious for enkindling Thy love in our hearts, for animating us to the practice of all kinds of virtues, and for making us avoid sin. Grant us then the grace, O amiable Savior, so to compassionate Thy sufferings upon earth, that we may hereafter merit to participate in Thy triumph in heaven. Amen.

———————

## Prayer
To Entreat for the Triumph of the Church
By Means of the Holy Face
Taken from the Scriptures
(Dan., IX, 13, 14, 17, 18, 19)

Lord, we have not entreated Thy Face that we might turn from our iniquities, and think on Thy truth. And the Lord hath watched upon the evil, and hath brought it upon us: the Lord our God is just in all His works which He hath done: for we have not hearkened to His voice. Now, therefore, O our God, hear the supplication of Thy servant, and his prayers: and show Thy Face upon Thy sanctuary which is desolate, for Thy own sake. Incline, O my God, Thy ear, and hear; open Thy eyes, and see our desolation, and the city upon which Thy Name is called: for it is not for our justifications that we present our prayers before Thy Face, but for the multitude of Thy tender mercies. O Lord, hear: O Lord, be appeased: hearken and do: delay not for Thy own sake, O my God: because Thy Name is invoked upon Thy city, and upon Thy people. But there is no one who invokes this powerful Name; there is none who lifts himself up to Thee, and who endeavors by his supplications to restrain the effects of Thy anger. Therefore, Thou hast turned away Thy Face from us, and Thou hast bruised us under the weight of our iniquities. Lord, look upon us in pity, keep no longer silent, and do not leave us prey to such sharp sorrows. O if

Thou wouldst open the heavens and come down! The mountains would tremble before Thy Face. Thy Name would be known amongst Thy enemies, the nations would be struck with terror. Cast Thy eyes upon us, and remember that we are Thy people. Amen.

---

# Prayers to the Holy Face

Extracted from the Writings of the Venerable Mr. Dupont*

### I. Elevation of the Heart to Jesus for the Outrages Offered to His Holy Face

Who can say how greatly our Divine Savior is offended by blasphemy! Placed as He is between His Father and sinners, the outrages which cannot rise as high as heaven fall in a rain of ignominy upon His Divine Face.

O Jesus! Thou must be God, since Thou art patient enough still to remain in our midst! If Thou couldst but find a sufficiency of friends possessed of the courage to interpose between Thee and the miserable people who conduct Thee back to Calvary!

But, as on the day of Thy Passion, Thou art alone amongst Thy enemies. Alas! do we not run the risk of losing all? If illuminated by the light of faith which enables us to see what Thou art O Jesus, do we not at least imitate the witness of Thy death in their lively contrition? If it be not given to all of us to weep like Saint Peter, grant that we may strike our breasts like the populace which returned to Jerusalem distracted with grief at recognizing the proof of a deicide.

O Holy Ghost! Thou who didst enlighten the apostles and didst reanimate their courage so energetically, inflame us with Thy Divine fire, and put into our mouths burning words after having enkindled in our hearts the fire of Thy love. So that becoming new men, we may feel ourselves possessed of sufficient courage to throw ourselves into the midst of the ranks of the enemy. Give us grace to vanquish them and to oblige them to love Thee.

## II. Prayer of Reparation to the Holy Face

Lord Jesus! after having contemplated Thy features, disfigured by grief; after having meditated upon Thy Passion with compunction and love, how can our hearts help being inflamed with a holy hatred of sin, which even now, still outrages Thy adorable Face? But, not allowing ourselves to be content with mere compassion, give us grace to follow Thee so closely on this new Calvary, that the opprobrium destined for Thee may rebound upon us, O Jesus, and that we may at least have some small share in the expiation of sin. Amen.

## III. Offering of the Holy Face to the Eternal Father

Almighty God, Eternal Father, contemplate the Face of Thy Son, our Lord Jesus Christ. We present It to Thee with confidence for the glory of Thy Holy Name, for the exaltation of Thy holy Church, and for the salvation of the world. Most merciful Advocate, He opens His mouth to plead our cause; listen to His cries, behold His tears, O my God, and Thou wilt be touched with compassion towards the poor sinners who ask of Thee grace and mercy. Amen.

## IV. Prayer to the Holy Face for the Feast of the Dedication

O God! who on the day of the dedication of the Temple, in an effusion of merciful goodness, didst promise to listen, from the height of heaven, to those who should invoke Thy Name, and who should seek Thy Face; grant to the associates of the Work of Reparation of blasphemy, prostrate before Thy adorable Face, the graces of which they have need in order to efficaciously work out their own salvation and to convert blasphemers, for whom Thy Holy Name is invoked with confidence. Thou, who livest and reignest forever and ever. Amen.

*(Office of the Dedication.)*

## V. Aspiration towards the Glorious Face of Our Lord

Lord! at the thought of the blessings which the vision of Thy Face could not but shed upon the earth, the Prophet exclaims in a holy transport: "Happy the people who joyfully declare Thy glory..." O Lord! permit us to aspire to this Divine discipline, grant us to walk in the light of Thy Face, and to rejoice in the praises which we will offer by day and night to Thy Holy Name.

(Ps. LXXXVIII, 15, 16, 17.)

*\*Note: During the Pontificate of Pope Pius XII, Mr. Leo Dupont was declared Venerable. The term "Venerable" has thus been added since he was referred to as only "Mr. Dupont" in the original manuals.*

---

# Prayers of the Venerable Mr. Dupont

O Savior Jesus! at the sight of Thy most Holy Face, disfigured by grief, and at the sight of Thy Sacred Heart so full of love, I cry out with Saint Augustine: Lord Jesus, impress upon my heart Thy sacred wounds, that I may read therein at once Thy sorrow and Thy love; Thy sorrow, in order to suffer every affliction for Thee; Thy love, in order to despise every other love except Thee. Amen.

Lord Jesus! when presenting ourselves before Thy adorable Face to entreat Thee for the graces of which we have need, we beseech Thee, above all things, to order the interior dispositions of our hearts, that we may never refuse Thee what Thou Thyself askest of us every day through Thy holy commandments and by Thy Divine inspirations. Amen.

O good Jesus, who hast said: *"Ask, and you shall receive; seek, and you shall find; knock, and it shall be opened to you,"* give us, if it be Thy will, the faith which supplies all, or else supply Thyself all that is wanting in us of faith; grant us, by the sole effect of Thy charity and for Thy eternal glory, the graces of which we stand in need and which we look for from Thine infinite mercy. Amen.

Be merciful to us, O my God! do not reject our prayers, when, in the midst of our afflictions, we call upon Thy Holy Name and seek with love and confidence Thy adorable Face. Amen.

We thank Thee, O Lord, for all Thy benefits, and we entreat Thee to engrave in our hearts feelings of love and of gratitude, putting upon our lips songs of thanksgiving for Thy eternal praise. Amen.

---

# Formulæ

Which Venerable Mr. Dupont use when Anointing
The Sick with Oil

*Unctiones sanitatis conficiat et perficiat ipse Deus. In nomine Patri, etc.*

*In English.* May the Lord Himself deign, together with us, to anoint this sick person and to restore him to health. In the name of the Father, etc.

*Or*: May the Holy Names of Jesus, of Mary and of Joseph be known, blessed and glorified throughout the whole earth. Amen.

*Or*: Crux sacra, sit tibi lux et sanitas, benedictio et voluntas Domini nostri Jesu Christi. Amen.

---

# Act of Resignation for the Sick*

Resolution to Confess Our Sins before Asking for a Cure

Thy word, Lord Jesus, granted to the happy paralytic, in the Gospel, the remission of his sins, before Thou saidst to him: *"Arise."* (Mark, II, 2.) Therefore I, a miserable sinner, knowing and firmly believing, that Thou hast given to Thy priests power to remit sins, resolve to descend at once into the sacred bath of penitence, before calling upon the eyes of Thy mercy, to look upon my corporal infirmities. Then submitting myself, heart and soul, to Thy most holy will, I will await, in peace, O Lord, the accomplishment of my wishes here on earth, with the hope of contemplating, blessing, and praising Thy adorable Face forever and ever in heaven. Amen.

*(Recommended by the Venerable Mr. Dupont.)*
*(Imprimatur: ✚ N. J. Perché, Archbishop of New Orleans from 1870-1883.)

# Cry of Love

Pardon, pardon, O my God, for the innumerable souls which are being lost, every day, around us. The devil rushes forth from the abyss, hurrying to make horrible conquests; he excites the infernal band; he exclaims: "Souls! Souls! Let us hasten to ruin souls!" And souls fall like autumn leaves into the eternal abyss.

We also, O my God, we will cry: "Souls! Souls!" We must have souls, wherewith to acquit the debt of gratitude we have contracted towards Thee; we ask them of Thee by the wounds of Jesus, our Savior. These adorable wounds cry out to Thee like so many powerful prayers. The King crowned with thorns demands subjects torn from the devil; we ask them from Thee, together with Him and by Him, for Thy greater glory, and by the intercession of the most holy Virgin Mary, conceived without sin. Amen.

---

# Prayer of Pope Pius IX

O my Jesus! cast upon us a look of mercy; turn Thy Face towards each one of us, even as Thou didst turn to Veronica, not that we may see It with the eyes of our body, for we do not deserve to do so, but turn It towards our hearts, that being sustained by Thee, we may ever draw from that powerful source, the vigor necessary to enable us to wage the combats we have to undergo.

*(Audience given to three parishes of Rome, 10 March 1872. This prayer was indulged by several French bishops.)*

---

# Aspirations

Eternal Father, we offer Thee the adorable Face of Thy well beloved Son for the honor and glory of Thy Holy Name and for the salvation of all men. (Sister Marie de Saint-Pierre.)

May I expire, burning with an ardent thirst to see the desirable Face of Our Lord Jesus Christ! (*Prayer of Saint Edme (Edmund), which Mr. Dupont often repeated during the latter portion of his life.*)

(With approbation of the Archbishop of Tours, dated August 26, 1876.)

————

# Praises of the Holy Face

Blessed be Jesus!

Blessed be the Holy Face of Jesus!

Blessed be the Holy Face in the majesty and beauty of Its heavenly features!

Blessed be the Holy Face through the words which issued from Its Divine mouth!

Blessed be the Holy Face through all the glances which escaped from Its adorable eyes!

Blessed be the Holy Face in the Transfiguration of Tabor!

Blessed be the Holy Face in the fatigues of Its apostolate!

Blessed be the Holy Face in the bloody sweat of the agony!

Blessed be the Holy Face in the humiliations of the Passion!

Blessed be the Holy Face in the sufferings of death!

Blessed be the Holy Face in the splendor of the Resurrection!

Blessed be the Holy Face in the glory of light eternal!

————

# Benediction of Saint Francis of Assisi

Through the Holy Face
(Blessing of the High-Priest Aaron)

Benedicat tibi Dominus et custodiat te;
Ostendat Dominus Faciem suam tibi et misereatur tui;
Convertat Dominus vultum suum ad te et det tibi pacem.

*The Lord bless thee, and keep thee;*
*The Lord show His Face to thee, and have mercy on thee;*
*The Lord turn His countenance towards thee, and give thee*
*peace. (Numbers VI, 24-26)*

---

# Quarantine of Saint Louis

Union of Prayers
From 16th of July to the 25th of August (inclusive
For the Necessities of the Church and of the State

## MAY GOD ARISE AND MAY HIS ENEMIES BE SCATTERED!

Three Pater Nosters, three Ave Marias, three Gloria Patris.

Saint Michael and all the holy angels, pray and fight for us!

Saint Peter and all the holy apostles, intercede for us!

St. Ignatius, St. Teresa and all the inhabitants of the
heavenly Jerusalem, pray for us!

*Aspirations During the Day*

May Thy Name, O Lord, be known and blessed at all times,
and in all places! Holy Mary, reign over us, thou and thy
Son Jesus!!! Amen.

---

# Divine Praises

Praises to the Holy Name of God, Jesus Christ, and Mary
In Reparation for Blasphemies

Blessed be God.
Blessed be His Holy Name.
Blessed be Jesus Christ, true God and true man.
Blessed be the Name of Jesus.
Blessed be His Most Sacred Heart.*
Blessed be His Most Precious Blood.*
Blessed be Jesus in the Most Holy Sacrament of the Altar.
Blessed be the Holy Ghost, the Paraclete.*
Blessed be the great Mother of God, Mary most Holy.
Blessed be her Holy and Immaculate Conception.
Blessed be her Glorious Assumption.*
Blessed be the name of Mary, Virgin and Mother.
Blessed be Saint Joseph her most chaste spouse.*
Blessed be God in His Angels and in His Saints.

Indulgence of a year each time;
plenary once a month with the usual conditions.
(Rescripts of Pius VII, 23rd of July 1801,
and of Pius IX, 8th of August 1847.)

*These five praises were not included in the prayer
as printed in the original manuals, however they are part of
the Divine Praises, and have been added for completeness.

---

# The Golden Arrow

Act of Praises for the Reparation of Blasphemies
Against the Holy Name of God
Dictated by Our Lord to Sister Marie de Saint-Pierre

May the most Holy, most Sacred, most Adorable, most Incomprehensible and Ineffable Name of God, be forever praised, blessed, loved, adored and glorified, in heaven, on earth and in hell, by all the creatures of God, and by the Sacred Heart of Our Lord Jesus Christ in the most Holy Sacrament of the Altar. Amen.

(40 days indulgence may be gained, by saying this act of praise in honor of the three Persons of the Blessed Trinity *three times*.)

✝ CHARLES, Archbishop of Tours, Good Friday, 15th of April 1881.

## Another version of the Golden Arrow:*

May the most Holy, most Sacred, most Adorable, most Incomprehensible and Unutterable Name of God be forever praised, blessed, loved, adored, and glorified in heaven, on earth, and in the hells, by all the creatures of God and by the Sacred Heart of our Lord Jesus Christ in the Most Holy Sacrament of the Altar. Amen.

*(This act of praise, in honor of the three Persons of the Holy Trinity, is to be repeated three times.)*

**\*The version above was not printed in the 1885 and 1887 manuals. However in some versions of the Life of Sister Marie de Saint-Pierre, she is quoted as saying that Our Lord specifically used the plural form of hell ("in the hells").**

Note (From the 1887 *Manual of the Archconfraternity of the Holy Face*):

I.  HISTORICAL RECITAL. — The Sister (Marie de Saint-Pierre) says in her writings: "Our Lord opened to me His Heart, and I heard these words: *My name is everywhere blasphemed, even children blaspheme it.*

"Then He made me understand how painfully this frightful sin wounded His Divine Heart, even more than any other; for, by blasphemy, the sinner curses Him to His Face, attacks Him openly, annihilates the Redemption, and pronounces himself his own condemnation and judgment. Blasphemy is like a poisoned arrow which continually wounds His Heart, and He told me He would give me a golden arrow wherewith to wound It sweetly, and to heal the malicious wounds inflicted on Him by sinners.

"This is the form of praise which He indicated to me, in spite of my great unworthiness, for the reparation of blasphemies against His Holy Name, and which He gave me, as a golden arrow, assuring me that each time I should say it, I should wound His Heart with a wound of love. He added: *Pay attention to this favor, for I will ask an account of it from you.* At that moment it seemed to me as though I saw, coming forth from the Sacred Heart of Jesus, wounded by this golden arrow, torrents of graces for the conversion of sinners."

Mr. Dupont, the holy man of Tours, had a great devotion for the *golden arrow*, and looked upon it as the basis of works of reparation.

II.  THEOLOGICAL AND MORAL EXPLANATION. — The words, *and in hell*, need not astonish us. They recall those of Saint Paul: "At the name of Jesus let every knee bow, in heaven, on earth, and in hell." The most rigorous theology approves of the sense. Recently (10 March 1886) a man of

God, a Religious very much looked up to in his Order and a learned theologian, gave us, in addition, this just and beautiful explanation:

"Men upon earth, the souls in purgatory, and the elect in heaven may transport themselves in spirit into hell, and there praise, bless, love, adore, and glorify the most Holy Name of God. They can there specially love and praise His Justice. In order to love and praise God anywhere, it is not necessary to be there physically and substantially; it suffices that God should be there and that we should be there ourselves through love, and in thought. In one of his psalms the Psalmist says to his soul: 'In all places of His dominion, bless the Lord, O my soul,' and yet the Psalmist could not physically be in all places of God's dominion; but, according to philosophers, the soul is more in what it loves, than in what it animates."

"Find," says St. Augustine (*Enar. in Ps.* CII, 22), "a place where God is not, and where He is not blessed. *Sic ubique est, ut ubique benedicatur.*"

When giving us this explanation, the eminent Religious added: "As a historian, be resolute in upholding a text which bears all the characters of a real revelation. As for me, I love and admire the *Golden Arrow* more and more every day, and the prayer seems to me incomparable."

# Fourth Part
# EXERCISES OF DEVOTION
# AND DIFFERENT PRACTICES

# Stations of the Cross of the Holy Face
## Preparatory Prayer

O adorable Face of my Jesus, humbly prostrate in Thy presence, I prepare myself to contemplate Thee upon the path of Calvary, in the sufferings and humiliations which Thou hast endured for my sins. Inspire me with the same sentiments of faith, of love, and of compassion, with which Our Lady of Sorrows, and the pious Veronica were overwhelmed. I purpose to compensate Thee, in as much as in me lies, for the sufferings and outrages which are caused Thee every day by blasphemers against Thy Name and by the sinners who profane Sunday. Why cannot I, O Jesus, mingle my tears with Thine, and give Thee the whole of my blood in expiation for so many crimes? Penetrate me, at least, with the thoughts of Thy Divine Heart; cast upon my soul the light of Thy countenance, that, touched with the unction of Thy Spirit, it may draw forth abundantly treasures of grace and salvation, from out Thy sacred wounds.

## I
## Jesus is Condemned to Death

The sentence pronounced against our Savior was as unjust as it was ignominious. He was led as a criminal before a pagan judge, He, the King of Heaven, the Sovereign Judge of Angels and of men! He was condemned to suffer the penalty of death as a factious man and a blasphemer, He who was innocence and goodness itself. Let us admire His perfect submission. According to Sister Saint-Pierre, when Pilate pronounced this terrible sentence, the Face of Jesus preserved the serenity habitual to It, and lost nothing of Its calm and sweetness. His adorable Face did not blush, because He knew that He was accomplishing the will of His Father, and that by submitting to this unjust death, He would obtain our salvation.

O Jesus! grant that whilst practicing my faith I may never blush at Thy doctrine nor at Thy example, but that I may perform my duties with a calm and serene countenance, and in the peace of a good conscience, being unmoved by mockery, and not fearing the injustice of those who can kill the body but who can do nothing to the soul, so that hereafter, when I appear before Thy tribunal, Thou mayst not need to blush for me before the angels, and that I may be admitted into the number of Thy elect.

## II
## Jesus is Laden with His Cross

A double burden is laid on Jesus; first the heavy wood of His Cross, the instrument of His punishment, with which His executioners brutally load His shoulders, and secondly the ignominious burden of our iniquities, which He takes upon Himself in order to expiate them. The latter Cross is the more painful; He feels the grief and the shame of it; His Face is sorrowfully bowed down, like that of a man in disgrace, laden with maledictions, condemned to bear a weight of ignominy. He blushes at the stigma inflicted on Him by the crimes with which He is covered. But as a great act of reparation is in question and one in which the glory of His Father and our salvation are concerned, He lovingly accepts it all.

It is just, O Jesus! that I should bear the weight and the shame of my sins. Give me a contrite and humble heart; that interior disposition which the Prophet asked of Thee, and which Thou hast promised not to reject; that, appropriating to myself the merits of Thy adorable Face, I may make amends for the contempt I have shown for Thy law, and the shame my sins have caused Thee.

# III
## Jesus Falls Beneath the Weight of His Cross

The Holy Face has already endured many outrages and sufferings. Here, it is a fresh outrage which is inflicted upon It: Jesus falls upon the ground, He wounds Himself by the violence of His fall, and when He rises, His august Face is soiled with mud, with dust and with blood, which excites the mocking laughter of the crowd, and the raillery of His enemies.

O Jesus! Thou dost thus expiate my weakness, my want of courage in bearing my cross, my criminal attachment to the pleasures and to the goods of this world, which are nothing more than a little mud and vile dust. Make me stronger, more mortified, more generous, in order that I may aspire more and more to the riches of grace and the eternal treasures which Thou dost promise me in heaven.

# IV
## Jesus Meets His Holy Mother

Our blessed Lady of Dolors here finds herself face to Face with the Man of Sorrows. The mother gazes on the Face of her Son. What an aspect it bears! No one else could have recognized Jesus! His beautiful and radiant Face is obscured, soiled, and like to that of a leper! The sight pierces the heart of the Blessed Virgin. She falls into the arms of the holy women who accompany her. On His side, Jesus has recognized His mother; their eyes have met. Those two souls, already so closely united, have found in their common anguish a more intense and still stronger element of attraction; they have embraced, clinging together as though they had been fused into one to offer one and the same sacrifice, and to form but one and the same victim.

O Jesus! O Mary! admit me into the community of Thy sacrifice. May I contemplate Thee! May I love Thee! May I imitate Thee! May I share in Thy sentiments and in Thy inmost feelings! May I never be separated from Thy trials, and Thy sufferings here below, in order that I may merit to be united with Thee forever, and to see Thee face to Face in eternity!

## V

## The Cyrenean Helps Jesus to Carry His Cross

A pious stranger, who was passing by, comes to the aid of Jesus Christ. This unexpected auxiliary is not allowed to be without a recompense.

To show him how grateful this service is to His Heart, Jesus turns from time to time towards him, and shows him His Face. Then, from that kind and grateful Face issues a ray of light, which touches the heart of the Cyrenean, enlightens him, inflames him, and strengthens him in the labor of love, which he has undertaken.

O Jesus! behold me ready to follow Thee, and to serve Thee. What obstacle could avail to hinder me?...the seductions of hell?...the mockery of the world?...the murmurs of the flesh and of the senses?...the attractions of pleasure?...Ah! to serve Thee is to reign. To aid Thee in Thy work of reparation is a happiness and a glory. Only do Thou look upon me. One of Thy glances, falling from Thy adorable Face on the face of my poor soul, is worth more to me than an empire; it is a ray of celestial joy, it is Paradise itself.

# VI
## A Pious Woman Wipes the Face of Jesus

This courageous woman is a perfect pattern for the adorers of the outraged Face of Jesus. See how resolutely she advances, with a firm and intrepid heart, in spite of the disdain of the crowd and the brutality of the executioners. Arrived in the proximity of the Savior, in presence of that obscured and disfigured Face, of which she nevertheless, perceives the majesty and Divine beauty, she feels herself to be moved with compassion, respect and love. Detaching the soft white veil made of fine Egyptian linen, which covers her face, she applies it to, and spreads it gently over the Face of Christ; she wipes It and solaces It; it is more than a homage which she renders It, it is a real service which soothes Its sufferings, refreshes It and revivifies It. We know what the reward was which Jesus granted her. He left her, when she retired from Him, that precious impression of His Face possessed by the Vatican and venerated by the whole world, that veil of which we here possess an authentic facsimile, and which will forever be the object of a sacred devotion.

O Jesus! I envy the happiness of that heroic woman. Grant that I may procure for Thee the like homage of reparation. But what Thou didst for Veronica will not suffice for me. Grant me, in addition, that Thy Divine features may be impressed upon my soul, disfigured and obscured with sin; render to it its first innocence and all the splendor of Thy grace.

# VII
## Jesus Falls on the Ground a Second Time

Jesus, like to a victim bearing the wood for the sacrifice, is a prey to weakness and exhaustion. He falls down a second time, with His Face to the ground, being unable to rise; He remains unaided stretched out, powerless, and given up to the tender mercy of His executioners, who furious and impatient, raise Him up again, while inflicting heavy blows upon Him. His meek and modest Face is not spared; they find a cruel pleasure in adding fresh wounds to It and making It bleed still more.

Behold the image of the blasphemer and the impious who make game of the seeming weakness of the Church, who outrage it in its doctrine and who persecute it in its ministers. To outrage the Church, to outrage the Holy Father, to outrage priests and religious, to outrage the servants of God and good Catholics, is to strike Jesus in the Face, it is to wound His adorable countenance.

O God! be our protector, behold the insolent pride of our enemies. Look on the Face of Thy Christ which they outrage. And Thou, adorable Face, show Thyself to the heavenly Father, disarm His anger; let the Church be delivered and triumphant; let blasphemers themselves be saved.

## VIII
### Jesus Consoles the Daughters of Israel
### Who Follow Him

Those daughters of Israel are the picture of Christian souls devoted to good works, who with the eyes of faith, seeing Jesus in the poor, Jesus in His suffering members, Jesus in the priest, Jesus in the Eucharist, Jesus in the Church, are ready to serve Him on all occasions and to follow Him generously, even along the path to Calvary. The holy women receive a very sweet recompense. Jesus pauses, turns His adorable Face towards them, and through the cloud of sorrow with which It is covered, bestows on them a smile of approbation together with words of consolation and of holy counsel.

O Jesus! inspire us with zeal for good works and the heroic courage of holy love. We do not desire, in compensation, either the treasures of this world, or earthly consolations; grant to us only some of the spiritual joys and instructive inspirations which flow from Thy Face upon those who contemplate It and do It homage. Shed them more and more upon us; grant that we may make haste to walk along the way of perfection and of salvation.

## IX
### Jesus Falls for the Third Time

It is for the third time that Our Lord inflicts on His adorable Face this species of suffering and of humiliation. The first fall was occasioned by the weight and the shame of our sins, the second was caused by our weakness; in this His third fall, He expiates our discouragement, those cowardly and criminal weaknesses which ruin souls and lead them little by little into the abyss of despair. Reaching Calvary and perceiving the place of His punishment, Jesus immediately thinks of the innumerable poor sinners who, failing in faith and in confidence, refuse to have recourse to the sacraments of His Church, render His Passion and His death useless, and cast themselves in despair into eternal misery. This thought fills Him with profound sorrow and cruel depression. As in His agony in the garden, He falls prostrate on His Face, bathed in sweat, exhausted and almost dying.

O Jesus! Thy weakness is my strength and my support. I have recourse to the merits of Thy Holy Face, have pity on me, preserve me from despair. No, whatever may happen to me, I will not be discouraged anymore, I will not despair. The sight of Thy adorable Face, the symbol of mercy and of reparation, will be my hope forever.

# X
## Jesus is Despoiled of His Raiment

Jesus is here the figure of the first sinner. After his fall, Adam was ashamed of himself; he endeavored to hide from the eyes of God and to flee far away from His irritated Face. This is the reason why Jesus submits to the ignominious spoliation which His executioners inflict upon Him by tearing off His garments, and above all by snatching away that virginal robe, without seam, which had been woven for Him by His august mother. Then Jesus closes His eyes through shame and sorrow. His adorable Face is moved and troubled. He longs to withdraw from the gaze of His heavenly Father.

O Jesus! rather turn away Thy eyes from the sight of my sins, do not look upon the sad state to which my soul is reduced; give back to it its robe of innocence and the beauty of grace, in order that with youth renewed and worthily clothed, it may more perfectly reproduce Thy features, and rejoice Thy eyes.

# XI
## Jesus is Attached to the Cross

Stretched upon the tree of sacrifice, Jesus holds out His hands and His feet; the executioners transpierce them and nail them to the wood by dint of violent and brutal efforts; the blood gushes forth and flows abundantly. In vain He seeks repose by leaning His Head upon the Cross; the thorns of His crown, which the executioners have left upon Him and which He will keep until the end, sink more and more deeply into His flesh and make Him suffer dreadful torments. His adorable Face, upon this bed of ignominy, nevertheless maintains Its serenity and peace; It is turned towards heaven and pleads our cause. Jesus does not curse, He does not murmur; He prays, He adores, He loves, He suffers sweetly and in silence; the expression of His Face is that of the Lamb; He is really the Lamb of God, giving His blood and His life to efface the sins of the world.

Who then can henceforth separate us from the love of a God so good?...Persecution?...The sword?... Death? With our eyes fixed on the loving Face of the Divine Crucified, let us say with the apostle: "I am nailed to the Cross with Christ my Savior, I will live and die in Him."

## XII
### Jesus Dies on the Cross

Let us contemplate the agonized Face of the Redeemer, raised on the Cross, suspended between heaven and earth. Before breathing Its last sigh, that merciful Face raises Its eyes to the heavenly Father, imploring of Him our pardon: "*Father, forgive them.*" Then It bends down towards Mary, whose children Jesus makes us in His stead: "*Behold Thy children.*" Then towards St. John, the beloved disciple, giving to him the mother, who is also to be ours: "*Behold thy Mother.*" Lastly It turns towards the crucified thief on His right, promising him an immediate entrance, together with the just, into heaven: "*Today thou shalt be with Me in Paradise.*" It fixes Its gaze upon Its executioners themselves, not in order to curse them, but to bless them and to ask for them the grace of conversion and of salvation which It obtains.

O dying Face of Jesus, so mercifully inclined upon the Cross, I implore Thee as Thy disciple and a child of the Church, above all as a sinner, to give me a share in the benediction of that supreme moment; do not refuse me the greatest blessing of all, even though I am utterly unworthy of that sweet kiss of peace which shall reconcile me with Thy Father, and assure me His friendship forever.

# XIII
## Jesus is Taken Down from the Cross and Given to His Mother

Our Lady of Sorrows knows the worth of the incomparable treasure which is confided to her. She contemplates, one after another, the wounds of the Divine Crucified, His hands and His feet pierced by the nails, His open side, His head torn and wounded. But the tender eyes of the Virgin rest more especially upon the Face of the Redeemer, cold and inanimate as It is now. She gazes on His dim eyes, His closed mouth, His pale features, that mute and insensible physiognomy which death has disfigured, but in which the glory of the Divinity and the splendor of the Father are, as always, reflected. What a touching and sublime contemplation! And she who contemplates Him thus, is it a mother? Is it an Archangel? Is it a Seraphim? It is all these in Mary, and it something far more. Never was such a holy reparatory adoration offered to the Face of Jesus.

O Blessed Virgin, our Lady of the Seven Dolors, associate me with your sentiments, obtain for me that by means of an assiduous and profound meditation, that I may penetrate more and more deeply into the hidden mysteries of that adorable Face, in order that I may draw from It, for myself and for the souls who are dear to me, the treasures of merit and of satisfaction contained in It.

## XIV
## Jesus is Placed in the Sepulchre

The disciples and the holy women embalm the body of their dear Master. They take care to wrap It in a white winding sheet, and upon His adorable Face they reverently place a shroud which covers and entirely conceals It. This sepulchre shroud will preserve the impress of the inanimate Face of the Savior and will, later on, become an object greatly venerated by the Church. And now let us also, draw near to the tomb of Jesus; let us enter therein in thought and in heart. Let us do homage to His winding sheet, to the spices used for His sepulchre. Let us above all honor that precious shroud enriched by the Holy Face with a privilege similar to that which decorates the veil of Veronica.

O adorable Face of my Jesus, hide me in Thy sacred wounds and in Thy Divine obscurity. May I be of the number of those of whom the Prophet King says: "Thou shalt hide them in the secret of Thy Face, from all earthly sounds and worldly agitations!" May my dwelling be in Thy tomb and in Thy tabernacle! May I hide myself there, may I die there, may I be buried there with Thee, through a mortified and annihilated life, so that I may merit hereafter to share in the joy of Thy Face, when it shall shine in the splendor of the resurrection.

## On Returning to the Altar

O amiable Face of my Jesus, I thank Thee for the graces with which Thou hast favored me during this exercise. Attract me more and more towards Thee, ravish my heart in order that I may never cease to contemplate Thee, to love Thee, and to render to Thee the homage which is

Thy due. I consecrate to Thee my life. Whilst waiting until I can follow Thee once more upon the way to Calvary, I will apply myself to walk in Thy presence, and to make, of every one of my actions, an offering of praise and of reparation. O adorable Face, be my treasure in my needs, my strength in weakness, my light in doubts, my consolation and my guide in this valley of tears. My supreme recompense will be that which Thou hast promised me of seeing Thee hereafter as Thou art, and of sweetly enjoying Thy ineffable perfections throughout eternity. Amen.

---

# Short Way of the Cross
# Of the Holy Face
In a Spirit of Reparation and for the Wants of the Church

### Preliminary Prayer

O adorable Face of Jesus, hanging so pitifully on the tree of the Cross, at the time of the Passion for the redemption of the world! Have mercy on us miserable sinners even at this day, look upon us with compassion, and grant us the kiss of peace. O my Jesus, mercy!

## 1st Station
## Jesus is Condemned to Death

And He is silent! He who is innocence itself; He whose words have the power of giving life! His adorable Face loses nothing of Its dignity and sweetness. What a lesson this is for me! O my God, forgive me all those words I have uttered contrary to charity, humility, modesty and piety! And grant that in my trials I may honor Thee by my resignation and patience.

## 2nd Station
## Jesus Carries His Cross

And He receives it with joy and love, and He holds it to His Heart. He presses His Holy Face, His brow and His lips upon it. O how much He loves us! My good Master, forgive me the murmurs and complaints with which I have received the sorrows sent me in Thy mercy, and teach me to count myself fortunate in having something to suffer for Thee.

## 3rd Station
## Jesus Falls Beneath the Weight of His Cross

And He bruises His Face with the violence of His fall. He rises, His Face covered with mire, dust and blood! Holy Father, I offer Thee the fall of my Savior in expiation of those faults by which I have disedified and scandalized my neighbor. Because of Jesus humiliated and suffering, have mercy on me. In reparation I purpose to strive to prevent evil, and to win hearts to Thee.

## 4th Station
## Jesus Meets His Most Holy Mother

What a moment! What sorrow! What looks I behold, exchanged between this Man-God and His tender mother! What tears bathe their Faces! O Heavenly Father, I offer Thee these tears in expiation of all my self-indulgence and the little resignation I show to Thy holy will. Grant me, as Thou didst Mary, to encounter the look and the Face of Jesus in all my sorrows.

## 5<sup>th</sup> Station
## Simon, the Cyrenean, Helps Jesus to Carry His Cross

Does a stranger help my Master to carry His Cross?! Whilst I, His child, the object of His tenderness, refuse to do so by endeavoring to escape the contradictions and disappointments with which life is strewn! O how ingrateful am I! Pardon, my God, forget the past, turn Thy Face towards me. Hereafter, I will share Thy sorrows, at least, in accepting mine with a Christian spirit.

## 6<sup>th</sup> Station
## A Holy Woman Wipes the Face of Jesus

And should I not also, following her example, cause Thee to forget, by my reparation, the outrages Thou receivest from so many sinners? Is it not for me to make amends by greater fidelity and love? O this is what I wish to do, my God, to find my glory in Thy humiliations and sorrows!

## 7<sup>th</sup> Station
## Jesus Falls for the Second Time beneath the Weight of His Cross

O to what a state of abasement and opprobrium do I see Thee reduced, my Savior Jesus! A God prone in the dust! The executioners raise Him with blows! They do not spare even His beautiful Face! And why? To expiate my thoughts of vanity and self-esteem. O with what horror should they fill me, since Jesus has suffered so much to obtain their forgiveness! My God! My God! Have mercy! Let my heart be truly humble.

## 8<sup>th</sup> Station
## Jesus Comforts the Women of Israel Who Follow Him

O blessed Master! In the midst of His sufferings, He is interested in those which cause the tears of the good women to flow! He teaches them how to make their tears useful for themselves, and deigns to console them by turning towards them His adorable Face which consoles and blesses them! O my Savior, teach us how to weep for our sins, which are the true cause of Thy sufferings. Grant me more especially a sincere sorrow for my own sins; let my last tear be one of repentance and love.

## 9<sup>th</sup> Station
## Jesus Falls for the Third Time

He again inflicts upon His Face the same pain and humiliations as before. At the sight of Calvary, He rises, if one may so speak, with renewed courage and renewed love! His Heart bids Him make haste to die for His children. O tender Heart of my God, what a poor return do I make Thee! At the approach of the slightest pain, or the smallest sacrifice I am frightened and discouraged. Pardon, my Jesus, pardon! I will rise up with Thee, and as an encouragement to follow Thee, I will say to myself in every sorrow: The mercy of God calls me!

## 10<sup>th</sup> Station
## Jesus is Stripped of His Garments

Strip me, my God, of all that displeases Thee in me; take from me more especially self-love. Wash me in the blood that flows from Thy wounds, and may this innocent blood cause the virtues of purity, sweetness, charity, and a penitential spirit to take root in my heart!

May my soul be pleasant to Thy eyes and rejoice Thy Holy Face!

## 11<sup>th</sup>Station
### Jesus is Bound to the Cross

O my God, I know that it is not sufficient to become detached from myself, but I must practice attachment and unite myself to Thee. Alas! I understand, it is only possible in this world by suffering. I submit Lord, without delay and without reserve. Stretch me on the Cross which Thy Providence prepares for everyone in this world, that I may become conformable to Thee! O suffering Face of my Jesus, suspend between heaven and earth, draw me up to Thee and elevate me to Thy height that I may become worthy of Thy eternal glory.

## 12<sup>th</sup>Station
### Jesus Dies upon the Cross

Holy Father, most powerful and eternal God, I offer Thee the sufferings of my Jesus, His aching Face, His sacred wounds, His adorable blood, His last words and last sigh, in thanksgiving for the benefits which Thou hast heaped upon me, and in expiation of my sins, and more especially to implore of Thee the three following grace:

- For me and mine, a perfect contrition, with a firm will to belong only to Thee.
- For the conversion of poor sinners, and for the holy Church, our Mother. Accord to her the help she expects from Thy bounty, in the terrible ordeal through which she is passing!
- Look not upon our sins, O Lord, but look upon the Face of Thy Christ! Look upon the Heart that has loved us so much, and because of Him, have mercy on us.

## 13<sup>th</sup>Station
## Jesus is Placed in the Arms of His Mother

O Mary, my tender Mother, it is I who have made thee suffer! Let me then, at least, weep with thee; let me adore the suffering and wounded Face of my dear Redeemer! Requite thyself, beloved mother, it is but just, yet requite thyself like a mother! Ask for me of thy Divine Son such love as may enable me to drink with entire willingness, the few drops reserved for me in the chalice of His Passion, and let me repeat with Magdalene: O how sweet it is to recover one's innocence through tears of repentance and of love!

## 14<sup>th</sup>Station
## Jesus is Placed in the Sepulchre

O my Jesus, my Savior, Thou shalt not be there alone! Permit Thy child to be buried with Thee! Again this is not enough; enfold me in the mystery of Thy Face and the wounds of Thy Heart, it is there, I wish to take up my abode, to be seen by Thee alone. "My God! My God! Cause me to live but for Thee!!!"

---

# Prayer of Reparation
To the Outraged Divinity of Our Lord Jesus Christ

O Lord Jesus, after contemplating Thy features, disfigured by anguish, and after meditating upon Thy Passion, how can my heart not be consumed with love for Thee, and hatred for those sins which, even at this day, wound Thy adorable Face? Permit me not, O Lord to feel merely compassion alone! Make of me a worthy child of Mary, and accord me the grace, as Thou didst to Thy Divine Mother, to follow Thee so closely on this new

Calvary, that the insults destined for Thee, O Jesus may fall upon me, a member of Thy Holy Church, and cause me to undertake with courage the duty of expiation and of love. Amen.

---

# Prayers and Exercises
# Suitable for Acts of Reparation

(From the Writings of Sister Marie de Saint-Pierre)

## Prayer to the Eternal Father

O Almighty and Eternal God, it is by the Heart of Jesus, Thy Divine Son, my Way, my Truth and my Life, that I draw near to Thee. I come, through this adorable Heart, in union with the holy angels, and with all the saints, to praise, bless, adore and glorify Thy Holy Name, despised and blasphemed by so great a number of sinners. Accompanying, by my desires, the blessed Spirits, ministers of Thy mercy, I circle the world in order to seek for souls bought by the blood of Thy only Son. I offer them all to Thee by the hands of the holy Virgin and of glorious Saint Joseph, under the protection of the angels and of all the saints, begging of Thee, in the Name and through the merits of Jesus our Savior, to convert all blasphemers and all who profane the holy day of Sunday, in order that we may all with one voice, one soul and one heart, praise, bless, love, adore and glorify Thy Holy Name, in the heights, the depths, the breadths, the immensity, the fullness of the honor, the praise and the infinite adorations that the Sacred Heart of Thy well beloved Son renders to Thee; that Heart which is the organ and the delight of the most Holy Trinity, and which alone knows and perfectly adores Thy Holy Name in spirit and in truth. Amen.

## Prayer to the Eternal Father

For a Country

Eternal Father, we offer Thee the adorable Face of Thy well-beloved Son for the honor and glory of Thy Holy Name and for the salvation of France *(or the name of the country you are praying for)*.

# Twenty-Four Acts of Adoration

For the Reparation of the Blasphemies Uttered
During the Twenty-Four Hours of the Day

*The Magnificat is said at the beginning.*

1. In union with the Sacred Heart of Jesus:
   Come let us adore the admirable Name of God which is above every name.
2. In union with the Holy Heart of Mary:
   Come let us adore the admirable Name of God which is above every name.
3. In union with the glorious Saint Joseph:
   Come let us adore the admirable Name of God which is above every name.
4. In union with St. John the Baptist:
   Come let us adore the admirable Name of God which is above every name.
5. In union with the choir of the Seraphim:
   Come let us adore the admirable Name of God which is above every name.
6. In union with the choir of the Cherubim:
   Come let us adore the admirable Name of God which is above every name.
7. In union with the choir of the Thrones:
   Come let us adore the admirable Name of God which is above every name.

8. In union with the choir of the Dominations:
   Come let us adore the admirable Name of God which is above every name.
9. In union with the choir of the Virtues:
   Come let us adore the admirable Name of God which is above every name.
10. In union with the choir of the Powers:
    Come let us adore the admirable Name of God which is above every name.
11. In union with the choir of the Principalities:
    Come let us adore the admirable Name of God which is above every name.
12. In union with the choir of the Archangels:
    Come let us adore the admirable Name of God which is above every name.
13. In union with the choir of the Angels:
    Come let us adore the admirable Name of God which is above every name.
14. In union with the seven Spirits which are before the throne of God and the twenty-four ancients:
    Come let us adore the admirable Name of God which is above every name.
15. In union with the choir of the Patriarchs:
    Come let us adore the admirable Name of God which is above every name.
16. In union with the choir of the Prophets:
    Come let us adore the admirable Name of God which is above every name.
17. In union with the choir of the Apostles and the four Evangelists:
    Come let us adore the admirable Name of God which is above every name.

18. In union with the choir of Martyrs:
Come let us adore the admirable Name of God which
is above every name.
19. In union with the choir of holy Pontiffs:
Come let us adore the admirable Name of God which
is above every name.
20. In union with the choir of holy Confessors:
Come let us adore the admirable Name of God which
is above every name.
21. In union with the choir of holy Virgins:
Come let us adore the admirable Name of God which
is above every name.
22. In union with the choir of holy Women:
Come let us adore the admirable Name of God which
is above every name.
23. In union with all the Heavenly Court:
Come let us adore the admirable Name of God which
is above every name.
24. In union with the whole Church and in the name of all
men:
Come let us adore the admirable Name of God which
is above every name, and let us prostrate ourselves
before Him. Let us weep in the presence of the God
who has made us, because He is the Lord our God;
we are His people and the sheep of His pasture.

## Salutation to Our Lord Jesus Christ

In Order to Repair the Blasphemies Committed
Against His Sacred Name

In union with the whole Church, by the hearts of
Mary and of Joseph all burning with love, and in the name
of all men, I salute Thee, I adore Thee, and I love Thee, O
Jesus of Nazareth! King of the Jews, full of meekness and
of humility, of grace and of truth. Mercy and justice

are with Thee; love is Thy substance; Thou art the Christ, the only Son of the living God, and the blessed fruit of the womb of the glorious Virgin Mary.

O Jesus! Good Shepherd, who hast given Thy life for Thy sheep, by all Thy sacred wounds, Thy precious blood, Thy Divine tears and beloved sweat, by all the sighs, the groans, the sorrows, the love, the merits of the thirty-three years of Thy holy life, enclosed in the ineffable sanctuary of Thy most loving Heart, have pity on us, poor and miserable sinners; convert all the blasphemers and profaners of the holy day of Sunday, and give us a share in Thy Divine merits, now and at the hour of our death. Amen.

*(This salutation above should be repeated three times in order to honor His Divine life, His glorious life, and His mortal life.)*

## Aspirations

Eternal Father, I offer Thee the body and blood of our Lord Jesus Christ, in expiation for our sins and for the needs of the Holy Church.

Amiable Heart of Jesus, our mediator, appease Thy Father, and save sinners.

Powerful heart of Mary, refuge of sinners, stay the arrows of Divine justice.

Saint Michael, pray for us.
Saint Martin, pray for us.
Saint Louis, pray for us.

*O God our Protector, behold us and cast Thine eyes upon the Face of Thy Christ.* (Ps. LXXXIII, 9.)

# A Crown of the Glory of the Holy Name of God For the Reparation of Blasphemies

*Instead of the* Credo, *say:*
We adore Thee, O Jesus, and we bless Thee, because
Thou hast redeemed the world by Thy holy Cross.

*Upon the three small beads of the Cross, say:*

1. May the most Holy Name of God be glorified by the
   most Holy Soul of the Incarnate Word.
2. May the most Sacred Name of God be glorified by
   the Sacred Heart of the Incarnate Word.
3. May the most adorable Name of God be glorified by
   all the wounds of the Incarnate Word.

*Upon the five large beads, say:*

We invoke Thee, O Sacred Name of the living God,
by the mouth of Jesus in the most Holy Sacrament, and
we offer Thee O my God, by the blessed hands of
Mary Immaculate, all the Sacred Hosts which are
upon our altars as a sacrifice of reparation for all the
blasphemies which outrage Thy Holy Name.

*Upon each small bead of the ten, say:*

1. Hail, O Sacred Name of the living God, through the
   Heart of Jesus in the most Holy Sacrament.
2. I revere Thee, O Sacred Name of the living God,
   through the Heart of Jesus in the most Holy
   Sacrament.
3. I adore Thee, O Sacred Name of the living God,
   through the Heart of Jesus in the most Holy
   Sacrament.

4. I glorify Thee, O Sacred Name of the living God, through the Heart of Jesus in the most Holy Sacrament.

5. I praise Thee, O Sacred Name of the living God, through the Heart of Jesus in the most Holy Sacrament.

6. I admire Thee, O Sacred Name of the living God, through the Heart of Jesus in the most Holy Sacrament.

7. I celebrate Thee, O Sacred Name of the living God, through the Heart of Jesus in the most Holy Sacrament.

8. I exalt Thee, O Sacred Name of the living God, through the Heart of Jesus in the most Holy Sacrament.

9. I love Thee, O Sacred Name of the living God, through the Heart of Jesus in the most Holy Sacrament.

10. I bless Thee, O Sacred Name of the living God, through the Heart of Jesus in the most Holy Sacrament.

# Offering of the Infinite Merits
# Of Our Lord Jesus Christ to God the Father

In Order to Appease His Justice and
Draw His Mercy upon Our Country

Eternal Father, turn away Thy angry gaze from our guilty people, whose face has become hideous in Thy eyes, and look upon the Face of Thy Son which we offer to Thee. It is Thy well beloved Son in whom Thou art well pleased. Listen, we beseech Thee to the voice of His blood and of His wounds which call for mercy from Thee.

Eternal Father, look upon the Incarnation of Jesus, Thy Divine Son, and His sojourn in the womb of His Divine Mother. We offer them to Thee for the honor and glory of Thy Holy Name and for the salvation of our country.

Eternal Father, look upon the birth of Jesus in the stable at Bethlehem and the mysteries of His most Holy Infancy. We offer them to Thee for the honor and glory of Thy Holy Name and for the salvation of our country.

Eternal Father, look upon the poor, hidden and laborious life of Jesus at Nazareth. We offer them to Thee for the honor and glory of Thy Holy Name and for the salvation of our country.

Eternal Father, look upon the baptism of Jesus and His retreat of forty days in the desert. We offer them to Thee for the honor and glory of Thy Holy Name and for the salvation of our country.

Eternal Father, look upon the journeys, the vigils, the prayers, the miracles and the teachings of Jesus. We offer them to Thee for the honor and glory of Thy Holy Name and for the salvation of our country.

Eternal Father, look upon the last supper Jesus partook of with His disciples, washing their feet, and instituting the august sacrament of the Eucharist. We offer them to Thee for the honor and glory of Thy Holy Name and for the salvation of our country.

Eternal Father, look upon the agony of Jesus in the Garden of Olives and the bloody sweat which covered His body and ran down to the ground. We offer them to Thee for the honor and glory of Thy Holy Name and for the salvation of our country.

Eternal Father, look upon the outrages which Jesus underwent before His judges and His condemnation to death. We offer them to Thee for the honor and glory of Thy Holy Name and for the salvation of our country.

Eternal Father, look upon Jesus, laden with His Cross and proceeding to the place where He was to be immolated. We offer them to Thee for the honor and glory of Thy Holy Name and for the salvation of our country.

Eternal Father, look upon Jesus crucified between two thieves, and made to drink gall and vinegar, blasphemed, and dying in order to repair Thy glory and to save the world. We offer them to Thee for the honor and glory of Thy Holy Name and for the salvation of our country.

Eternal Father, look upon the five wounds of Jesus. We offer them to Thee for the honor and glory of Thy Holy Name and for the salvation of our country.

Eternal Father, look upon the sacred head of Jesus, crowned with thorns. We offer It to Thee for the honor and glory of Thy Holy Name and for the salvation of our country.

Eternal Father, look upon the adorable Face of Jesus, wounded with blows and covered with spittle, with dust, with sweat and with blood. We offer It to Thee for the for the honor and glory of Thy Holy Name and for the salvation of our country.

Eternal Father, look upon the adorable Body of Jesus, taken down from the Cross. We offer It to Thee for the honor and glory of Thy Holy Name and for the salvation of our country.

Eternal Father, look upon the heart, the soul and the Divinity of Jesus, the holy victim, who when dying triumphed over sin. We offer them to Thee for the honor and glory of Thy Holy Name and for the salvation of our country.

Look, O Eternal Father, on all that Jesus Christ, Thy only Son did during the thirty-three years of His mortal life, in order to accomplish the work of our redemption; look upon all the mysteries of that most holy life. We offer them to Thee for the honor and glory of Thy Holy Name and for the salvation of our country.

Look, O Eternal Father, on all the desires, all the thoughts, the words, the actions, the virtues, the perfections, the prayers of Jesus Christ, as well as upon all His sufferings and humiliations. We offer them to Thee for the honor and glory of Thy Holy Name and for the salvation of our country.

Look, O Eternal Father, on the crib and the swaddling clothes used at the birth of Jesus. We offer them to Thee for the honor and glory of Thy Holy Name and for the salvation of our country.

Look, O Eternal Father, on the Cross, the nails, the crown of thorns, the reed, the bloody scourges, the pillar, the lance, the sepulchre, the holy shroud, and all the instruments used in the Passion of Jesus. We offer them to Thee for the honor and glory of Thy Holy Name and for the salvation of our country.

# Affectionate Aspirations to Our Lord

In Order to Repair Blasphemies

O Jesus, eternal truth and wisdom, who wast treated as a seducer and a madman, I adore Thee and I love Thee with all my heart.

O Jesus, in whom are all the treasures of Divine knowledge, but who wast looked upon as an ignorant man and the son of a carpenter, I adore Thee with all my heart.

O Jesus, fountain of life, who didst hear the impious say of Thee: *Will he then kill himself,* because Thou saidst to them: *You cannot come where I go,* I adore Thee with all my heart.

O Jesus, the Divine Word, who wast called a man possessed by a devil and a Samaritan, I adore Thee with all my heart.

O Jesus, God thrice holy, who wast treated as a sinner by the chief priests, I adore Thee with all my heart.

O Jesus, model of sobriety, whom Thy enemies accused of loving wine and of feasting, I adore Thee with all my heart.

O Jesus, enemy of sin, but full of mercy towards the guilty, who wast called the friend of publicans and sinners, I adore Thee with all my heart.

O Jesus, the splendor of the Father and the image of His substance, who wast represented as a flagitious man, and a false prophet, I adore Thee with all my heart.

O Jesus, enemy of lies, who didst hear the impious cast doubts upon the veracity of Thy words, when they ironically exclaimed: *Thou art not yet fifty years old, and Thou hast seen Abraham!* I adore Thee with all my heart.

O Jesus, God all powerful, who, in order to render Thyself conformable to our nature, with which Thou wast clothed, didst hide Thyself and leave the Temple, to avoid being stoned by Thy enemies, I adore Thee with all my heart.

O Jesus, only Son and faithful worshiper of the living God, who wast accused by the High-Priest of having blasphemed and wast judged by him to be worthy of death, I adore Thee with all my heart.

O Jesus, King of Glory, who full of meekness and of humility, didst allow Thy eyes to be blindfolded, Thy Face to be spit upon, and wounded by blows and buffets, I adore Thee with all my heart.

O Jesus, who dost search our hearts and our reins, and from whom nothing is hidden, who without complaint didst allow those insulting words to be addressed to Thee: *Prophesy unto us, O Christ, who is he that struck thee?* I adore Thee with all my heart.

O Jesus, pacific King, accused of perverting the nation, of hindering the payment of tribute, of exciting the people to rebel, and of calling Thyself King and Messiah, I adore Thee with all my heart.

O Jesus, King of kings, despised by Herod and by his court, and clothed in derision, with a white robe as a madman, I adore Thee with all my heart.

O Jesus full of love, who didst hear the people cry out: *Put this man to death, and give up to us Barabbas... May His blood fall on us and upon our children,* I adore Thee with all my heart.

O Jesus, King of heaven and earth, crowned with thorns, insolently struck and cruelly outraged by the words: *Hail King of the Jews,* I adore Thee with all my heart.

O Jesus, infinite goodness, the source of all creation, the sovereign master of the world, who didst listen to that sentence of death: *away with him; away with him; crucify him; we have no king but Caesar;* I adore Thee with all my heart.

O Jesus, worthy of all praise, who wast blasphemed on the Cross by the passersby, by the bad thief, by the chief priests, by the ancients of the people, by the scribes and by the soldiers, I adore Thee with all my heart.

O Jesus, holy victim of sinners, who didst hear Thy enemies say: *He saved others, himself he cannot save. Let Christ the King of Israel come down now from the Cross, that we may see and believe,* I adore Thee with all my heart.

O Jesus, full of love, of confidence and of reverence for Thy Divine Father, who wast wounded with the most poignant anguish when the people cried out at the sight of Thee expiring: *He confided in God; let Him now deliver him if He will have him; for he said: I am the Son of God,* I adore Thee, and I love Thee with all my heart.

## Prayer

Reparation for the Innumerable Insults Inflicted on the Savior

O my Savior Jesus Christ, I feel bitter compassion for the grief experienced by Thy Divine Heart on hearing the blasphemies vomited by Thy enemies against Thee and against Thy heavenly Father.

But, O Jesus, what must be Thy affliction at seeing, after having given Thy life to the very last drop of Thy blood for the salvation of men, that Thou wouldst in the lapse of centuries, have fresh enemies who would reiterate those blasphemies a thousand times! Receive, O sweetest

those blasphemies a thousand times! Receive, O sweetest Jesus, the ardent desire we have of repairing all the outrages and the contempt which Thou hast received, and which Thou dost still receive every day from heretics and impious men. O why is it not given to us to withdraw Thee from the rage of those who hate Thee and who are leagued together against Thee and against the Holy Church, Thy spotless spouse?! Repeat with us, O merciful Jesus, that touching prayer which Thou didst address to Thy Divine Father before Thou didst utter Thy last sigh: *Father, forgive them, for they know not what they do.* We offer to Thee, in reparation for all the innumerable insults inflicted on Thee, all the glory, all the honor, all the praises, and all the gladness which are and which will be given to Thee by the most blessed Virgin and Saint Joseph, the angels, the saints, and all the elect, in time and in eternity. Amen.

# Crown
# In Honor of the Most Holy Name of Jesus
For the Reparation of the Blasphemies and the
Injuries Inflicted on Him by the Crowning with Thorns

*Instead of the* Credo *say:*
Hail, Word of the Father, Savior of men; I adore Thee, Sacred Host, true and living flesh, perfect Divinity, true God and true man. O Jesus who hast given me life, I adore Thee, and I love Thee with all my heart!

*On the three small beads of the Cross say:*
We give Thee glory O Jesus, and we call upon
Thy Holy Name.

*On the five large beads say one:*
Gloria Patri, Pater Noster, and an Ave.

*On each of the small beads say:*
Our Father who art in heaven,

1.	May the Holy Name of Jesus be adored!
2.	May the Holy Name of Jesus be contemplated!
3.	May the Holy Name of Jesus be admired!
4.	May the Holy Name of Jesus be manifested!
5.	May the Holy Name of Jesus be loved!
6.	May the Holy Name of Jesus be glorified!
7.	May the Holy Name of Jesus be exalted!
8.	May the Holy Name of Jesus be reverenced!
9.	May the Holy Name of Jesus be invoked!
10.	May the Holy Name of Jesus be blessed and celebrated in time and in eternity!

# Prayer
## To Our Lord Jesus Christ
The True Repairer of the Outrages
Committed against the Glory of His Father

O Jesus, at the sight of the blasphemers of the sacred Name of God, we beseech Thee to repeat with us the prayer Thou didst once address to Thy Divine Father, and which has been given to us by Saint John, Thy beloved disciple: *Father, glorify Thy Name.* Then, O Divine Jesus, came a voice from heaven saying: *I have glorified It already, and I will glorify It again.*

May that voice resound throughout the earth, we entreat Thee by Thy sacred wounds and by Thy adorable Face! As for us, forgetting at this moment our own interests, in order to defend the glory of Thy Father's Name, we will keep in mind the three first petitions of the prayer Thou Thyself hast taught us: *Our Father, who art in heaven, hallowed be Thy Name: Thy kingdom come; Thy will be done on earth as it is in heaven. Amen.*

# Little Scapular
# Of the Holy Face

The scapular of the Holy Face is a small picture of that adorable Face, printed upon linen, which the faithful wear from devotion, as a testimony of love towards our Lord and a preservative against temptations and the dangers of the soul and body.

It may be fastened upon the scapular of our Lady of Mount Carmel or upon any other which is worn; it is not necessary to have recourse to a priest in order to receive it, and there is no liturgical form to be complied with; when taking it to wear, no other obligation is contracted than that of wearing it in a spirit of faith and of reparation. It is a small copy of the veil of Saint Veronica which has touched the great relic at Rome.

---

# Little Chaplet
# Of the Holy Face

The little chaplet of the Holy Face has for its object the honoring of the five senses of our Lord Jesus Christ, and of entreating God for the triumph of His Church.

This chaplet is composed of a Cross, of thirty-nine beads, six of which are large, and thirty-three small, and of a medal of the Holy Face. It is well to recite it every day, in order to obtain from God, by means of the Face of His well beloved Son, the triumph of our Mother the Catholic Church, and the downfall of her enemies. The Cross recalls to us the mystery of our Redemption; we must sign ourselves with it and make the invocation: *Deus, in adjutorium meum intende: Domine, ad adjuvandum me festina (Incline unto my aid, O God; O Lord, make haste to help me);* followed by the *Gloria Patri.*

The thirty-three small beads represent the thirty-three years of the mortal life of Our Lord. The first thirty recall to mind the thirty years of His private life, and are divided into five parts of six beads each, with the intention of honoring the five senses of the *touch,* of the *hearing,* of the *sight,* of the *smell,* and of the *taste* of Jesus, which have their seat principally in His Holy Face, and of rendering homage to all the sufferings which our Lord endured in His Face, through each one of these senses.

Each of these six beads is preceded by a large bead in honor of the sense which it is intended to honor, and is followed by a *Gloria Patri.* The set of three small beads recall to mind the public life of the Savior and have for their object the honoring of all the wounds of His adorable Face; these are also preceded by a large bead, to be followed by a *Gloria Patri,* for the same intention.

On each large bead is said: *My Jesus, mercy!* (100 days' indulgence). On each small bead is said: *Arise, O Lord, and let Thy enemies be scattered, and let all that hate Thee flee before Thy Face.*

The Gloria is repeated seven times, in order to honor the Seven Last Words of Jesus upon the Cross, and the Seven Dolors of the Immaculate Virgin. The Chaplet is concluded by saying on the medal: *God, our Protector, look down upon us, and cast Thine eyes upon the Face of Thy Christ.*

The little chaplet comes to us from Sister Saint-Pierre, and the little scapular from the Venerable Mr. Dupont.

---

# Rosary
# In Honor of the Holy Face

*(From the 1887 Manual of the Archconfraternity)*
*N.B. — The recitation of the Rosary, or of the Chaplet,*
*so strongly recommended at the present day by the*
*Sovereign Pontiff Leo XIII, may be made with great*
*consolation and benefit, if each of the fifteen mysteries,*
*which must be meditated upon in the spirit of Saint*
*Dominic, be said in reference to the most Holy Face of Our*
*Lord.*

## JOYFUL MYSTERIES

### 1st Mystery — THE ANNUNCIATION

I adore Thee, O Jesus, who, having the Divine nature, didst deign to take upon Thyself our likeness in order to conform us all to Thy semblance. Imprint more and more deeply in our souls, by a lively faith, the seal of Thy Divine resemblance.

Pardon, mercy, for all unhappy pagans who are enemies of the Gospel, and rebel to the grace of Thy Incarnation.

### 2nd Mystery — THE VISITATION

I adore Thee, O Jesus, Divine sun, whose rays, though veiled, reaches him, "who is one day to walk before Thy Face." May the light of Thy Face, which descended upon us at the moment of baptism, enlighten, warm, and continually vivify our souls.

Pardon, mercy, for all ungrateful men who desire to efface from their foreheads the mark of a Christian; for heretics who are not blessed by Thy luminous presence in the bosom of the true Church.

### 3rd Mystery — THE NATIVITY

I adore Thee, O Jesus, little Infant laid in a crib. Thy Face, so full of graces, inspires angelic songs, and ravishes the shepherds and the Magi. All Thy features wear an expression of benignity: *Apparuit benignitas*. O beauty of the Holy Face, O goodness of Jesus, captivate all hearts!

Pardon, mercy, for the many indifferent men who misunderstand Thy sweet attractions, who shut their hearts to the excess of Thy charity.

### 4th Mystery — THE PRESENTATION

I adore Thee, O Jesus, presented in the Temple by the hands of Mary. Thou art the victim without spot, alone worthy of all the complaisance of the Father. May we like the holy old man Simeon, after having known and contemplated Thee with the eyes of faith, no longer cling to this world, but turn our eyes and our hearts to Thee alone.

Pardon, mercy, for so many poor madmen, who are captivated and seduced by the figure of this world which passes away.

### 5th Mystery — FINDING OF JESUS IN THE TEMPLE

I adore Thee, O Jesus, found again in the temple in the midst of the Doctors. How beautiful was the ray of Divine light, emanating from Thy august Face upon those who listened to Thee! Make that wisdom, which Thou camest to bring down upon earth, and which Thou hast placed within the reach of all, shine upon us.

Pardon, mercy, for the voluntarily blind who obstinately refuse Thy light, and for the victims of an education without God.

# SORROWFUL MYSTERIES

### 1st Mystery — THE AGONY IN THE GARDEN

Hail, adorable Face of my Savior, bowed to the earth under the weight of the sins of the world which cover Thee with confusion. Take away from us all human respect, all culpable shame.

Eternal Father, I offer Thee the Face of Thy Son, covered with the sweat of agony, obscured by the shades of death; may Thy justice be appeased at the sight of so affecting a spectacle; mayest Thou have mercy on our country in spite of all the crimes that are committed against Thee therein.

### 2nd Mystery — THE FLAGELLATION

Hail, adorable Face of my Savior, disfigured by the scourges of the executioners filled with fury against their innocent victim. Repair the injuries inflicted upon my soul by sin, which, as a hideous leprosy, disfigures and withers it.

Eternal Father, I offer Thee the bleeding Face of Thy Son in reparation for the innumerable, abominable sins, which imprint their shameful marks even upon the face of men.

### 3rd Mystery — THE CROWNING WITH THORNS

Hail, adorable Face of my Savior, ignominiously blindfolded, covered with spittle, crowned with thorns, wounded with blows. Efface from amongst us every trace of that devastating scourge, the impious and satanic pride of our times.

Eternal Father, I offer Thee the Face of Thy Son which has become unrecognizable. Spare us, and our nation which has committed so many blasphemies, so many profanations, so many audacious revolts against Thee.

### 4th Mystery — THE BEARING OF THE CROSS

Hail, adorable Face of my Savior, miraculously impressed upon the veil of St. Veronica. May my soul bear the impress of the features of Thy humiliation, in order that it may be one day clothed with Thy glory!

Eternal Father, I offer Thee the Face of Thy Son still wiped by so many faithful Veronicas, by so many reparatory souls. For the sake of these souls which are so pleasing to Thee, stay Thy chastisements, and do not hurl Thy avenging thunders upon our unhappy people.

### 5th Mystery — THE CRUCIFIXION

Hail adorable Face of my Savior on the Cross. Before Thee the sun is veiled, the earth is moved and is covered with darkness, all the nature mourns. O features of the dying Jesus, features of crucified love, the ineffable expression of which has ravished all the Saints! May you be imprinted deeply in my heart!

Eternal Father, I offer Thee the Face of Thy expiring Son. *Respice in Faciem Christi tui!* "Look on the Face of Thy Christ." May Thou be moved, and may the flood of Thy mercy inundate the whole earth.

## GLORIOUS MYSTERIES

### 1st Mystery — THE RESURRECTION

Glory to Thee, O Lord, risen Jesus, who didst appear with radiant Face to Thy mother, to the holy women, to the assembled disciples. It is no longer Calvary with its horrors. What beauty, what splendor, what gladness!

By that glory of Thy Face, give back to our souls that beauty of which sin has deprived them; give back to them their Christian characteristics.

## 2nd Mystery — THE ASCENSION

Glory to Thee, Lord Jesus, ascending to heaven, with Thy Face turned towards the shores of Thy blessed home. Thou wilt hereafter descend once more with the angry Face of the Judge, and in presence of Thy Majesty, every proud head shall prostrate itself before Thee.

O sweet Face of Jesus, going to prepare a place for us, draw our eyes, raise our gaze towards Thee! We desire to belong "to the generation of those who, thirsting, seek the Face of the God of Jacob."

## 3rd Mystery — THE DESCENT OF THE HOLY GHOST

Glory to Thee, Lord Jesus, seated at the right hand of the Father. Thou wilt appear continually before the Face of God to plead our cause. A thousand and a thousand thanksgivings for that perpetual intercession.

After having obtained the full effusion of the Holy Ghost upon the apostles, pray to Thy Father to let the same Holy Ghost reign over us, let it brood upon the face of the great waters, upon the nations of the earth agitated, like an ocean, by the tempests of atheism.

## 4th Mystery — THE ASSUMPTION

Glory to Thee, Lord Jesus, the new Solomon coming to meet Thy mother. How beautiful Thou art, how gracious, how full of infinite amiability in presence of the Holy Ark introduced by Thee into the heavenly Jerusalem amidst celestial songs!

O smiling Face of Jesus, appear to us at the hour of death, and may the horrible form of the devil disappear at Thy aspect.

5th Mystery — THE CROWNING OF THE VIRGIN

Glory to Thee, Lord Jesus, crowning Thy mother, and making her sit down beside Thee. The eyes of all the Blessed are fixed on Thy Face and on that of Thy mother. Those two Faces shine like two suns, and shed joy throughout the whole of Paradise.

O Jesus, O Mary, grant us the grace so greatly to be desired, the grace of graces, that of contemplating Thee thereafter face to Face in the eternal vision of the elect.

---

## The Little Sachet or The Little Gospel

This devotional object was composed by Sister Marie de St. Pierre after a special communication from our Lord. It consists of a leaflet on which is printed the Gospel of the Circumcision, which is short, and in which is made mention of the Name of Jesus, given to the Savior. On the same leaflet is ngraved, at the top of it, the figure of the Divine Child and the initials of His adorable Name, and below the Gospel, some pious invocations calculated to excite confidence in the Name of Jesus, together with the lines:

When Jesus was named,
Vanquished Satan was disarmed.

The leaflet is folded in two and enclosed in a little piece of cloth on which is embroidered a Cross with the Sacred Heart, so that it resembles a medal suitable to be worn on the person.

There is no other blessing needed, in order to receive it, than that which is attached to the Holy Name of Jesus. In honor of the five letters of this Divine Name, and by virtue of the five wounds, Our Lord has promised to grant special graces to those who shall embrace this devotion with faith and piety: firstly to preserve them from lightning; secondly from the cunning and the malice of the devil; thirdly from sudden and unprovided death; fourthly to enable them to walk readily along the path of virtue; fifthly to grant to them final perseverance.

Our Lord is pleased to manifest the power of His Holy Name by many other spiritual and temporal graces: conversions, cures, etc. The sachet is principally employed with success in the case of dying sinners.

This devotion to the Holy Name of Jesus is attached to the great work of the Reparation of blasphemies and to that of the Holy Face.

---

## Explanations
## The Medal of Saint Benedict

The Cross, so called, of Saint Benedict, engraved upon a medal for many ages past, has some little resemblance, in its form, to the Cross of the Holy Order of Jerusalem; it is particularly recommended because of its efficacy.

The letters in relief on the medal represent an equal number of Latin words, of which the following is the meaning. Between the four limbs of the Cross, are the initials C. S. P. B., which signify: "Crux sancti Patris Benedicti," or, in English: *The Cross of our holy father Benedict.*

Upon the vertical line of the Cross is engraved: C. S. S. M. L., which stand for: "Crux sacra sit mihi lux," or, in English: *May the holy Cross be my light.*

Upon the horizontal line of the same Cross the letters N. D. S. M. D. signify: "Non Draco sit mihi dux," or, in English: *May the dragon never be my guide.*

Upon the band of the ellipse, commencing at the top and turning to the left of the Cross, are the initials: V. R. S. N. S. M. V. S. M. Q. L. I. V. B.: "Vade retro Satana; numquam suade mihi vana; sunt mala quæ libas, ipse venena bibas," or, in English: *Begone Satan; never tempt me with your vanities. What you offer me is evil, drink thy poison thyself.*

In the upper portion of the ellipse, is seen upon some medals a Cross ✠; upon others the monogram IHS: both of them indicating that the virtue of this devotion depends entirely upon faith in Jesus Christ. Still other medals have the word "Pax," or, in English: *Peace.*

Upon the margin of the medal, encircling the figure of Saint Benedict is "Eius in obitu nostro praesentia muniamur," or, in English: *May we be strengthened by his presence in the hour of our death.*

By a brief of Pope Benedict XIV, dated the 12th of March 1742, the use of the medal was sanctioned and encouraged by the richest indulgences; but this favor, added to the graces of which the medal is already the instrument, requires, in order to its application, the special benediction of a priest authorized to that effect by the Holy See. The Benedictines of the Congregation of Monte Cassino and those of the French Congregation enjoy this right, with the power of delegating it to priests who may make a request for it. The same Brief describes the medals, known by the name of the Cross of Saint Benedict, as presenting on one side the figure of the holy Patriarch, and on the other a Cross with the letters or characters already described.

A long experience has proved how useful this medal is for delivering human bodies, houses, even animals from all diabolic influences; for curing those attacked by pestilence, and many other infirmities; for preservation from all danger of lightening; for fortifying us in temptations, and preserving purity of the mind and the heart.

The way in which to make use of this holy medal is to wear it, or to apply it to the persons or objects in which we are interested, praying to God always through the intercession and the merits of the most holy Patriarch. The Italian Fathers recommend that, in such circumstances, 5 *Glorias* should be recited in honor of the Passion of our Lord Jesus Christ, 3 *Aves* to the most Blessed Virgin Mary, and 3 *Glorias* in honor of Saint Benedict.

They also advise that those who can make it convenient to do so, should recite these prayers every day, or, at least, every Tuesday, because that day is specially consecrated to the memory of Saint Benedict in the whole of the monastic Order. We propose to add to these prayers the aspirations attached to the medal, that is to say:

*Crux sacra, sit mihi lux, non draco sit mihi dux. Vade retro, Satana; numquam suade mihi vana: Sunt mala, quæ libas; ipse venena bibas.*

But let no one confound this exhortation with the practices which are prescribed. For, to gain the indulgences attached to this devotion, it suffices to wear the medal of Saint Benedict, which ought to be made entirely of gold, of silver, of copper, or of some solid metal, and not of cardboard, or any other material, under penalty of nullity of the benediction and of the application of the indulgences.

Saint Benedict having promised to assist, at the hour of death, anyone who should have invoked him during their life, we may make sure of this favor by every day reciting the following prayer, to which Pope Clement XIV has attached a plenary indulgence.

*Prayer*

My beloved Father Saint Benedict, in consideration of the dignity with which the Lord has deigned to
honor you and to beatify you by so glorious and end, I beg
of you to deign to be present at my death, and to fulfill
towards me all the promises you made to the virgin Saint
Gertrude. Amen.

---

# Exercise
## In Honor of Our Lady of Seven Dolors

*Indulgence of 300 days.* (Pope Pius VII, 14th Jan. 1815

I.    I deeply compassionate, O Mary, Mother of
Sorrows, the affliction suffered by thy tender heart, on
hearing the prophecy of the old man Simeon. Dearest
Mother, by thy greatly afflicted heart, obtain for us the
virtue of humility and the grace of the fear of God.
*Ave, Maria...*

II.    I deeply compassionate, O Mary, Mother of
Sorrows, the anguish suffered by thy most sensitive heart
during the flight and the sojourn in Egypt. Dearest Mother,
by thy afflicted heart, obtain for us the virtue of
generosity and of liberality above all towards the poor
and the gift of piety.
*Ave, Maria...*

III.    I deeply compassionate, O Mary, Mother
of Sorrows, the cruel grief felt by thy tender heart, at the
loss of thy dear son Jesus.  Dearest Mother, by thy holy
heart so keenly tried, obtain for us the virtue of chastity
and the gift of knowledge.
*Ave, Maria...*

IV.    I deeply compassionate, O Mary, Mother of Sorrows, the consternation which thy maternal heart experienced when thou didst meet Jesus bearing His Cross. Dearest Mother, by thy sensitive heart so steeped in grief, obtain for us the virtue of patience and the gift of fortitude.
*Ave, Maria...*

V.    I deeply compassionate, O Mary, Mother of Sorrows, the martyrdom endured by thy courageous heart at witnessing Jesus in His agony. Dearest Mother, by thy heart, so cruelly martyred, obtain for us the virtue of temperance and the gift of good counsel.
*Ave, Maria...*

VI.    I deeply compassionate, O Mary, Mother of Sorrows, the wound received by thy tender heart when the side of Jesus was opened, and His Heart pierced by the lance. Dearest Mother, by thy heart so sorrowfully transpierced, obtain for us the virtue of fraternal charity and the gift of understanding.
*Ave, Maria...*

VII.    I deeply compassionate, O Mary, Mother of Sorrows, the lively anguish with which thy tender heart was torn at the burial of Jesus. Dearest Mother, by thy Immaculate Heart, so cruelly overwhelmed by sorrow, obtain for us the virtue of diligence and the gift of wisdom.
*Ave, Maria...*

V. Pray for us, O most sorrowful Virgin.
*R. That we may be made worthy of the promises of Christ*

### Prayer

Lord Jesus, we implore now and at the hour of our death, the intercession of the most Blessed Virgin Mary, Thy mother, whose holy soul was transpierced with a sword of sorrow at the hour of Thy Passion. Grant us this grace, O Savior of the world, Thou who livest and reignest with the Father and the Holy Ghost forever and ever. Amen.

# The Seven *Aves*, In Honor of Mary Mother of Dolors

Anyone who will recite, with a contrite heart, seven *Aves,* adding, after each one of them this invocation: *Holy Mother, engrave the wounds of my Savior in my innermost heart*, will gain: firstly an indulgence of 300 days, once a day; secondly a plenary indulgence, once a month, if recited every day.

---

## Chaplet of Our Lady of Seven Dolors (Sorrows)

This chaplet is divided into seven sevens, each one of which is composed of a Pater Noster and seven Aves. At the end, three Aves are added in honor of the tears shed by the Blessed Virgin during the Passion.

An indulgence of two hundred days for each Pater and Ave, on the feast of the Compassion of the Blessed Virgin; on all Fridays throughout the year, and during Lent; and of one hundred days for every other day during the year; second, a plenary indulgence once a month for those who recite it every day, and once a year for those who recite it, at least, four times a year.

The chaplet which is used must be blessed by a priest, who has received powers to do so. In order to sustain attentiveness and nourish piety, it will be well to meditate upon the seven mysteries of the dolors of Mary, indicated in the first exercise. We give an abstract of them here.

1st dolor: Saint Simeon predicts that a sword of sorrow shall pierce her soul.

2nd dolor: She is forced to fly into Egypt with Jesus and St. Joseph

3rd dolor: She loses the infant Jesus and searches for Him during three days.

4th dolor: She meets Jesus ascending to Calvary.

5th dolor: She sees Him attached to the Cross and dying.

6th dolor: She receives His body on Its descent from the Cross.

7th dolor: She accompanies Him to the sepulchre.

## *Prayer*

Lord Jesus, we implore now and at the hour of our death, the intercession of the most Blessed Virgin Mary, Thy mother, whose holy soul was transpierced with a sword of sorrow at the hour of Thy Passion. Grant us this grace, O Savior of the world, Thou who livest and reignest with the Father and the Holy Ghost forever and ever. Amen.

---

# The Gospel of the Holy Face

Recited over the Head of Pilgrims upon Request

In illo tempore, summus sacerdos interrogavit Jesum et dixit ei: Tu es Christus Filius Dei benedicti? Jesus autem dixit illi: Ego sum; et videbitis Filium hominis sedentem a dextris virtutis Dei et venientem cum nubibus cœli. Summus autem sacerdos, scindens vestimenta sua, ait: Quid adhuc desideramus testes? Audistis blasphemiam: quid vobis videtur? Qui omnes condemnaverunt eum esse reum mortis. Et cœperunt quidam conspuere eum, et velare Faciem ejus, et colaphis eum cædere et dicere ei: Prophetiza; et ministri alapis eum cædebant.

At that time, the high priest asked Jesus, and said to Him: Art Thou the Christ the Son of the Blessed God? and Jesus said to him: *I am. And you shall see the Son of Man sitting on the right hand of the power of God, and coming with the clouds of heaven.* Then the high priest, rending his garments saith: What need we any any further witnesses? You have heard the blasphemy. What think you? Who all condemned Him to be guilty of death. And some began to spit on Him, and to cover His Face, and to buffet Him and to say to Him: Prophesy: and the servants struck Him with the palms of their hands.

## ANTIPHONA

Insurrexerunt in me viri iniqui; absque misericordia quæsierunt me interficere, et non pepercerunt in Faciem meam spuere.

## ANTIPHON

Impious men have risen up against Me, having no pity; they sought to put Me to death, and they did not spare Me, but spit upon My Face.

*V.* Protector noster, aspice Deus;

*R.* Et respice in Faciem Christi tui.

*Oremus.* Concede, quæsumus, omnipotens et misericors Deus, ut qui Faciem Christi tui propter peccata nostra in Passione deformatam veneramur, eamdem in cœlesti gloria fulgentem contemplari perpetuo mereamur. Per eumdem. Amen.

V. Sanctissima Facies Christi Jesu,

*R.* Miserere ei (or nobis).

*V.* O God, our Protector, cast Thy eyes upon us;

*R.* And look upon the Face of Thy Christ.

*Let us pray.* Almighty and merciful God, grant, we beseech Thee, that whilst venerating the Face of Thy Christ disfigured in the Passion because of our sins, we may merit to contemplate It forever, shining in celestial glory. Through the same Jesus Christ. Amen.

V. Most Holy Face of Christ Jesus,

*R.* Have mercy upon him (*o*r her *o*r us).

———————

# Mass
## In Honor of the Most Holy Face
## Of Our Lord Jesus Christ Disfigured in
## His Passion

### INTROIT

Propter te, Domine, sustinui opprobrium; operuit confusio Faciem meam; et factus sum illis in parabolam. *Ps.* Salvum me fac, Deus; quoniam intraverunt aquæ usque ad animam meam.

V. Gloria Patri. Propter te...

It is for Thy glory, O Lord, that I have suffered opprobrium, that My Face has been covered with confusion, and that I have become a mockery to them. *Ps.* Save me, O God, because the waters of tribulation have entered into my soul.

V. Glory be to the Father. It is...

### COLLECT

Concede, quæsumus, omnipotens et misericors Deus, ut qui Faciem Christi tui propter peccata nostra in passione deformatam veneramur, eamdem in cœlesti gloria fulgentem contemplari perpetuo mereamur. Per eumdem.

Almighty and merciful God, grant, we beseech Thee, that whilst venerating the Face of Thy Christ disfigured in the Passion because of our sins, we may merit to contemplate It eternally in the splendor of heavenly glory. Through the same Jesus Christ. Amen.

# EPISTLE

## Lesson from the Prophet Isaias, ch. LII et LIII.

Sicut obstupuerunt super te multi, sic inglorius erit inter viros aspectus ejus, et forma ejus inter filios hominum. Iste asperget gentes multas, super ipsum continebunt reges os suum: quia quibus non est narratum de eo, viderunt: et qui non audierunt, contemplati sunt. Quis credidit auditui nostro? et brachium Domini cui revelatum est? Et ascendet sicut virgultum coram eo, et sicut radix de terra sitienti: non est species ei, neque decor; et vidimus eum, et non erat aspectus, et desideravimus eum. Despectum et novissimum virorum, virum dolorum, et scientem infirmitatem: et quasi absconditus Vultus ejus et despectus, unde nec reputavimus eum. Vere languores nostros ipse tulit, et dolores nostros ipse portavit.

Even as many have been astonished at Thee, so shall His visage be inglorious among men, and His form among the sons of men. He shall sprinkle many nations, kings shall shut their mouth at Him: for they to whom it was not told of Him, have seen: and they that heard not, have beheld. Who hath believed our report? and to whom is the arm of the Lord revealed? And He shall grow up as a tender plant before Him, and as a root out of a thirsty ground: there is no beauty in Him, nor comeliness: and we have seen Him, and there was no sightliness, that we should be desirous of Him: despised, and the most abject of men, a man of sorrows, and acquainted with infirmity: and His look was as it were hidden and despised, whereupon we esteemed Him not. Surely He hath our infirmities and carried our sorrows.

# GRADUAL

Confusio Faciei meæ cooperuit me a vocee exprobrantis et obloquentis, a facie inimici et persequentis.

The confusion of My Face hath covered Me at the voice of him that reproacheth and detracteth Me: at the face of the enemy and persecutor.

*V.* Cœperunt conspuere Jesum, et velare Faciem ejus, et colaphis eum cædere et dicere ei: Prophetiza: et ministri alapis eum cædebant.

*V.* They began to spit upon Jesus, to cover His Face, and to buffet Him and to say to Him: Prophesy: and the servants struck Him with the palms of their hands.

# TRACT

Improperium expectavit cor meum, et miseriam. Et sustinui qui simul constristaretur, et non fuit: et qui consolaretur, et non inveni. Et dederunt in escam meam fel: et in siti mea potaverunt me aceto.

My heart hath expected reproach and misery. And I looked for one that would grieve together with Me, but there was none: and for one that would comfort Me, and I found none. And they gave Me gall for My food, and in My thirst they gave Me vinegar to drink.

*V.* Quem tu percussisti, persecuti sunt: et super dolorem vulnerum meorum addiderunt.

*V.* They have persecuted Him whom Thou hast smitten; and they have added to the grief of My wounds.

## ☩ GOSPEL

### According to St. Mark, ch. XIV, v. 61 to 65.

In illo tempore: Summus sacerdos interrogavit Jesum et dixit ei: Tu es Christus Filius Dei benedicti? Jesus autem dixit illi: Ego sum: et videbitis Filium hominis sedentem a dextris virtutis Dei, et venientem cum nubibus cœli. Summus autem sacerdos scindens vestimenta sua, ait: Quid adhuc desideramus testes? Audistis blasphemiam: quid vobis videtur? Qui omnes condemnaverunt eum esse reum mortis. Et cœperunt quidam conspuere eum, et velare Faciem ejus, et colaphis eum cædere, et dicere ei: Prophetiza: et minisri alapis eum cædebant.

At that time: the high priest asked Him, and said to Him: Art Thou the Christ the Son of the blessed God? and Jesus said to him: *I am. And you shall see the Son of Man sitting on the right hand of the power of God, and coming with the clouds of heaven.* Then the high priest, rending his garments, saith: What need we any further witnesses? You have heard the blasphemy. What think you? And they all condemned Him to be guilty of death. And some began to spit upon Him, and to cover His Face, and to buffet Him, and to say unto Him: Prophesy: and the servants struck Him with the palms of their hands.

## OFFERTORY

Suscitatur falsiloquus adversus Faciem meam contradicens mihi. Aperuerunt super me ora sua, et exprobantes percusserunt maxillam meam. Satiati sunt pœnis meis. Hæc passus sum, cum haberem mundas ad Deum preces.

A false speaker riseth up against My Face, contradicting Me. They have opened their mouths upon Me, and reproaching Me they have struck Me on the cheek, they are filled with My pains. These things have I suffered when I offered pure prayers to God.

## SECRET

Averte, misericors Deus, Faciem tuam a peccatis nostris, et respice in Faciem Christi tui, qui tibi semetipsum pro nobis hostiam obtulit, et lavit nos a peccatis nostris in sanguine suo. Per eumdem... Qui tecum vivit, etc.

God of mercy, turn away Thy Face from our crimes, and cast Thy eyes upon the Face of Thy Christ, who has offered Himself to Thee as a victim for us, and has washed us from our sins in His own blood. Through the same Jesus Christ, who liveth and reigneth, etc.

## PREFACE OF THE CROSS

Vere dignum et justum est, æquum et salutare, nos tibi semper, et ubique gratias agere: Domine sancta, Pater omnipotens, æterne Deus. Qui salutem humani generis in ligno crucis constituisti: ut, unde mors oriebatur, inde vita resurgeret: et qui in ligno vincebat, in ligno quoque vinceretur, per Christum Dominum nostrum. Per quem majestatem tuam laudant Angeli, adorant Dominationes, tremunt Potestates. Cœli, cœlorumque Virtues, ac beata Seraphim, socia exsultatione concelebrant. Cum quibus et nostras voces, ut admítti jubeas, deprecamur, supplici confessione dicentes:

It is truly meet and just, right and for our salvation, that we should at all times, and in all places, give thanks unto Thee, O holy Lord, Father almighty, everlasting God: Who didst establish the salvation of mankind on the tree of the Cross; that whence death came, thence also life might arise again, and that he, who overcame by the tree, by the tree also might be overcome: Through Christ our Lord. Through whom the Angels praise Thy Majesty, the Dominations worship it, the Powers stand in awe. The heavens and the heavenly hosts together with the blessed Seraphim in triumphant chorus unite to celebrate it. Together with these we entreat Thee, that Thou mayest bid our voices also to be admitted while we say with lowly praise:

# COMMUNION

Exeamus ad Jesum extra castra, improperium ejus portantes.

Let us go forth from the camp, and let us go to Jesus, bearing the ignominy of His Cross.

## POST-COMMUNION

Adorantibus, Domine, Vultum tuum olim in ignominia Passionis quasi absconditum, et in hoc amoris tui Sacramento nunc velatum, concede propitius: ut et opprobria tua debita veneratione compensemus in terris, et gloriæ tuæ participes esse mereamur in cœlis. Qui vivis, etc.

Deign, O Lord to grant to those who adore Thy Face, once hidden under the ignominy of the Passion and now veiled in the Sacrament of Thy love, grace to compensate Thee for Thy opprobrium upon earth by reverential homage and to merit to share in Thy glory in heaven. Thou who livest etc.

---

# Hymn to the Holy Face

### I

O Face Divine of Jesus,
In ages long ago
Prophets and sages prayed that Thou,
On earth, Its light would show;
Most Holy Face, I cry to Thee,
Like them, that I Its beams may see.

### II

O radiant Face of Jesus,
Transfigured in the sight
Of Thy Apostles, on the Mount,
Shining with heaven's own light;
Most Holy Face, I cry to Thee,
Thus to reveal Thyself to me.

### III

O pitying Face of Jesus,
Thine eyes on Peter rest,
And bitter tears the Apostle sheds,
Contrite and sore distressed;
Most Holy Face, I cry to Thee,
Whene'er I sin, look so on me.

### IV

O suffering Face of Jesus,
Bleeding, and soiled, and torn,
Its temples and Its brow transpierced
By many a cruel thorn;
Most Holy Face, I cry to Thee,
Offer Thy wounds to God for me.

## V

O Face benign of Jesus,
The thief with sorrowing eyes
Gazed at It, and repentant went
With Christ to Paradise;
Most Holy Face, I cry to Thee,
In loving kindness look on me.

## VI

O dying Face of Jesus,
Upon the accursed tree,
Crying aloud: Ah! why, my God,
Hast Thou forsaken me?
Most Holy Face, I cry to Thee,
Plead by Thine agony for me.

## VII

O risen Face of Jesus,
Never was face like Thine,
Where Godhead joins with manhood,
In unity Divine;
Most Holy Face, I cry to Thee,
Turn not away Thy gaze from me.

## VIII

O awful Face of Jesus,
How shall I bear Thy sight
When, at the judgment, all my sins
Reveal themselves to light;
Most Holy Face, I cry to Thee,
In that dread hour to pity me.

## IX

O glorious Face of Jesus,
If, after I have died,
My soul but in Thy likeness wake,
I shall be satisfied;
Most Holy Face, I cry to Thee,
More like Thee ever make Thou me.

---

# Hymn to the Holy Face

For the use of the Archconfraternity

### I

O Lord our God, and Brother, bruised
For us beneath a load of grief,
Before Thy solitary Face,
We come, to give our tears relief.

*Refrain*

O Face adorable, august,
Of our Redeemer, see
A guilty people come to make
Reparation unto Thee.

### II

Look on that forehead pierced with thorns,
And contemplate that Face Divine:
Its eyes bedimmed with tears and blood,
Savior! can it indeed be Thine?
(*Refrain*)

### III

"When our eyes saw Him," prophets said,
"Beauty and glory He had none.
Bowed down, like storm tossed reed He was,
Or leper which the world doth shun."
(*Refrain*)

## IV

He, loveliest of the sons of men,
He, of Gods rays the mirror clear,
Behold Him now! And we, ah! we,
To be His hangmen do not fear.
*(Refrain)*

## V

Upon that cruel night, when scorned
And outraged was that Holy Face,
And the most high, thrice holy, God
Was yielded up to menials base.
*(Refrain)*

## VI

We too were there: our sinful hands
Perchance, on Him fierce blows did wreak,
Or else, alas! we left Him alone,
Friends faithless found, companions weak.
*(Refrain)*

## VII

Forgive us, Jesus, victim dear,
Forgive, ungrateful though we be;
When prostrate we confess our crimes,
Thy Face, Redeemer, let us see.
*(Refrain)*

## VIII

O Face adored! Be Thine our sighs,
Our secret tears, by day and night;
The world runs after treasures frail,
Thy Face alone is our delight.
*(Refrain)*

### IX

We keep Thee, and Thou keepest us,
Thy blood and tears to us belong,
Our brows grow pure beneath Thy gaze.
And near to Thee, our hearts are strong.
(*Refrain*)

### X

O Face desirable, august,
Ceaseless we march on earth to Thee,
Face of our God awaiting us,
Soon we in heaven Thyself shall see.
(*Refrain)*

---

## Devout Addresses to the Sacred Face

O Face Divine!
Face most sorrowful yet so benign!
So beauteous still in grief, towards me incline!

Sacred Eyes!
On which the weight of dreaded anguish lies,
That look must break the heart which Christ denies.

Lips so Meek!
Unless their all-absolving word I seek,
Those lips one day eternal doom will speak.

Sacred Face!
Which mortal hand has dared with prayer to trace,
Thee on my heart with throbs of awe I place.

O Face Divine!
Give me of love returned some blissful sign;
O Face Divine, in grief towards me incline.

---

# Canticles
## In Honor of the Needs of the Holy Face
From the French Writings of Sister Marie de Saint-Pierre

### Canticle – First

#### I

From out the sanctuary's silence
What sighs are those I hear?
What bitter cry is breaking
From Thy soul, Savior dear?
"Alas! the whole world wounds Me
With blasphemy's swift dart;
My love hath lost its power
O'er man's forgetful heart.

#### II

"With deadly hatred banded,
Schism walks forth today,
The holiest laws defying,
Impatient of their sway;
And My Face, that highest rapture
In the vision of the blest,
With a constant memory cruel
Of their outrage is impressed.

#### III

"O ye to whose brave spirits
My glory is so near,
To whom My victory cometh,
My triumph is so dear,
Ye are My cherished spouses;

My Name e'er holy keep,
Asking ever for the guilty
Pardon and sorrow deep.

### IV

"Of old, before My Passion,
Veronica, with love's great power,
Clad with courage, seemed to soften
All the anguish of that hour.
Another Veronica I now long for
Who, adoring night and day,
On My bleeding brow unceasing
The veil of her true love shall lay.

### V

"And Veronica, the faithful,
My grateful memory knew;
Of My Holy Face forever
She kept the Image true.
To ye also I now leave it;
Let thine hearts be impressed deep,
And with love's tender homage
A fervent incense keep.

### VI

"In this Countenance Divine
The Godhead is concealed;
'Tis the mirror where His beauty
Eternal is revealed.
Ah! Christian soul, if only
Thou knewest the holy spell
Of that Face, what supreme rapture
Would in thy spirit swell!

### VII

"On the Brow behold the Father,
From the Lips list to the Son,
In the Eyes' pure light the Spirit
Of the Holy Three-in-One.
And these sacred tresses, countless,
The symbols seem to be
Of the attributes surrounding
The God-like Trinity.

### VIII

"This Holy Face reflecting
My blest Humanity
Is for thee the precious ransom
Paid for thine eternity.
None have ever met denial
Who looked to its priceless worth,
That Face of treasures holiest
That await the elect of earth.

### IX

"Alas! blasphemy's outrage
Wounds Me on every side;
Have I no brave defenders
In whom I may confide?
Avenge Me, faithful virgins,
My cruel wrongs repair;
Be thine the gentle vengeance
Of love and tears and prayer.

### X

"Within thine hearts My Image
Deeply shall ye enshrine,
Till its beauty shall enkindle
The fires of love Divine.

And this Face for e'er adored
The sign and the seal shall be
Of the grace which shall be thy greeting
In a blest eternity."

## Canticle – Second

### I

Lord Jesus, our God, our Brother,
We have grieved Thee, Savior above;
Before Thy Face, God-like and lonely,
We pour out our tears and our love.

*Refrain*
Face ever adored,
Behold 'neath Thee now
A people most sinful
In penitence bow.

### II

See the Brow, where the thorns are piercing,
And the Face — ah! God, is it Thine?
The tears and the blood of Redemption
Are veiling those Eyes Divine.
(*Refrain*)

### III

"We have seen Him," crieth the prophet,
"Without beauty, deserted, alone,
As a reed all bruised by the tempest,
As a leper cast forth from His own."
(*Refrain*)

## IV

Of the sons of men the fairest,
Bright Mirror of splendors Divine.
Behold Him, for thou art, sinner,
His tormentor; the lashes are thine.
(*Refrain*)

## V

Holy Face, on that night most cruel
Thou with infamous blows wast stained;
The Most High, the God thrice holy,
By the fury of wretches profaned.
(*Refrain*)

## VI

We were there; our hands have wounded
Our Christ. Ah! sinners, 'tis true;
We were the faithless companions,
False friends — we deserted Him, too.
(*Refrain*)

## VII

Forgive us, Jesus, our Victim!
Forgive them that slight Thee, we pray;
When before Thee we kneel in sorrow,
Thy Face, Lord, turn not away.
(*Refrain*)

## VIII

Holy Face, our days and our vigils,
Our vows and our tears, are Thine;
The world seeks its false pleasures,
We are shielding the Face Divine.
(*Refrain*)

## IX

We shield Thee, and Thou wilt shield us
Thy sorrows to us belong;
Our brows are pure when Thou lookest,
And near Thee our hearts are strong.
(*Refrain*)

## X

Face Divine, Face ever desired,
Our steps turn ceaseless to Thee;
Face of God, forever adored,
Where Thou waitest soon let us be.
(*Refrain*)

## Canticle to St. PeterRepenting

### I

Before the Altar, where the soul repenteth
Beholding God, with sin and sorrow crushed,
Remembers and adores Love immolated,
The heart dejected, powerless, is hushed.

*First Refrain*
O! holy tears,
Heart-voices flow,
Telling its fears,
Regrets, and woe.

### II

Ah! fruitful tears, how oft our souls have sought ye,
How oft we waited for ye, all in vain;
Bring forth from their deep sources, mighty Patron,
Of love repentant bring our tears, blest rain.
(*First Refrain*)

### III

Thrice in that night of blasphemy had Peter
Faltered, and, alas! his Lord denied.
Ah! sinners, let us weep — weep for ourselves
And for the countless sins we cannot hide;
*(First Refrain)*

### IV

When Peter saw Its look on him as a sinner,
He was the first conquest of the Holy Face;
Already wounded but Divine forever,
It blest and pardoned him with mercy's grace.
*(First Refrain)*

### V

And when his Lord had once looked on Peter
Grief smote him, and, with swift, repentant cry,
He wept for his sin; and those dews penitential
Dwelt ever in his eyes till life's last sigh.
*(First Refrain)*

### VI

But one blest day the stream that o'er his spirit
In sorrow flowed a sweeter measure traced;
The triple sin was blotted out forever
Was by the triple oath of love effaced.
*(First Refrain)*

### VII

"Thou knowest, Lord, I love Thee," vows the Apostle,
And from Christ's feet arises, all the weight
The supreme burden bearing of Chief Shepherd;
His tears of love crown him and consecrate!

*Second Refrain*
Oh! sweet tears, flow;
Come, fervor true,
Your power show,
And our hearts subdue.

## VIII

Thou who thyself didst know one human weakness,
Thou who thy God's forgiveness sweet didst taste,
Thou whom He vested with His wondrous powers
To open for us heaven's riches, haste!
(*Second Refrain*)

## IX

The Church, alas! like Christ at the Tribunal,
Ever on dread Calvary's Mount appears.
Around our Mother's feet, then, let us sorrow;
But let hope strengthen, make sweet our tears.
(*Second Refrain*)

## X

For we have loved her, holy Church immortal,
Where Thou dost live again, the Three-in-One.
She keeps Thy faith; help us, God! To give her
Our tears and blood, even as Thou hast done.
(*Second Refrain*)

---

# A Rhythm

Pope John XXII, elected Sovereign Pontiff at Avignon in 1316, wrote the following prayer in honor of the Most Holy Veil, and granted an Indulgence of twenty-five years and twenty-five quarantines to the faithful who would recite it. To those who cannot read, the same Indulgence is granted provided five Our Fathers, five Hail Marys, and the Gloria be said for the same intention.

### I

Hail, token of love to Veronica given!
Stamped Divinely on linen, without spot or stain,
Pure and bright with the splendor that comes but from
heaven; Features most sacred of Jesus, all hail!

### II

Hail, glory of earth, of Thy faithful the Mirror!
'Tis to see Thy blest Face Thrones and Virtues aspire!
Send afar from us all the dark stains of error,
That with Thee at last we may find our desire.

### III

Hail, features most sacred! Hail, Face of my Savior!
O! shed on us here the sweet light of Thy love.
From on High Thou receiv'dst the Omnipotent favor
Of freeing our senses from all but Thy love.

### IV

Hail, rampart of Faith! Be with us forever;
Before Thee dread Heresy's poisonous dart
Is dispelled. Bless Thy people; O! let us ne'er sever
Our eyes from Thy features, our love from Thy Heart.

### V

Hail, refuge in sorrow, and help in our way!
Through this lifetime of danger O! be our tried friend;

Call us ever, blessed Image, to heaven away,
Where Thy radiant Face beckons us to ascend.

### VI

Hail, Jesus Divine! Hail, diamond most bright!
O'er the light of the firmament shines Thy soft ray.
God Himself formed these lines, beauteous, fair in His sight,
And without mortal aid bid these blest Features to stay.

### VII

Hail, Reflection unchanging, of joy without end!
The glory Divine which on Thee appears
Is ever as pure as when first to us given;
Beauty e'er new, Thou fad'st not in years.

### VIII

Hail, Essence of Majesty, Sacred yet kind!
Thy Face the calm impress of purity bears;
O! let us not *Justice* but sweet *Mercy* find,
And grant us in heaven a rest from our fears!

### IX

O! be our loved Refuge, our Help, and our Star;
Be a soft, soothing balm to our hearts, till above,
In the calm rest eternal of Thy heaven afar,
We may praise Thee forever and ever in love.
Amen.

### *Let us pray*

Give joy to the countenance of Thy servants, O my Lord, and save our souls from the darkness of hell, that, being protected by the contemplation of Thy adorable Face, we may trample on all carnal desires, and see Thee, O Lord Jesus, our Savior, face to Face, without fear, when the clouds of heaven will open to admit us to Thy judgment. Amen.

---

# A Rhythm

The following prayer was composed by Pope Clement VI, at Avignon. His Holiness granted an indulgence of three years to all those who would recite it before a *Vera Effigies*, or authentic facsimile of the Veil of St. Veronica.

### I

O venerated Features, hail!
On the bleeding altar of the Cross,
Alas! how altered and how pale!
Thou look'st so sorrowful and sad,
Staining with Thy Sweat and Blood
This precious Veil and wood!

### II

Token of Thy Passion sad,
This Veil is brightest even now;
'Twas stamped and given for our Redemption,
Inflame my soul, sweet Jesus, teach
My heart the fire of Thy love;
Reveal to us Thy Features fair above.

### III

O! grant me, at the end of life,
Of God the beauty for ever to see;
Give to my then transported soul
The bliss of heaven's felicity. Amen.

*V.* Make the light of Thy Countenance, O Lord, to shine upon us,
*R.* Thou hast given gladness to my heart.
*V.* Save Thy servant.
*R.* Trusting in Thee, O my God.
*V.* Save me in Thy mercy, O Lord.

*R.* Let me not be confounded, for I have called upon Thy Name.

*V.* Make Thy Face to shine upon Thy servant.

*R.* And teach me Thy way upon earth.

*V.* O Lord God of Hosts, convert us.

*R.* And show Thy Face, and we shall be saved.

*V.* O Lord, hear my prayer.

*R.* And let my cry come unto Thee.

### *Let us pray*

O God, who hast shed upon us the light of Thy Face, and who wast pleased, through Veronica, to leave us Thy Holy Image imprinted on this veil as an eternal token of Thy love, grant us by Thy Passion and Cross the grace so to honor, adore and glorify Thee here below, through this mystical Veil, that we may without fear meet Thy gaze when Thou wilt receive and judge us in heaven. Amen.

O Eternal and Omnipotent God, whose Divine Features are revealed through this precious Image to Thy people here assembled, grant us the pardon of our sins, and direct our actions, words, senses, and faculties. We trust in Thy mercy, O Lord, who liveth and reigneth with Thee in the unity of the Holy Ghost, one God, world without end. Amen.

---

# Act of Reparation
# For Blasphemy and Irreverence

To be recited at the monthly meeting of the Confraternity

O God, infinitely worthy of all adoration and love, I prostrate myself at Thy feet, filled with grief for the blasphemies uttered against Thy Holy Name, and for the offenses committed against Thy Divine worship and the observances of Thy Church.

O my God, this blasphemy is the profanation of that which is most holy in the height of Thine inaccessible sanctuary; it is an attack upon Thine infinite majesty; an outrage against the Face of Thy Divine Son; a crime without excuse, without any other motive than that wickedness which hates Thee, O God, infinitely worthy of all love!

We beg pardon, O Lord, a thousand times pardon, for these blasphemies. Would that we could prevent them by the sacrifice of all that we are or that we possess! At least it is in the sincerity of our hearts that we desire with all our power to combat this horrible crime, and for all we hear or know to offer instantly, by the merits of the Face of Thy Christ, our humble and sorrowful expiation.

But that which is most grievous to us is that, while blasphemy and infidelity daily increase, the adoration due to Thee diminishes. Alas! now, even more than in the days of the prophet Ezekiel, men neglect and profane Thy holy days, because their hearts are given to idols. Slaves of avarice and of pleasure, they have no longer time for Thy worship nor attraction to Thine altars. The days set apart for Thy service are profaned by their worldliness or pleasure. They abandon Thy house; they fly from the preaching of Thy word; they despise the sacraments and graces of the sanctuary to give themselves to labors forbidden or to amusements still more criminal.

O Lord, grant us the grace to make reparation for this contempt and forgetfulness of Thee by the zeal and fervor of our adoration. Bless this Confraternity established under the invocation of the adorable Face of Jesus Christ, that by its prayers and sacrifices it may bring back to Thy worship and to the observances of Thy Church the unfaithful who have strayed from Thee. Receive our vows and promises never to transgress Thy sacred precepts, neither in our own persons nor by those who are under our charge; and in every way possible to us, to procure the obedience and honor which are due to Thee.

> May the most adorable Name of the Lord be glorified forever!
> May the holy days of Thy Church be sanctified by all men! Amen.
> Saint Michael, Pray for us.
> Saint Peter, Pray for us.
> Saint Martin, Pray for us.
> Saint Louis, Pray for us.
> Saint Veronica, Pray for us.
> O God, our protector, look upon the Face of Thy Christ, and we shall be saved!

---

# An Offering

Of the Infinite Merits of Our Lord Jesus Christ to His Eternal Father
In Order to Appease the Divine Justice and Draw Mercy on France†
*(†Substitute with the name of the country you are praying for)*

Eternal Father, turn Thine offended eyes from culpable France†, whose face has become hideous in Thy eyes, and look upon the Face of Thy Son which we offer Thee — this well-beloved Son, in whom Thou art well pleased. Listen, we beseech Thee, to the voice of His blood and His wounds, which cry out for mercy.

Eternal Father, behold the Incarnation of Jesus, Thy Divine Son, and His sojourn in the womb of His Blessed Mother. **We offer this to Thee for the honor and glory of Thy Holy Name and for the salvation of France.†**

Eternal Father, behold the birth of Jesus in the stable of Bethlehem and the mysteries of His most Holy Infancy. We offer them to Thee, etc.

Eternal Father, behold the poor, hidden, and laborious life of Jesus at Nazareth. We offer it to Thee, etc.

Eternal Father, behold the baptism of Jesus and His forty days' retreat in the desert. We offer these to Thee, etc.

Eternal Father, behold the journeys, the vigils, the prayers, miracles, and sermons of Jesus. We offer them to Thee, etc.

Eternal Father, behold the Last Supper which Jesus made with His disciples, at which He washed their feet and instituted the august sacrament of the Eucharist. We offer this to Thee, etc.

Eternal Father, behold the agony of Jesus in the Garden of Olives, the sweat of blood which covered His Body and flowed to the ground. We offer this to Thee, etc.

Eternal Father, behold the outrages which Jesus received before His judges, and His condemnation to death. We offer them to Thee, etc.

Eternal Father, behold Jesus burdened with His Cross and walking towards the place where He is to be immolated. We offer Him to Thee, etc.

Eternal Father, behold Jesus crucified between two thieves, tasting gall and vinegar, blasphemed, and dying to repair Thy glory and to save the world. We offer Him to Thee, etc.

Eternal Father, behold the Sacred Head of Jesus crowned with thorns. We offer it to Thee, etc.

Eternal Father, behold the adorable Face of Jesus bruised with buffets, covered with sweat, dust, and blood. We offer it to Thee, etc.

Eternal Father, behold the adorable Body of Jesus taken down from the Cross. We offer it to Thee, etc.

Eternal Father, behold the Heart, Soul, and Divinity of Jesus, this Holy Victim who in dying has triumphed over sin. We offer them to Thee, etc.

Eternal Father, behold all that Jesus Christ, Thy only Son, has done during the thirty-three years of His mortal life to accomplish the work of our Redemption. Behold all the mysteries of His Holy Life. We offer them to Thee, etc.

Eternal Father, behold all the desires, all the thoughts, words, actions, virtues, perfections, and prayers, of Jesus Christ; also all His sufferings and humiliations. We offer them to Thee, etc.

Eternal Father, behold the crib, the swaddling-bands which have served Jesus at His birth. We offer them to Thee, etc.

Eternal Father, behold the Cross, the nails, the crown of thorns, the reed, the bloody scourge, the column, the lance, the sepulchre, the winding-sheet, and all the instruments which were used in the Passion of Jesus, Thy Divine Son. We offer them to Thee, etc.

———————

# One Hundred Offerings Of Our Lord Jesus Christ to His Eternal Father

*Thirty-three Offerings of Jesus Christ in His Infancy and Hidden Life*

1. Eternal Father, I offer Thee Jesus, Incarnate in the womb of the Virgin Mary for the salvation of men.
2. Eternal Father, I offer Thee Jesus, sanctifying St. John the Baptist in the womb of His mother, St. Elizabeth.
3. Eternal Father, I offer Thee Jesus, a captive for nine months in the chaste womb of His Blessed Mother.
4. Eternal Father, I offer Thee Jesus, rejected by the inhabitants of Bethlehem.
5. Eternal Father, I offer Thee Jesus, coming forth from the womb of His Mother and born in a poor stable.
6. Eternal Father, I offer Thee Jesus, wrapped in swaddling-clothes and laid in a manger.
7. Eternal Father, I offer Thee Jesus, trembling with cold and warmed by the breath of an ox and a donkey.
8. Eternal Father, I offer Thee Jesus, weeping for our sins in the manger.

9. Eternal Father, I offer Thee Jesus, by the hands of Mary and St. Joseph, for the salvation of the world.

10. Eternal Father, I offer Thee Jesus, nursed by Mary.

11. Eternal Father, I offer Thee Jesus, adored by angels in the stable of Bethlehem.

12. Eternal Father, I offer Thee Jesus, adored by the poor shepherds.

13. Eternal Father, I offer Thee Jesus, circumcised and named Jesus, beginning to fulfill the office of Savior in offering Thee the first-fruits of His Blood.

14. Eternal Father, I offer Thee Jesus, receiving the gifts and adorations of the Magi.

15. Eternal Father, I offer Thee all the glory that Jesus has rendered Thee during the forty days He dwelt in the stable of Bethlehem.

16. Eternal Father, I offer Thee Jesus, brought to the Temple by Mary and Joseph, and received with great joy by the holy old man Simeon and the prophetess Anna.

17. Eternal Father, I offer Thee Jesus, who offers Himself to Thy Divine justice to be the repairer of Thy outraged glory and the holy victim of sinners.

18. Eternal Father, I offer Thee Jesus, fleeing into Egypt to avoid the murderous hand of Herod.

19. Eternal Father, I offer Thee Jesus, poor and unknown in His exile, but tenderly loved and profoundly adored by Mary, Joseph, and the angels.

20. Eternal Father, I offer Thee Jesus, carried in the arms of Mary and Joseph and submitting to all the trials of infancy.

21. Eternal Father, I offer Thee Jesus, nursed by His Divine Mother for fifteen months.

22. Eternal Father, I offer Thee the first steps, the first words, the first actions of Thy Divine Son Jesus.

23. Eternal Father, I offer Thee all that Jesus suffered in the seven years of His exile in Egypt.

24. Eternal Father, I offer Thee Jesus, returning to Nazareth between Mary and Joseph.

25. Eternal Father, I offer Thee Jesus, growing in age and in wisdom before God and men.

26. Eternal Father, I offer Thee Jesus, conducted to the Temple at the age of twelve years to celebrate the Passover.

27. Eternal Father, I offer Thee Jesus, remaining three days in the Temple in the midst of the Doctors of the Law, and filling them with admiration.

28. Eternal Father, I offer Thee Jesus, found by Mary and Joseph, returning to Nazareth, and being perfectly submissive to them.

29. Eternal Father, I offer Thee Jesus, hiding His glory in the workshop of St. Joseph, and seeming to be only a carpenter.

30. Eternal Father, I offer Thee Jesus, working for His support by the sweat of His brow.

31. Eternal Father, I offer Thee Jesus, assisting St. Joseph during His last illness and at the hour of His death.

32. Eternal Father, I offer Thee Jesus, consoling Mary, His Blessed Mother, for the death of her holy spouse.

33. Eternal Father, I offer Thee all the glory that Jesus has rendered Thee during the thirty-three years of His hidden and laborious life, also all the merits He has acquired for us.

Eternal Father, I offer Thee all the glory that our Divine Savior Jesus has rendered Thee during the thirty years of His hidden and laborious life, and all the merits He has acquired for us from the moment of His Divine Incarnation until His evangelical Life. I make this offering for the honor and glory of Thy Holy Name, in reparation for the indignities offered our Savior; finally, for the wants of the Holy Church, the Salvation of France (*or the country you are praying for*), and the Work of Reparation.

*Thirty-three Offerings of Jesus in His Evangelical Life*

34.  Eternal Father, I offer Thee Jesus, baptized in the river Jordan by St. John the Baptist.

35.  Eternal Father, I offer Thee Jesus, led by the Spirit into the desert, and suffering there hunger and thirst.

36.  Eternal Father, I offer Thee Jesus, spending His nights in the desert among wild beasts.

37.  Eternal Father, I offer Thee Jesus, passing days and nights in prayer, watering the ground with His Divine tears, in expiation for our sins.

38.  Eternal Father, I offer Thee Jesus, tempted by the evil spirit to change stones into bread.

39.  Eternal Father, I offer Thee Jesus, carried by Satan to the top of the Temple, and tempted by this evil spirit to cast Himself down.

40.  Eternal Father, I offer Thee Jesus, carried by Satan to the top of a high mountain with the promise of all the kingdoms of the world.

41.  Eternal Father, I offer Thee Jesus, triumphing over the temptations of the evil spirit and confronting him with the words of Holy Scripture.

42.  Eternal Father, I offer Thee Jesus, in the desert taking the food ministered by the angels.

43.  Eternal Father, I offer Thee all the glory that Jesus has rendered Thee in the desert and all the merits He has acquired for us.

44. Eternal Father, I offer Thee Jesus, coming forth from the desert and going to make known to His Blessed Mother the mission He was about to commence.

45. Eternal Father, I offer Thee Jesus, choosing poor fishermen for His Apostles.

46. Eternal Father, I offer Thee Jesus, going from city to city, from town to town, preaching everywhere the Kingdom of God, and making known His Divine Father.

47. Eternal Father, I offer Thee Jesus, followed by immense crowds even to the desert.

48. Eternal Father, I offer Thee Jesus, multiplying the loaves and fishes to feed the multitude.

49. Eternal Father, I offer Thee Jesus, consoling the afflicted.

50. Eternal Father, I offer Thee Jesus, curing the sick and raising the dead.

51. Eternal Father, I offer Thee Jesus, driving out the evil spirit from those who were possessed.

52. Eternal Father, I offer Thee Jesus, giving sight to the blind and hearing to the deaf.

53. Eternal Father, I offer Thee Jesus, curing the lame and making the dumb to speak.

54. Eternal Father, I offer Thee Jesus, converting sinners and doing good to all.

55. Eternal Father, I offer Thee Jesus, weeping for the death of Lazarus and raising Him to life.

56. Eternal Father, I offer Thee Jesus, converting Mary Magdalene.

57. Eternal Father, I offer Thee Jesus, weary by the . wayside and seated on Jacob's Well.

58. Eternal Father, I offer Thee Jesus, asking drink of the Samaritan woman, converting her, and making known to her that He was the promised Messiah.

59. Eternal Father, I offer Thee Jesus, confounding His enemies with an admirable wisdom when they presented before Him a woman taken in adultery.

60. Eternal Father, I offer Thee Jesus, driving the sellers out of the Temple.

61. Eternal Father, I offer Thee Jesus, transfigured on Mt. Tabor, conversing with Moses and Elias on the greatness of the sorrows of His Passion.

62. Eternal Father, I offer Thee Jesus, embracing and blessing little children, bidding us to become as one of them to enter the Kingdom of Heaven.

63. Eternal Father, I offer Thee Jesus, entering the city of Jerusalem in triumph, and received as a King by the people.

64. Eternal Father, I offer Thee Jesus, weeping for the sins of Jerusalem.

65. Eternal Father, I offer Thee Jesus alone and abandoned, obliged on the evening of the Feast to seek the hospitality of Martha and Mary, at Bethany.

66. Eternal Father, I offer Thee all the glory that Jesus has rendered Thee during the three years of His Divine preachings.

Eternal Father, I offer Thee all the glory that Jesus, our Divine Savior, has rendered Thee, all the infinite merits He has acquired for us from the moment of His evangelical life until His Passion. I make this offering for the honor and glory of Thy Holy Name, to repair the outrages offered our Divine Savior; finally, for the wants of the Holy Church, the salvation of France (*or country you are praying for*), and the extension of the Work of Reparation.

67. Eternal Father, I offer Thee Jesus, sold for thirty pieces of silver by the traitor Judas.

68. Eternal Father, I offer Thee Jesus, taking His Last Supper with His Apostles.

69. Eternal Father, I offer Thee Jesus, humbling Himself unto washing the feet of His Apostles.

70. Eternal Father, I offer, Thee Jesus, instituting the adorable Sacrament of the Eucharist and ordaining His Apostles priests of the New Law.

71. Eternal Father, I offer Thee Jesus, praying and in an agony in the Garden of Olives.

72. Eternal Father, I offer Thee Jesus, suffering in His Divine Heart all the sorrows of His Passion and watering the earth with a profuse sweat of blood.

73. Eternal Father, I offer Thee Jesus, sorrowful unto death in the Garden of Olives, burdened with all the sins of the world, and accepting the chalice from Thy Hand.

74. Eternal Father, I offer Thee Jesus, betrayed and kissed by the perfidious Judas, delivering Himself up to His enemies to be bound and blindfolded for our sins.

75. Eternal Father, I offer Thee Jesus, abandoned by His disciples, maltreated and outraged by the soldiers, and led to the house of the high-priest Annas.

76. Eternal Father, I offer Thee Jesus, interrogated and receiving a blow from a servant.

77. Eternal Father, I offer Thee Jesus, conducted to the house of Caiaphas and accused by false witnesses.

78. Eternal Father, I offer Thee Jesus, treated as a blasphemer because He declared to His enemies that He was the Son of God.

79. Eternal Father, I offer Thee Jesus, despised, struck, and spit upon during that horrible night, and treated as the vilest slave.

80. Eternal Father, I offer Thee Jesus, conducted in chains to Pilate's house.

81. Eternal Father, I offer Thee Jesus, led to the court of Herod and despised by that impious king.

82. Eternal Father, I offer Thee Jesus, reconducted to the house of Pilate, treated with contempt and humiliations on the streets of Jerusalem by a nation which He had overwhelmed with benefits.

83. Eternal Father, I offer Thee Jesus, tied to the column and torn by the stripes of the scourge.

84. Eternal Father, I offer Thee Jesus, covered with wounds and blood, trampled upon by His executioners.

85. Eternal Father, I offer Thee Jesus, arrayed as a mock-king, crowned with thorns, robed in a scarlet mantle, His arms tied, and a reed for a scepter in His hand.

86. Eternal Father, I offer Thee Jesus, outraged, despised, and then shown to the people.

87. Eternal Father, I offer Thee Jesus, rejected by His people, who with loud voices demanded His death and preferred to Him an infamous thief, Barabbas.

88. Eternal Father, I offer Thee Jesus, condemned by Pilate to the death of the Cross.

89. Eternal Father, I offer Thee Jesus, given over to an insolent multitude, who vent upon this sweet Lamb, so meek and humble of Heart, all that the darkest malice could devise.

90. Eternal Father, I offer Thee Jesus, going forth from Pilate's hall between the two thieves, carrying the Cross upon His Divine Shoulders, bruised and bleeding.

91. Eternal Father, I offer Thee Jesus, exhausted by fatigue, falling several times under the heavy burden of His Cross, beaten and overwhelmed with injurious treatment by His executioners.

92. Eternal Father, I offer Thee Jesus on the summit of Calvary, despoiled of His garments and extending Himself on the tree of the Cross as a Lamb without stain.

93. Eternal Father, I offer Thee Jesus, nailed with heavy blows of the hammer to the Cross.

94. Eternal Father, I offer Thee Jesus, suspended for three hours between heaven and earth, satiated with revilings, partaking of gall and vinegar, and tasting with delight the intensity of interior and exterior sufferings.

95. Eternal Father, I offer Thee Jesus, asking forgiveness for His executioners, granting pardon to the good thief, and giving us His most Blessed Mother.

96. Eternal Father, I offer Thee Jesus, consummating His sacrifice and yielding up His Holy Soul into Thy Hands, uttering a loud cry to call all sinners to Him, inclining His Head to give them the kiss of peace and the last sigh of His Heart.

97. Eternal Father, I offer Thee Jesus, His Heart pierced by a lance, His Sacred Body covered with wounds and blood, taken down from the Cross and placed in the arms of His Divine Mother.

98. Eternal Father, I offer Thee Jesus, embalmed and shrouded by His Holy Mother, assisted by His faithful friends; then carried to the sepulchre and remaining therein three days, as He had foretold.

99. Eternal Father, I offer Thee Jesus, rising victorious from the tomb and visiting His Blessed Mother.

100.     Eternal Father, I offer Thee Jesus, appearing to
          His Apostles and the holy women for their
          consolation and instruction, gloriously ascending to
          heaven in their presence forty days after His
          Resurrection.

Eternal Father, I offer Thee all the glory that Jesus Christ, our Divine Savior, has rendered Thee, as well as all the merits He has acquired for us during His sorrowful and glorious life. I make this offering for the honor and glory of Thy Holy Name, in reparation for the indignities offered to our Savior — in fine, for the needs of the Holy Church, for the salvation of France *(or the country you are praying for)* and the entire world, and for the extension of the Work of Reparation.

*This is My well-beloved Son,*
*in whom I am, well pleased. Hear ye Him.*

*In truth I say to thee that all thou wilt ask the*
*Father in My Name He will grant.*
*Ask, and thou shall receive.*

———————

# The Sacred Humanity of Jesus

And the Holy use He made of His Senses, Offered to
The Eternal Father to Repair and Efface the Sins
We have Committed by Ours

Eternal Father, I offer Thee the Sacred Feet of Jesus, walking and traveling, and finally pierced by rough nails, to repair our criminal steps.

Eternal Father, I offer Thee all the devout and respectful prostrations of Jesus before Thy Divine Majesty, to repair all our irreverences in Thy holy presence.

Eternal Father, I offer Thee the Divine Hands of Jesus, which accomplished so many good works, and nevertheless were pierced by rough nails, to repair all the sins of our wicked hands and our iniquitous works.

Eternal Father, I offer Thee the Divine Arms of Jesus, fatigued by labor and torn by the whips of His executioners, to atone for our sins of sloth and all our other crimes.

Eternal Father, I offer Thee the Divine Head of Jesus, crowned with thorns, His hair covered with blood, to atone for our sins of pride and all our criminal thoughts.

Eternal Father, I offer Thee the adorable Eyes and looks of Jesus, full of sweetness and majesty, to atone for our sins of immodesty and curiosity.

Eternal Father, I offer Thee also His sleep, His vigils, His tears which flowed from His Divine Eyes, to merit the pardon of our faults.

Eternal Father, I offer Thee the mortification of the smell of Jesus, to atone for all the sins of sensuality of which we are guilty.

Eternal Father, I offer Thee the adorable Mouth of Jesus, His Divine words, and His admirable silence, to repair all the sins that our bad and unruly tongue has committed. I offer Thee also His fasts and His frugal meals, to repair all our sins of gluttony and intemperance.

Eternal Father, I offer Thee the adorable Face of Jesus, covered with spittle, sweat, dust, and blood, bruised by buffets, and His beard torn out, to repair the pride and vanity, also all the other sins, of worldlings.

Eternal Father, I offer Thee the prayers, praises, and thanksgivings of Jesus, to repair blasphemies and all sins committed against the glory of Thy Name.

Eternal Father, I offer Thee the Sacred Body of Jesus, covered with wounds, to repair all the sins of our corrupt flesh. We offer Thee the seven effusions of His precious Blood, to purify us from our crimes.

Eternal Father, I offer Thee the inflamed Heart of Jesus, pierced by a lance, to repair all the sins committed by our hearts. I offer also all the desires, sighs, thoughts, affections, prayers, and virtues, all the adorable perfections of this Divine Heart, to cover the poverty of our poor, miserable hearts.

Eternal Father, I offer Thee the holy Soul of Jesus, that sacrificed Itself for us and gave Itself into Thy hands at the moment of death. By the glory and merits of this most holy Soul, we pray Thee to pardon and justify our criminal souls.

Eternal Father, I offer Thee the Divine, glorious, and laborious life of Jesus. We beseech Thee, by the holiness of His interior life, to pardon our lives, spent in indifference and dissipation.

Eternal Father, I offer Thee the eternal birth of Jesus in the splendor of Thy glory. I offer also all the praises, honor, and eternal love He has for Thee, to repair all the impieties and blasphemies of poor blinded sinners.

Eternal Father, I offer Thee this Divine Jesus, to adore, love, and glorify in Him and by Him all Thy adorable perfections and Thy Sacred Name, which is unknown to creatures, but which expresses all that Thou art, and which Thy Divine Son Jesus alone knows and adores in spirit and in truth, in the name of all souls redeemed by His precious Blood.

I salute, adore, and love Thee, O God the Father and God the Son, in the ineffable embraces of Thy Divinity. I embrace with affection in the Sacred Heart of Jesus all creatures of heaven and earth, and I kiss Thee with the eternal kiss of the Holy Ghost.

God has so loved the world that He has given His only-begotten Son to be its Redeemer.

--------

## An Offering

To the Eternal Father of the things His
Adorable Son used during His Mortal Life
(The Precious Relics of Jesus)

Eternal Father, I offer Thee the manger and hay upon which Jesus was laid at His birth. I offer also His poor swaddling clothes and bands.

Eternal Father, I offer Thee the two little doves and five pieces of silver given by the Blessed Virgin and St. Joseph to redeem Jesus at His Presentation.

Eternal Father, I offer Thee the tunic which Mary wove for the Infant Jesus.

Eternal Father, I offer Thee the cup from which the Infant Jesus drank.

Eternal Father, I offer Thee the hammer, axe, saw, and other tools which the Divine Carpenter Jesus used.

Eternal Father, I offer Thee all the work He made.

Eternal Father, I offer Thee the scourge which Jesus made with His Divine Hands to drive the sellers from the Temple.

Eternal Father, I offer Thee the four drachmas which Jesus made St. Peter take from the fish's mouth to pay the tribute.

Eternal Father, I offer Thee the basin in which Jesus washed the feet of His Apostles, and the linen with which He was girded.

Eternal Father, I offer Thee the chalice which Jesus held in His Divine Hands after the Supper when He changed the wine into His precious Blood.

Eternal Father, I offer Thee the thirty pieces of silver with which Jesus was bought.

Eternal Father, I offer Thee the cords that bound Jesus in the Garden of Olives.

Eternal Father, I offer Thee the iron gauntlet from which Jesus received a buffet.

Eternal Father, I offer Thee the bands which blind-folded the eyes of Jesus.

Eternal Father, I offer Thee the gag which Jesus' enemies thrust into His mouth.

Eternal Father, I offer Thee all the instruments which were used to torment our Lord during the night of His bitter Passion.

Eternal Father, I offer Thee the white robe of scorn in which Herod clothed Jesus.

Eternal Father, I offer Thee the column of the flagellation, the cords which bound Jesus, and the fearful instruments with which they tore His flesh.

Eternal Father, I offer Thee the royal crown of thorns, the scarlet mantle, and the reed which He held in His Divine Hands.

Eternal Father, I offer Thee the steps which Jesus mounted and watered with His precious Blood when Pilate showed Him to the people, saying: "Behold the Man!"

Eternal Father, I offer Thee the cords which bound Jesus as a criminal.

Eternal Father, I offer Thee the sentence of death which was pronounced upon Thy only Son.

Eternal Father, I offer Thee the rods which were used to strike Jesus on the road to Calvary.

Eternal Father, I offer Thee the Veil of St. Veronica upon which Jesus impressed His Divine Features.

Eternal Father, I offer Thee the hammers used in the Crucifixion of Jesus.

Eternal Father, I offer Thee the vase from which Jesus tasted the bitter draught.

Eternal Father, I offer Thee the reed and sponge used to present Jesus the gall and vinegar.

Eternal Father, I offer Thee the Holy Cross of Jesus, empurpled with His blood, and the inscription Pilate had attached to it: *"Jesus of Nazareth, King of the Jews!"*

Eternal Father, I offer Thee the sacred vesture of Jesus, sanctified by His tears, sweat, and blood, and upon which the soldiers cast lots.

Eternal Father, I offer Thee the sandals worn by the Sacred Feet of Jesus.

Eternal Father, I offer Thee the garments of Jesus, covered with blood and divided in four parts by the soldiery.

Eternal Father, I offer Thee the lance which opened the Sacred Side of Jesus and pierced His most loving Heart, making it our place of refuge.

Eternal Father, I offer Thee all the instruments of torture used to accomplish the Passion of Thy Divine Son Jesus.

Eternal Father, I offer Thee the aromatics and perfumes which embalmed the Sacred Body of Jesus.

Eternal Father, I offer Thee the holy winding sheet and the bands which were honored in shrouding the Sacred Body of Jesus.

Eternal Father, I offer Thee the Holy Sepulchre which enclosed the Sacred Corpse of Jesus, the Divine source of life.

Eternal Father, I offer Thee all the holy relics of Thy Divine Jesus, humbly praying Thee to look upon them with contentment. This Divine look will render them more honor than can be rendered by all angels and saints. It will be a very worthy reparation for the profanations of which they have been the object.

Arrest, O Divine Father, the instruments of Thy justice, ready to strike us! Behold the instruments of the most Sacred Passion of Jesus, red with His adorable Blood. May this sight change Thy justice to mercy, and move Thee to speak peace to France *(or the country you are praying for)* and the world.

---

# Prayers

I salute Thee, Jesus of Nazareth, King of the Jews. Thou art the blessed Wheat of Nazareth, the delicious Bread of Bethlehem, the Lamb of God immolated at Jerusalem. Feed us poor sinners now and at the hour of our death. Amen.

We give Thee glory, O most amiable Heart of Jesus, wounded by the impious of all ages. As a sword they have sharpened their tongues, and pierced Thee by their injuries, blasphemies, and sarcasms. We invoke Thee, and we celebrate Thy praises in a spirit of honor and Reparation.

Eternal Father, I offer Thee the most Holy Face of Thy Divine Son to appease Thy wrath. Remember His Divine Head has borne the thorns of our sins and has set itself to receive the strokes of Thy justice, of which He still bears the marks. Behold these Holy Wounds! Incessantly they cry out to Thee: Mercy, mercy, mercy for the whole world!

Eternal Father, I offer Thee the Holy Face of Jesus for the spiritual needs of poor sinners. It is the golden coin which alone can cancel their debts.

---

# Aspirations

Sacred Body of Jesus, that I have received in the most Blessed Sacrament of the Altar, preserve my soul unto eternal life.

Jesus, Son of Mary, who hast been crowned with cruel thorns, grant that we may arrive at union with Thee.

Jesus, Son of Mary, who hast three times inclined Thy Divine Face to the earth in the Garden of Olives, deign to incline towards the earth of my heart, and water it with Thy tears, Thy sweat, and Thy precious Bloody Spirit of Love. Tongue of Fire, impress upon my heart the thrice Holy Name of God.

Spirit of Consolation, by Holy Communion fill our souls with Thy gifts and fruits.

I salute Thee, O Mary. Spouse of the Holy Ghost, bid Him to come and dwell in us.

---

## A Prayer for the Church

O God, by Thy Holy Name have pity on us, protect us, and save us.

O good Jesus, in Thy sweet Name guard our Sovereign Pontiff; breathe into his soul the spirit of the Comforter.

Jesus, Thy Church is menaced with great trials! . . . Holy Father, by the virtue of Thy salutary Name protect the Church of Jesus Christ. This was the last will of Thy Divine Son; it is the holy prayer which love prompted towards the end of His life. *Holy Father, keep in Thy Name those Thou hast given Me. (John xxvii. 11.)*

O most holy and worthy Mother, refuge of the Church, intercede for us and save us by the Name of our Lord Jesus Christ.

St. Michael and the holy angels, guard the Bark of Peter; disperse its enemies by the holy Cross of our Lord Jesus Christ.

---

# A Little Exercise
# In Honor of the Five Wounds

*Wound of the Right Hand* — Jesus, Son of Mary, who hast the power to forgive sins, grant me the remission of my faults through the merits of Thy Holy Passion.

*Wound of the Left Hand* — Jesus, Son of Mary, who art a God of union, grant me the grace to communicate worthily.

*Wound of the Right Foot* — Jesus, Son of Mary, who art Infinite Mercy, cleanse me in Thy precious Blood.

*Wound of the Left Foot* — Jesus, Son of Mary, who art the light of the world, deign to breathe in my soul the spirit of the Comforter.

*Wound of the Sacred Heart* — Jesus, Son of Mary, who hast merited heaven for us, grant us eternal life.

Eternal Father, I offer Thee the Five Wounds of Thy Divine Son. We beseech Thee to infuse in our souls the Divine Spirit which proceeds from Thee and Him; by the merits of the Sacred Passion of Jesus nourish our souls with the Living Bread of the Blessed Sacrament of the Altar.

---

# Devotions
## In Honor of the Holy Infant Jesus
The Month of the Divine Infant

On the 15th of the month Sister Saint-Pierre celebrated the Espousals of the Blessed Virgin with St. Joseph. The 16th was consecrated to the mystery of the Incarnation. The nine following days she honored the Infant Jesus in the chaste womb of Mary, and accompanied the Blessed Virgin and St. Joseph in their journey to Bethlehem. On the 25th she celebrated the birth of the Holy Infant. On the 26th she adored Him with the shepherds; on the 27th in His Circumcision when He was named Jesus; on the 28th with the Three Kings; on the 29th in His Presentation in the Temple; on the 30th in His Flight into Egypt.

The first seven days of the following month were consecrated to the Infant Jesus in His place of exile; she honored there His first words, steps, actions, His purity and simplicity. On the 8th she celebrated the return of the Holy Family to Nazareth.

On the 9th she contemplated Jesus beginning to work with St. Joseph. On the 10th she honored the obedience of the Infant Jesus to His parents. On the 11th she recalled the filial attentions He showed to His Blessed Mother and the faithful Guardian of His Infancy. The 12th was consecrated to the journey of the Infant Jesus when at the age of twelve years He went with Mary and Joseph to celebrate the Pasch, and also to the loss of the Child Jesus. On the 13th she adored Him in the midst of the Doctors of the Law, maintaining the rights of His Father. On the 14th she rendered homage to the Child found in the Temple by Mary and Joseph, and His returning in their company to Nazareth, where He was subject to them.

*Admirabile nomen Jesu, quod est super omne nomen. Venite, adoremus* — "The Name which shall be called wonderful, the Name of Jesus, is the Name which is above every name. O! come, let us worship Him."

(Sister Saint-Pierre was accustomed to repeat this
beautiful invitatory thousands of times,
and received signal graces thereby.)

------

## Prayers
## In Honor of the Infant Jesus
## And His Blessed Mother

An Act of Adoration to the Incarnate Word in the August
Bosom of the Immaculate Virgin

O Word Divine, Incarnate for me, I adore Thee, and I love
Thee with all my heart!

Eternal Wisdom, come and teach us the way to heaven!

O King of kings, come and reign over the hearts of all men,
particularly over mine!

Come, all ye angels, all ye men; come, all creatures, and
unite with me in adoring a God so humbled!

O Holy Virgin, O Blessed St. Joseph, obtain for me such a
great purity of heart that this Divine Infant may not be
obliged to seek shelter in a stable on finding in my soul
obstacles to His graces!

May my heart be ever open to Him, may He make it His
throne, and may all the powers of my soul be submissive to
Him!

Open, ye heavens! O Mary, give us our King and our
Savior!

------

# Prayer to the Infant Jesus

O Divine Infant Jesus, by the love which impelled Thee to take Flesh in the bosom of Thy Holy Mother, and by that same love which made Thee find means to give Thyself to us, I pray Thee most humbly to pardon all my sins, to destroy in me the old man and clothe me with Thyself, so that I may no longer live but in Thee and for Thee, in honor of the abasement of Thy Divinity, which was united to our humanity.

---

## Offerings
## In Honor of the Divine Infant Jesus
(A Preparation for the Twenty-Fifth of Each Month)

*First Offering* — Eternal Father, I offer to Thy honor and glory, and for my own salvation and for the salvation of the whole world, the mystery of the birth of our Divine Savior.

*Gloria Patri*, etc.

*Second Offering* — Eternal Father, I offer to Thy honor and glory, and for my eternal salvation, the sufferings of the most Holy Virgin and St. Joseph in that long and weary journey from Nazareth to Bethlehem. I offer Thee the sorrows of their hearts when they found no place wherein to shelter themselves when the Savior of the world was to be born.

*Gloria Patri*, etc.

*Third Offering* — Eternal Father, I offer to Thy honor and glory, and for my eternal salvation, the sufferings of Jesus in the stable where He was born, the cold He endured, the swaddling-clothes which bound Him, the tears He shed, and His tender infant cries.

*Gloria Patri, etc.*

*Fourth Offering* — Eternal Father, I offer to Thy honor and glory, and for my eternal salvation, the pain which the Holy Child felt in His tender Body when He submitted to Circumcision. I offer Thee that Precious Blood which then, for the first time, He shed for the salvation of the whole human race.

*Gloria Patri*, etc.

*Fifth Offering* — Eternal Father, I offer to Thy honor and glory, and for my eternal salvation, the humility, mortification, patience, charity, all the virtues of the Child Jesus; and I thank Thee, and I love Thee, and I bless Thee without end for the ineffable mystery of the Incarnation of the Divine Word.

*Gloria Patri*, etc.

*V.* The Word was made Flesh.

*R.* And dwelt amongst us.

### Let us pray

O God, whose only-begotten Son was made manifest to us in the substance of our flesh, grant, we beseech Thee, that through Him, whom we acknowledge to be like unto ourselves, our souls may be inwardly renewed. Who liveth and reigneth with Thee forever and ever. Amen.

*(An Indulgence of one year to all the faithful who, with contrite heart and devotion, in public or in private, on any of the nine days preceding the twenty-fifth of the month, shall recite these five Offerings with the versicle and prayer.)*

_____

# Prayers to Excite Confidence in the Invocation of the Adorable Name of Jesus

"And after eight days were accomplished, that the Child should be circumcised, His name was called Jesus, which was called by the Angel before He was conceived in the womb." (Gospel of the Feast of the Circumcision: *Luke, ii. 21.*)

"For there is no other name under heaven given to men whereby we must be saved." (*Acts of the Apostles, iv. 12.*)

Divine Savior! Through the victory Thou hast gained over Satan by taking the Name of Jesus, deliver us from his snares.

> Jesus, Son of God! Have mercy on us!
> Jesus, Son of the Virgin Mary! Have mercy on us!
> O Jesus and Mary! Be propitious to us!*

Make us, O Lord! To have a continual fear and love of Thy Holy Name, because Thou dost never abandon the care of those who, by Thy grace, cease not to love Thee; who livest and reignest, one God, world without end, Amen. *(Examined and approved. Gentry, Vic.-Gen. Tours, July 24, 1848.)*

When Jesus was named, Satan, conquered, was disarmed.

* *An indulgence of twenty-five days for invoking the Holy Name of Jesus and Mary; fifty days indulgence to those who wear the Blue Scapular, plenary indulgence at the hour of death; twenty days for reverently bowing the head when pronouncing these sacred names; an indulgence of fifty days as often as two persons salute each other, the one saying, in any language whatever, "Praised be Jesus and Mary." and the other replying, "Now and forever." (Pius IX., Sept. 26, 1864.)*

*(Extract from the Life of Sister Saint-Pierre, Carmelite of Tours, France, written by herself, and published with the approbation of the Archbishops of Tours and New Orleans and with the approbation of the Most Rev. Archbishop Gibbons.)*

Jesus, be to me a Jesus!

## Prayer to the Holy Name

May the adorable Name of Jesus be the sweet and daily music of my soul and the joy of my heart; and when, in the agony and cold sweat of death, I give the last look for mercy, may the parting sigh of my soul be, Jesus! Jesus! Amen.

## Prayers in Honor of the Maternity of the Blessed Virgin Mary

O most holy and worthy Mother of God, impart abundantly to all mankind, thy children, the milk of grace and mercy.

Hail, Mary, conceived without sin, mysterious vine which has produced the Divine Grape, destined to be crushed in the wine-press of the Cross, whence issued a sacred wine that was deposited in the precious vase of thy Immaculate Heart, to be distilled upon the children whose Mother thou didst become upon Calvary's mount.

O Divine Infant Jesus, I adore Thee on Thy Blessed Mother's bosom. Yes, O Divine Infant, in this state of humiliation and littleness Thou art as worthy of our love, our homage, and adoration as when Thou didst cure the sick, raise the dead to life, and command the winds and waves.

Here do I contemplate Thee, silent and unknown, adoring Thy Eternal Father's counsels upon Thy life and sorrowful Passion. Already is the Cross planted in Thy Heart; Thou dost only await the hour marked by Thy Heavenly Father for Thee to fulfill His will.

Hail, Queen of Martyrs! whose precious blood, blanched by maternal piety, flowed for fifteen months from thy virginal bosom to fill the sacred veins of the King of Martyrs.

O holy Virgin, how pure and admirable thou art! The Holy Ghost seems ever occupied with thee. At thy birth I hear Him saying in His Divine Council: *"Our Sister is little . . . . What shall we do with our Sister in the day when she is to be spoken to?"*

O mystery ineffable! He who eternally reposes in the Bosom of the Father rests at the same time in the bosom of a humble Virgin. I adore Thee, most Holy Infant Jesus, in that royal shrine surrounded by roses and lilies; my soul experiences joy inexpressible at beholding Thee dwelling in that *House of Gold* built by Supreme Wisdom.

Come forth, O Divine Jesus, from the virginal prison where love holds Thee captive; give me the consolation of beholding and adoring Thee, and in a state that I may embrace Thee. Let us rejoice; the day of joy hath come at last, and the Angels sing in heavenly strains, "Glory be to God on high, and on earth peace to men of good will!" The hour of man's salvation has dawned. Behold the Savior, born of Mary. O earth, Thou didst become a heaven on that day eternally memorable. O glorious Mother of God, my hopes are realized, my yearning satisfied, now that I find Jesus, my Redeemer, in thy holy arms, resting upon thy maternal bosom, nourished with thy virginal milk. I hear the Heavenly Spouse felicitating thee on thy blessed maternity. Yes, thou art beautiful in the eyes of thy Spouse, because thou hast preserved intact the beautiful flower of virginity. While angels in heaven sing the eternal canticle of the thrice Holy God, we on earth sing the virginal canticle of the Mother thrice a virgin. O grandeur of Mary! O incomparable privilege! O mystery of love!

Hail Mary, full of grace, the Lord is with thee; blessed art thou amongst women, and blessed is the Fruit of thy womb, Jesus, whom thou didst nourish during fifteen months with thy virginal milk.

We give thee thanks, O Blessed Virgin. Mary, for the great love with which thou didst suckle the King of Heaven, and we bless thy maternal tenderness.

Eternal Father, we offer Thee the Incarnate Word, a babe at His Blessed Mother's breast, rendering Thee by this lowly action perfect praise for the honor and glory of Thy Holy Name.

O most holy and sweet Mother of God, remember thou art my Mother and that I am the little sister of the Holy Infant Jesus.

Thy Divine Son has left upon thy bosom the charming virtues of His Holy Infancy, and He sends me to gather this celestial dew, which will fill my soul with purity, innocence, and simplicity.

Receive, O Virgin and Mother, these fifteen salutations in memory of the fifteen months during which thou didst nurse the Lamb of God, born in the stable of Bethlehem.

O holy and august Mother, what dost thou do? "I give my milk to Him who hath given me being." And what will become of this milk? "It will become His Flesh and the Blood of His veins. This Flesh which I give Him will suffer the torments of His Passion, and this Blood obtained from me will be shed upon the Cross for the salvation of sinners."

O angels of heaven, what think ye of this prodigy? It was once your mission to give man delicious food on earth by showering manna from heaven, and this was truly a great miracle. But behold now, with admiration inexpressible, the Virgin Mother, your Queen, nourishing God Himself, her Creator and yours.

O Divine Blood of Jesus, refresh the earth that it may bring forth elect souls.

*(Our Lord promised that all who would thus honor Him should receive great blessings, that they would be especially assisted by His Blessed Mother, and that He would grant all their petitions. Holy Church keeps the Feast of the Maternity of the Blessed Virgin on the second Sunday in October. )*

———————

# Sister Saint-Pierre's Prayer
# To the Queen of Carmel for
# The House of Her Order

"O Holy Mary, sprinkle the flowers of Carmel with thy fruitful grace, that they may thus become so strongly rooted in this land of benediction as never to be eradicated by the demon."

The *O Gloriosa Virginum* seventy-two times
in honor of her Divine Maternity.

Come, Jesus, come! *Sit Nomen Domini benedictum.*

Mother most pure, pray for us. O Mary, Mother of God, source of all our joy for time and eternity, be thou our strength. Lead us to the arms of thy Divine Child and teach us His winning ways. When earth and sense shall fail show us thy gentle face, and in thy pure embrace let us meet the merciful gaze of our Savior Jesus. Amen.

---

# Our Lady of La Salette

On the 19th of September, 1846, Our Blessed Lady appeared upon an Alpine mountain called La Salette to humble little shepherds named Maximin and Melanie, two innocent children through whose mouths she reproached "her people" of France for their blasphemy and impiety. Tears were flowing from her eyes; the crucifix was fixed upon her heart. She was surrounded by the instruments of the Passion, and the cruel hammer and sharp pincers were the ornaments of her maternal bosom.

---

# Exercise in Honor of Our Lady of La Salette

1. I salute thee, blessed soul of Mary, image of the Divinity. *Ave Maria!*
2. I revere thee, sacred body of Mary, living temple of the Holy Ghost. *Ave Maria!*
3. I bless thee, precious blood of Mary, from which was formed the Body of the Man-God. *Ave Maria!*
4. I kiss with profound respect the charitable feet of Mary, which did not disdain to descend upon the mountain of La Salette for the salvation of France. *Ave Maria!*
5. I exalt thee, most pure hands of Mary, who for the first time offered to the Eternal Father the Host without stain. *Ave Maria!*
6. I venerate thee, chaste bosom of Mary, as the sanctuary of God, sacred ostensorium of the Incarnate Word. *Ave Maria!*
7. I invoke thee, Immaculate Heart of Mary, ardent furnace of charity. *Ave Maria!*
8. I solicit thee, blessed ears of Mary, always attentive and propitious to the cries of the unfortunate. *Ave Maria!*
9. I admire thee, beautiful eyes of Mary, full of sweetness and compassion, always open to our needs and ready to supply them. May we experience the virtue of thy charitable gaze. *Ave Maria!*
10. I regard thee with love, incomparable mouth of Mary, which pleads our cause without ceasing before the Sovereign Judge and continually obtains favorable judgment. *Ave Maria!*
11. I contemplate thee with joy, resplendent face of Mary, radiant with beauty and glory. Give to thy

children the kiss of maternal love as a pledge of the treaty of peace, which we pray thee to obtain from a God irritated on account of our crimes.
*Ave Maria!*

12. I salute thee, rainbow of mercy in the day of storm; appear before our terrified eyes and prevent the thunderbolt from striking our guilty heads.
Ave Maria!

*Memoráre* – Remember, O most gracious VirginMary, that never was it known, that anyone who fled to thy protection, implored thy help, or sought thy intercession was left unaided. Inspired with this confidence, I fly unto thee, O Virgin of virgins my Mother. To thee do I come; before thee I stand, sinful and sorrowful, O Mother of the Word Incarnate! Despise not my petitions, but in thy mercy hear and answer me. Amen.

Our Lady of the Holy Name of God, may thou be blessed in all times and all places.

(For connection between the devotion of the Holy Face and La Salette, see Life of Sister Saint-Pierre.)

---

## Forty Days' Prayer
## For the Needs of the Church and State

(Commenced by M. Dupont in 1843)

May God arise and His enemies be dispersed!

Say three *Paters (Our Father)*, three *Aves (Hail Mary)*, and three *Glorias (Glory be)*.

St. Michael and all the holy angels, pray and combat for us.

St. Peter and all the holy apostles, intercede for us.

St. Ignatius, St. Teresa, and all the inhabitants of the heavenly Jerusalem, pray for us.

# Aspiration during the Day

May Thy Holy Name, O Lord, be known and blessed in all times and places.

Blessed Virgin Mary, reign over us with thy Divine Son Jesus. Amen.

(This devotion is made from July 16th, Feast of Our Lady of Mt. Carmel, until August 25th, Feast of St. Louis, King and Protector of France.)

---

# Salutation
# To the Holy Veil of St. Veronica
### The Greater Relic of the Vatican Basilica

### Antiphon
My heart speaks to Thee; my eyes seek Thee; yes, Lord, I will always seek Thy Face. Do not hide Thy Face from me; do not turn away from Thy servant.

*V.* O Lord, Thou hast shown to me the light of Thy Face.

*R.* Thou hast given joy to my heart.

### *Let us pray*

Grant in Thy mercy, O Lord, that my soul, created by Thy wisdom and governed by Thy providence, may be filled with the light of Thy Holy Face, through our Lord Jesus Christ. Amen.

---

# Fifth Part
# LITTLE OFFICE OF THE HOLY NAME OF GOD

Explanation from the 1887 Manual of the Archcon-fraternity of the Holy Face: "*The little Office of the most Holy Name of God* is in great part due to the pen of Mr. Dupont. We first found it in a pamphlet entitled, *Association of prayers against blasphemy*, etc., which went through several editions, the last being dated 1867; but since then it has not been reprinted. This portion of the pamphlet deserves to be saved from oblivion. We publish it as a supplement to our *manual* of the Archconfraternity from which it will be easy to detach it and form of it a separate small tract.

It is a homage of reparation and of honor which we desire to offer to the most holy and most adorable Name of God, so strangely misunderstood and outraged at the present day. Already, as we are aware, fervent souls living in the world make a practice of reciting this *Little Office* every day. So praiseworthy an example cannot be too loudly praised, and we earnestly desire that it should have imitators, in sufficient number to stifle, by a sacred concert of praise, the horrible clamor which hell vomits forth at this time against God and His redoubtable Name."

| **PARVUM OFFICIUM** | **LITTLE OFFICE** |
| Santissimi Nominis Dei. | Of the Holy Name of God. |

### AT MATINS

The faithful soul, astonished at the patience of God in bearing with blasphemers, entreats Him to cover them with confusion, and thereby to cause their conversion.

| | |
|---|---|
| Pater noster… | Our Father… |
| *V.* Domine, labia mea aperies. | *V.* Lord, Thou wilt open my lips. |
| *R.* Et os meum exaltabit Nomen tuum. | *R.* And my mouth shall extol Thy Name. |

Usquequo, Deus, improperavit inimicus? irritat adversarius Nomen tuum in finem?

How long, O God, shall the enemy outrage Thee? Is the adversary to provoke Thy Name forever?

Nesciunt quia tu ipse es Deus noster, qui conteris bella, et Dominus Nome est tibi.

They know not that Thou art our God, who destroyest wars from the beginning, and that the Lord is Thy name.

Imple facies eorum ignominia, et quærent Nomen tuum, Domine.

Fill their faces with shame, and they shall seek Thy Name, O Lord.

Confiteantur Nomini tuo magno, quoniam terribile et sanctum est.

Let them give praise to Thy great Name: because it is terrible and holy.

Et benedicant Nomini gloriæ tuæ excelso, in omni laude et benedictione.

And blessed be the great Name of Thy glory with all blessing and praise.

Gloria Patri…

Glory be to the Father…

*Ant.* Expectemus a Domino misericordiam; forsitan enim indignationem suam abscondet, et dabit gloriam Nomini suo.

*Ant.* Let us wait for mercy from the Lord; for perhaps He will put a stop to His indignation, and He will give glory to His own name.

### CAPITULUM

Sanctificabo Nomen meum magnum, quod pollutum est inter gentes, dicit Dominus: et assumam zelum pro Nomine sancto meo, ut sciant gentes quia ego Dominus.

### CHAPTER

I will sanctify My great Name, which was profaned among the Gentiles, saith the Lord; and I will become jealous for the honor of My Holy Name in order that the nations may know that I am the Lord.

R. Deo gratias.

R. Let us give thanks to God.

*V.* Quis non timebit te, Domine?
R. Et magnificabit Nomen tuum?

*V.* Who shall not fear Thee, O Lord?
R. And who shall not magnify Thy Name?

### OREMUS

Deus, cujus sanctum et terribile Nomen jugiter tota die blasphematur, illumina oculos improperantium tibi, ut majestatem tui Nominis agnocentes, illud

### LET US PRAY

O God, whose holy and terrible Name is unceasingly profaned by blasphemers, lighten the eyes of those who outrage Thee, that confessing the majesty of Thy Name,

nobiscum et revereantur et ament.  Per Dominum.

they may, together with us, revere and love it. Through Jesus Christ Our Lord.

*V.* Sit Nomen Domini benedictum.
*R.* Ex hoc nunc, et usque in sæculum.  Amen.

*V.* May the Name of the Lord be blessed.
*R.* Now and forevermore. Amen.

## AT LAUDS

The faithful soul invites all creatures to unite in praising the Name of the Lord.

Pater noster...
*V.* Domine, labia mea aperies.
*R.* Et os meum exaltabit Nomen tuum.

Our Father...
*V.* Lord, Thou wilt open my lips.
*R.* And my mouth shall extol Thy Name.

Laudate Dominum de cœlis; laudate eum in excelsis.
Laudate eum, omnes angeli ejus; laudate eum, omnes virtutes ejus.
Laudate eum, sol et luna; laudate eum, omnes stellæ et lumen.
Laudate eum, cœli cœlorem; et aquæ omnes quæ super

Praise ye the Lord from the heavens: praise ye Him in the high places.
Praise ye Him, all His Angels: praise ye Him, all His Hosts.

Praise ye Him, sun and moon: praise Him, all ye stars and light.
Praise Him, ye heavens of heavens, and let all the waters that are above

cœlos sunt laudent
Nomen Domini.
Bestiæ et universa pecora,
serpentes et volucres
pennatæ;
Reges terræ et omnes
populi, principes et
omnes judices terræ;
Juvenes et virgines, senes
cum junioribus laudent
Nomen Domini, quia
exaltatum est Nomen
ejus solius.

Gloria Patri...

*Ant.* Jubilate Deo, omnis
terra; psalmum dicite
Nomini ejus; date gloriam
laudi ejus.

CAPITULUM

Benedictus es, Domine
Deus patrum nostrorum; et
laudabilis, et gloriosus, et
superexaltatus in sæcula,
et benedictum Nomen
gloriæ tuæ sanctum, et
laudabile, et
superexaltatum

the heavens praise the
Name of the Lord.
Praise Him, beasts and all
cattle, serpents and
feathered fowl;
Kings of the earth and all
people, princes and all
judges of the earth;
Young men and maidens:
let the old with the
younger, praise the
Name of the Lord, for
His Name alone is
exalted.
Glory be to the Father...

*Ant.* Sing to the Lord with
holy transports of joy, all
ye inhabitants of the earth:
sing canticles to the glory
of His Name: render to
Him, by your praises, the
homage due to Him.

CHAPTER

Blessed art Thou, O Lord,
God of our fathers; and
worthy to be praised, and
glorified, and exalted
above all forever; and
blessed is the Holy Name
of Thy glory: and worthy
to be praised, and exalted

in omnibus sæculis.

R. Deo gratias.
V. A solis ortu usque ad occasum.
R. Laudabile Nomen Domini.

OREMUS

Concede nobis, omnipotens Deus, ita Nomen sanctum tuum in terra venerari, ut cum angelis et sanctis tuis in cœlo ipsum laudare et exaltare mereamur. Per Dominum.

V. Sit Nomen Domini benedictum.
R. Ex hoc nunc, et usque in sæculum. Amen.

above all from century to century.

R. Thanks be to God.
V. From the rising to the setting of the sun.
R. The Name of the Lord shall be blessed.

LET US PRAY

Grant to us almighty God, grace so to venerate Thy Holy Name on earth, that we may merit to praise and bless it with the angels and saints in heaven. Through Our Lord Jesus Christ.

V. Blessed be the Name of the Lord.
R. Now and forevermore. Amen.

AT PRIME

The faithful soul, terrified at the thought of all the crimes, and above all the blasphemies which are committed, thereby provoking God to inflict chastisements, conjures Him, by His Holy Name, to have pity on His people.

| | |
|---|---|
| Pater noster... | Our Father... |

*V.* Doimne, labia mea aperies.
*R.* Et os meum exaltabit Nomen tuum.

*V.* Lord, Thou wilt open my lips.
*R.* And my mouth shall extol Thy Name.

Deus meus, aperi oculos, et vide desolationem nostram et civitatem super quam invocatum est Nomen tuum.
Exurge; quare obdormis, Domine? Exurge, Domine, adjuva nos, et redime nos propter Nomen tuum.
Noli meminisse iniquitatum patrum nostrorum, sed memento manus tuæ et Nominis tui in tempore isto.
Peccavimus cum patribus nostris; injuste egimus, et iniquitatem fecimus.

My God, open Thine eyes, and consider our desolation, and the city upon which Thy Name is invoked.
Arise, O Lord; why sleepest Thou? Arise, O Lord, help us and redeem us for Thy Name's sake.
Remember not the iniquities of our fathers, but think at this time upon Thy power and upon Thy name.
We confess that we have sinned with our fathers; that we have acted unjustly, and wrought iniquity.

Si iniquitates nostræ responderunt nobis, Domine, fac propter Nomen tuum; quoniam multæ sunt aversiones nostræ, et tibi peccavimus.

If our iniquities cry out against us, O Lord, nevertheless be merciful to us for Thy Name's sake, for our rebellions are many,

Adjuva nos, Deus salutaris noster, et propter gloriam Nominis tui libera nos, et propitius esto peccatis nostris, propter Nomen tuum.
Gloria Patri…

*Ant.* Exurge, Domine adjuva nos, et redime nos propter Nomen tuum.

CAPITULUM

Si conversus autem populus meus, super quos invocatum est Nomen meum, deprecatus me fuerit, et exquisierit Faciem meam, et egerit pœnitentiam a viis suis pessimis, et ego exaudiam de cœlo, et propitius ero peccatis eorum.

*R.* Deo gratias.

*V.* In eo lætabitur cor nostrum.
*R.* Et in Nomine sancto ejus speravimus.

OREMUS

we have sinned against Thee.
Help us, O God our Savior; deliver us for the glory of Thy Name, and forgive us our sins for Thy Name's sake.
Glory be to the Father…

*Ant.* Arise, O Lord, help us and redeem us for Thy Name's sake.

CHAPTER

And My people, upon whom My Name is called being converted, shall make supplication to Me, and seek out My Face, and do penance for their most wicked ways: then will I hear from heaven, and will pardon their sins.

*R.* Let us give thanks to God.
*V.* Our heart finds its joy in Him.
*R.* And we hope in His Holy Name.

LET US PRAY

Ineffabilem nobis, Domine, propter Nomen sanctum tuum, misericordiam tuam clementer ostende, ut simul nos, et a peccatis omnibus exuas et a pœnis quas pro his mereamur eripias. Per Dominum

Deign, O Lord, for Thy Name's sake, to show to us Thy mercy that we may be delivered, both from our sins and from the chastisements they have deserved. Through our Lord Jesus Christ.

*V.* Sit Nomen Domini benedictum.
*R.* Ex hoc nunc, et usque in sæculum. Amen.

*V.* Blessed be the Name of the Lord.
*R.* Now and forevermore. Amen.

## AT TIERCE

The faithful soul, having withdrawn into solitude blesses, invokes and glorifies the Holy Name of God.

Pater noster...
*V.* Domine, labia mea aperies.
*R.* Et os meum exaltabit Nomen tuum.

Our Father...
*V.* Lord, Thou wilt open my lips.
*R.* And my mouth shall extol Thy Name.

Exaltabo te, Deus meus Rex, et benedicam Nomini tuo in sæculum et in sæculum sæculi.
Et in conspectu angelorum psallam tibi; adorabo ad templum sanctum

I will extol Thee, O God my King: and I will bless Thy Name forever, yea forever and ever.
I will sing praise to Thee in the sight of the angels: I will worship

tuum, et confitebor Nomini tuo.

Per singulos dies benedicam tibi, et laudabo Nomen tuum, in sæculum et in sæculum sæculi.

Sic benedicam te in vita mea, et in Nomine tuo levabo manus meas.

Et tu, Domine, fac mecum propter Nomen tuum, quia suavis est misericorda tua.

Aspice in me, et miserere mei, secundum judicium diligentium Nomen tuum.

Exultabit cor meum in salutare tuo; cantabo Domino qui bona tribuit mihi, et psallam Nomini Domini altissimi.

Gloria Patri...

*Ant.* Exaltabo te, Deus meus Rex, et benedicam Nomini tuo in sæculum sæculi.

towards Thy holy temple, and I will give glory to Thy Name.

Every day I will bless Thee: and I will praise Thy Name forever, yea forever and ever.

I will bless Thee as long as I live: and in Thy Name I will lift up my hands to heaven.

And Thou, O Lord, defend me for Thy Name's sake: because Thy mercy is sweet.

Look upon me, O Lord, and have mercy on me, according to the judgment of them that love Thy Name.

My heart will thrill with joy in Thy salvation; I will sing to the Lord, who giveth me good things: yea I will sing to the Name of the Lord the most High.

Glory be to the Father...

*Ant.* I will praise Thee, O God my King, and I will bless Thy Name forever and ever.

Turris fortissima Nomen Domini: ad ipsum currit justus, et exaltabitur.

*R.* Deo gratias.
*V.* Benedic, anima mea, Domino.
*R.* Et omnia quæ intra me sunt, Nomini sancto ejus.

## OREMUS

Da nobis, omnipotens et sempiterne Deus, Nomen sanctum tuum ita pura mente benedicere et fiducialiter invocare, ut quodcumque sic petierimus obtinere mereamur. Per Dominum.

*V.* Sit nomen Domini benedictum.
*R.* Ex hoc nunc et usque in sæculum. Amen.

The Name of the Lord is a strong tower: the just runneth to it, and shall be exalted.

*R.* Thanks be to God.
*V.* Bless the Lord, O my soul.
*R.* And let all that is within me bless His Holy Name.

## LET US PRAY

Grant us, almighty and eternal God, grace to bless Thy Name with such pure heart and to invoke it with such confidence, that we may deserve to obtain all that we have asked of Thee. Through Jesus Christ.

*V.* Blessed be the Name of the Lord.
*R.* Now and forevermore. Amen.

The faithful soul is convinced, by its own experience, of the power of the Holy Name of God against the enemies of our salvation.

| | |
|---|---|
| Pater noster... | Our Father... |

*V.* Domine, labia mea aperies.
*R.* Et os meum exaltabit Nomen tuum.

*V.* Lord, Thou wilt open my lips.
*R.* And my mouth shall extol Thy Name.

Beatus vir cujus est
    Nomen Domini spes
    ejus, et non respexit in
    vanitates et insanias
    falsas.

Blessed is the man whose
    trust is in the Name of
    the Lord; and who
    hath not had regard to
    vanities, and lying
    follies.

Circumdantes
    circumdederunt me; et
    in Nomine Domini
    quia ultus sum in eos.

My enemies have
    surrounded me and
    compassed me about:
    and in the Name of the
    Lord, I have been
    revenged on them.

Circumdederunt me sicut
    apes, et exarserunt
    sicut ignis in spinis; et
    in Nomine Domini,
    quia ultus sum in eos.

They have surrounded me
    like bees, and they
    burned like fire among
    thorns: and in the
    Name of the Lord I
    was revenged on them.

Confitebor Nomini tuo,
    Domine, quoniam
    adjutor et protector

I will give glory to Thy
    Name, O Lord: for
    Thou hast been a

factus es mihi.

Et liberasti me, secundum multitudinem misericordiæ Nominis tui, de manibus quærentium animam meam.

Sperent in te qui noverunt Nomen tuum, quoniam non dereliquisti quærentes te, Domine.

Propterea confitebor tibi in nationibus, Domine, et Nomini tuo psalmum dicam.

Gloria Patri…
*Ant.* In Nomine tuo spernemus insurgentes in nobis.

CAPITULUM

Qui ambulaverit in tenebris et non est lumen ei, speret in Nomine Domini, et innitatur super Deum suum.

helper and protector to me.

And Thou hast delivered me, according to the multitude of the mercy of Thy Name from the hands of those who sought after my life.

Let those who know Thy Name trust in Thee: for Thou has not forsaken those who seek Thee, O Lord.

Therefore, O Lord, I will confess Thee among the nations; and I will sing a psalm to the glory of Thy Name.

Glory be to the Father…
*Ant.* In Thy Name we will despise those who rise up against us.

CHAPTER

Let him who hath walked in darkness and who hath no light, hope in the Name of the Lord, and lean upon his God.

*R.* Deo gratias.
*V.* In te, Domine,
   inimicos nostros
   ventilabimus cornu.

*R.* Et in Nomine tuo
   spernemus insurgentes
   in nobis.

OREMUS

Deus, qui in Nomine tuo
sperantes nunqam deseris,
concede fragilitati nostræ
præsidium, ut sancti
Nominis tui protectione
muniti, omnia salutis
nostræ adversantia
superare valeamus. Per
Dominum.

*V.* Sit nomen Domini
benedictum.
*R.* Ex hoc nunc et usque
in sæculum. Amen.

*R.* Thanks be to God.
*V.* In Thee, O Lord, we
   shall have strength to
   fight against our
   enemies.

*R.* And in Thy Name we
   will despise those who
   rise up against us.

LET US PRAY

O God, who never
forsakest those who hope
in Thy Name, grant us
Thy help in our weakness,
so that under the
protection of Thy Holy
Name we may triumph
over all the obstacles
which we may encounter
in the way of salvation.
Through Jesus Christ our
Lord.

*V.* Blessed be the Name
of the Lord.
*R.* Now and forevermore.
Amen.

The faithful soul admires the grandeur of the Holy Name of God, and begs that it may be known, feared and glorified by all men.

| Pater noster… | Our Father… |
|---|---|

*V.* Domine, labia mea aperies.
*R.* Et os meum exaltabit Nomen tuum.

*V.* Lord, Thou wilt open my lips.
*R.* And my mouth shall extol Thy Name.

Domine Deus noster,
    quam admirabile est
    Nomen tuum in
    universa terra!
Non est similis tui,
    Domine: magnus es tu,
    et magnum Nomen
    tuum in fortitudine.
Quis non timebit te, et
    magnificabit Nomen
    tuum?
Sit auris tua attendens
    adorationem servorum
    tuorum qui volunt
    timere Nomen tuum.

Tu exaudies de cœlo, in
    firmamento habitaculi
    tui, ut discant universi
    populi terrarum
    Nomen tuum timere,

O Lord our God, how
    admirable is Thy
    Name throughout the
    whole earth!
There is none like to Thee,
    O Lord: Thou art
    great, and great is Thy
    Name in might.
Who shall not fear Thee,
    O Lord, and magnify
    Thy Name?
Let Thy ear, Lord, be
    attentive to the prayer
    of Thy servants who
    desire to fear Thy
    Name.
Thou wilt hear us from the
    firmament where Thou
    dwellest, in order that
    all people, throughout
    the whole earth, may

sicut populus tuus Israël.

Et omnes gentes, quascumque fecisti, venient, et adorabunt coram te, et glorificabunt Nomen tuum.

Secundum Nomen tuum, sic et laus tua in fines terræ,

Et memores erunt Nominis tui in omni generatione et generationem.

Gloria Patri…

*Ant.* Quis non timebit te, Domine, et magnificabit Nomen tuum?

learn to fear Thy Name, like Thy people Israel.

And all the nations Thou hast made shall come and adore before Thee, O Lord: and they shall glorify Thy Name.

According to Thy Name O God, so also is Thy praise unto the ends of the earth.

And Thy Name shall be remembered from generation to generation.

Glory be to the Father…

*Ant.* Who shall not fear Thee, O Lord, and magnify Thy Name?

## CAPITULUM

Ab ortu solis usque ad occasum magnum est Nomen meum in gentibus, et in omni loco sacrificatur et offertur Nomini meo oblatio munda, quia magnum est Nomen meum in gentibus, dicit Dominus exercituum.

## CHAPTER

From the rising to the setting of the sun, My Name is great among the Gentiles, and in every place there is sacrifice, and there is offered to My Name a clean oblation: for great is My Name, among the Gentiles, saith the Lord of Hosts.

| | |
|---|---|
| *R.* Deo gratias. | *R.* Thanks be to God. |
| *V.* Sanctum et terribile Nomen ejus. | *V.* Holy and terrible is His Name. |
| *R.* Initium sapientiæ timor Domini. | *R.* The fear of the Lord is the beginning of wisdom. |

| OREMUS | LET US PRAY |
|---|---|
| Sancti Nominis tui, Domine, timorem pariter et amorem fac nos habere perpetuum, quia nunquam tua gubernatione destituis, quos in soliditate tuæ dilectionis instituis. Per Dominum. | Make us, O Lord, to have a perpetual fear and love of Thy Holy Name, for Thou never ceasest to govern those whom Thou dost solidly establish in Thy love. Through Jesus Christ our Lord. |
| *V.* Sit nomen Domini benedictum. | *V.* Blessed be the Name of the Lord. |
| *R.* Ex hoc nunc et usque in sæculum. Amen. | *R.* Now and forevermore. Amen. |

AT VESPERS

The faithful soul engages all Christians to assemble in the holy place, to glorify the Name of the Lord after the example and under the auspices of the most holy Virgin.

| | |
|---|---|
| Pater noster… | Our Father… |
| Ave, Maria… | Hail, Mary… |

*V.* Domine, labia mea aperies.
*R.* Et os meum exaltabit Nomen tuum.

Magnificate Dominum mecum, et exaltemus Nomen ejus in idipsum.

Introite portas ejus in confessione, atria ejus in hymnis; confitemini illi, laudate Nomen ejus.

Illuc enim ascederunt tribus, tribus, Domini, testimonium Israël ad confitendum Nomini Domini.

Afferte Domino gloriam et honorem, afferte Domino gloriam Nomini ejus; adorate Dominum in atrio sancto ejus.

Cantate Domino, et benedicite Nomini ejus; annuntiate de die in diem salutare ejus.

Cantate Deo, psalmum dicite Nomini ejus; iter

*V.* Lord, Thou wilt open my lips.
*R.* And my mouth shall extol Thy Name.

Magnify the Lord with me, and let us extol His Name together.

Go ye into His temple with praise, and into His courts with hymns: glorify Him: and praise ye His name.

For thither did the tribes go up, the tribes of the Lord: the testimony of Israel, to praise the Name of the Lord.

Bring to the Lord glory and honor: bring to the Lord glory to His Name: adore ye the Lord in His holy court.

Sing ye to the Lord and bless His Name: show forth His salvation from day to day.

Sing ye to God, sing a psalm to His Name: make a way for Him

facite ei qui ascendit super occasum: Dominus Nomen illi. Modulamini illi psalmum novum; exaltate et invocate Nomen ejus. Gloria Patri…

*Ant.* Bonum est confiteri Domino et psallere Nomini tuo, Altissime.

CAPITULUM

Elegi et sanctificavi locum istum, dicit Dominus, ut sit Nomen meum ibi in sempiternum, et permaneant oculi mei et cor meum ibi cunctis diebus.

*R.* Deo gratias.

CANTICUM<br>BEATÆ MARIÆ VIRGINIS

Magnificat anima mea Dominum,
Et exultavit spiritus meus in Deo salutari meo.

Quia respexit humilitatem ancillæ suæ; ecce enim

---

who ascendeth upon the west: the Lord is His Name.
Sing ye to Him a new psalm, extol and call upon His Name.
Glory be to the Father…

*Ant.* It is good to give praise to the Lord: and to sing Thy Name, O most High.

CHAPTER

I have chosen and I have sanctified this place, saith the Lord, that My Name may be there forever, and that My eyes and My heart may remain there perpetually.

*R.* Thanks be to God.

CANTICLE<br>OF THE BLESSED VIRGIN

My soul doth magnify the Lord,
And my spirit hath rejoiced in God my Savior.
Because He hath regarded the humility of His

ex hoc beatam me
dicent omnes
generationes.

Quia fecit mihi magna qui
potens est, et sanctum
Nomen ejus.

Et misericordia ejus a
progenie in progenies
timentibus eum.

Fecit potentiam in brachio
suo: dispersit superbos
mente cordis sui.

Deposuit potentes de sede,
et exaltavit humiles.

Esurientes implevit bonis,
et divites dimisit
inanes.

Suscepit Israël puerum
suum, recordatus
misericordiæ suæ.

Sicut locutus est ad patres
nostros, Abraham et
semini ejus in sæcula.

Gloria Patri...

handmaid; for behold
from henceforth all
generations shall call
me blessed.

Because He that is mighty,
hath done great things
to me; and holy is His
Name.

And His mercy is from
generation unto
generation, to them
that fear Him.

He hath showed might in
His arm: He hath
scattered the proud in
the conceit of their
heart.

He hath put down the
mighty from their seat,
and hath exalted the
humble.

He hath filled the hungry
with good things; and
the rich He hath sent
empty away.

He hath received Israel
His servant, being
mindful of His mercy.

As He spoke to our
Fathers: to Abraham
and to his seed forever.

Glory be to the Father...

*Ant.* Fecit mihi magna qui potens est, et sanctum Nomen ejus.

*V.* Adorabo ad templum sanctum tuum.
*R.* Et confitebor Nomini tuo, Domine.

OREMUS

Respice, quæsumus, Domine, super famulos tuos in Nomine tuo congregatos, et concede illis ut operibus, et non tantum verbis, injurias sancto Nomini tuo illatas reparare valeant. Per Dominum.

*V.* Sit nomen Domini benedictum.
*R.* Ex hoc nunc et usque in sæculum. Amen.

*Ant.* For He that is mighty hath done great things to me; and holy is His Name.

*V.* I will worship towards Thy holy temple.
*R.* And I will give glory to Thy Name, O Lord.

LET US PRAY

Lord, we beseech Thee, look upon Thy family which is gathered together in Thy Name and grant to them that, not only by their words, but by their actions, they may make reparation for the outrages committed against Thy Holy Name. Through Jesus Christ our Lord, etc.

*V.* Blessed be the Name of the Lord.
*R.* Now and forevermore. Amen.

AT COMPLINE

The faithful soul excites itself more and more to praise the Holy Name of God, in the hope of glorifying It in a still more perfect manner in heaven.

| | |
|---|---|
| Pater noster... | Our Father... |

*V.* Domine, labia mea aperies.
*R.* Et os meum exaltabit Nomen tuum.

*V.* Lord, Thou wilt open my lips.
*R.* And my mouth shall extol Thy Name.

Confitebor tibi in
    sæculum, et expectabo
    Nomen tuum, quoniam
    bonum est in
    conspectu sanctorum
    tuorum.

I will praise Thee forever,
    O Lord; and I will wait
    on Thy Name for it is
    good in the sight of
    Thy saints.

Gloriabuntur in te omnes
    qui diligunt Nomen
    tuum, quoniam tu
    benedices justo.

All those who love Thy
    Name shall glory in
    Thee: for Thou wilt
    bless the just.

Quoniam tu, Deus meus,
    exaudisti orationem
    mean; dedisti
    hæreditatem
    timentibus Nomen
    tuum.

Because Thou hast heard
    the voice of my prayer,
    O Lord my God: Thou
    hast given a heritage to
    those who fear Thy
    Name.

Ut annuntient in Sion
    Nomen Domini, et
    laudem ejus in
    Jerusalem.

That they may declare the
    Name of the Lord in
    Sion: and publish His
    praise in Jerusalem.

Et laudent Nomen ejus in
    choro; in tympano et
    psalterio psallant ei.

Let them praise His Name
    in holy songs; let them
    sing to Him with
    instruments of music.

Voluntarie sacrificabo tibi,
    et confitebor Nomini

Then I will freely sacrifice
    to Thee, and I will

tuo, quoniam bonum est.

Sic psalmum dicam Nomini tuo in sæculum sæculi, ut reddam vota mea de die in diem.

Confitebor tibi, Domine Deus meus, in toto corde meo; et glorificabo Nomen tuum in æternum.

Spiritus tuus bonus deducet me in terram rectam; propter Nomen tuum, Domine, vivificabis me in æquitate tua.

Educ de custodia animam meam ad confitendum Nomini tuo: me expectant justi donec retribuas mihi.

Gloria Patri…

*Ant.* Non nobis, Domine non nobis; sed Nomini tuo da gloriam.

give praise to Thy Name: for it is good.

I will sing a psalm to Thy Name forever and ever: that I may pay my vows from day to day.

I will praise Thee, O Lord my God, with my whole heart, and I will glorify Thy Name forever.

Thy Good Spirit shall lead me into the right Land: for the sake of Thy Name, O Lord, Thou wilt quicken me in Thy justice.

Bring my soul out of prison, that I may praise Thy Name: the just wait for me until Thou reward me.

Glory be to the Father…

*Ant.* Not to us, O Lord, not to us, but to Thy Name give glory.

CAPITULUM

Ecce Agnus stabat super montem Sion, et cum eo centum quadraginta quatuor millia habentes

CHAPTER

Then I saw the Lamb standing upon Mount Sion, and with Him one hundred and forty-four

Nomen ejus, et Nomen Patris ejus scriptum in frontibus suis.

R. Deo gratias
V. Gloriabuntur in te omnes qui diligunt Nomen tuum.
R. Quoniam tu benedices justo.

OREMUS

Repleatur os nostrum laude, omnipotens Deus, ut semper benedicentes te, dum peregrinamur exules, canticum æternum cantare mereamur in cœlis, habentes scriptum in frontibus nostris Nomen sanctum tuum et Nomen Filii tui. Qui tecum vivit et regnat in unitate Spiritus sancti Deus, per omnia sæcula sæculorum. Amen.

V. Sit Nomen Domini benedictum.
R. Ex hoc nunc et usque in sæculum.

thousand persons who had His Name, and the Name of His Father, written on their foreheads.

R. Thanks be to God.
V. Let all who love Thy Name, glorify themselves in Thee.
R. Because Thou wilt bless the just.

LET US PRAY

Grant, O almighty God, that our mouths may not cease to celebrate Thy glory, and that having blessed Thee during our exile here on earth, we may deserve to praise Thee eternally in heaven, having written on our foreheads Thy Holy Name and the Name of Thy Son Jesus Christ; who liveth and reigneth with Thee, in the unity of the Holy Ghost forever and ever. Amen.

V. Blessed be the Name of the Lord.
R. Now and forevermore.

*V.* Erue nos in mirabilibus tuis.
*R.* Et da gloriam Nomini tuo Domine.

Dei Patris omnipotentis Verbum, te, Domine Jesu Christe, deprecamur ut nos in Fide Nominis tui robores per spei perseverantiam, et caritatis excellentiam. Qui vivis et regnas cum Deo Patre in unitate Spiritus sancti Deus, per omnia sæcula sæculorum. Amen.

*V.* Deliver us by Thy miraculous power.
*R.* And give glory to Thy Name, O Lord.

O Word of the omnipotent God, our Lord Jesus Christ, we beg of Thee to fortify us in the faith of Thy Name by the hope of perseverance and by the excellence of charity, Thou who livest and reignest with God the Father in the unity of the Holy Ghost forever and ever. Amen.

---

# Sixth Part
# SUPPLEMENT

The following prayers and information on the devotion to the Holy Face were not contained in the original manuals. Some of the prayers that follow are included for the reader who may not be familiar with the prayers in full (e.g. Pater, Ave, Gloria), since they are included in some of the prayers in the preceding sections. There are additional prayers to the Holy Face which appeared in a 1950 printing *Handbook of the Holy Face* which were not in the original manuals, but are being included in this supplement. The Fatima prayers are also included in this supplement as they are prayers of reparation for the salvation of souls.

### Pater Noster

Pater Noster, qui es in cœlis, sanctificétur Nomen tuum, advéniat regnum tuum, fiat volúntas tua, sicut in cœlo et in terra. Panem nostrum quotidiánum da nobis hódie; et dimítte nobis débita nostra, sicut et nos dimíttimus debitóribus notris, et ne nos indúcas in tetatiónem, sed libra nos a malo. Amen.

### The Our Father

Our Father, who art in heaven, hallowed be Thy Name. Thy kingdom come, Thy will be done on earth as it is in heaven. Give us this day our daily bread, and forgive us our trespasses, as we forgive those who trespass against us, and lead us not into temptation, but deliver us from evil. Amen.

### Ave Maria

Ave María, grátia plena, Dóminus tecum; benedícta tu in muliéribus, et

### The Hail Mary

Hail Mary, full of grace, the Lord is with thee; blessed are thou amongst

benedíctus fructus ventris tui, Jesus. Santa María, Mater Dei, ora pro nobis peccatóribus, nunc et in hora mortis nostræ. Amen.

women, and blessed is the fruit of thy womb, Jesus. Holy Mary, Mother of God, pray for us sinners, now and at the hour of our death. Amen.

## Glória Patri

## Doxology to the Blessed Trinity

Glória Patri, et Fílio, et Spirítui Sancto. Sicut erat in princípio, et nunc, et semper, et in saécula sæculórum. Amen.

Glory be to the Father, and to the Son, and to the Holy Ghost. As it was in the beginning, is now, and ever shall be; world without end. Amen.

## Credo

## The Apostle's Creed

Credo in Deum, Patrem omnipoténtem, Creatórem cœli et terrae; et in Jesum Christum, Fílium ejus únicum, Dóminum nostrum; qui concéptus est de Spíritu Sancto, natus ex María Virgine; passus sub Póntio Piláto, crucifixus, mórtuus et sepúltus; descéndit ad ínferos, tértia die resurréxit a mórtuis, ascéndit ad cœlos; sedet ad déxteram Dei Patris omnipoténtis, inde ventúrus est

I believe in God, the Father Almighty, Creator of heaven and earth; and in Jesus Christ, His only Son, our Lord, who was conceived by the Holy Ghost, born of the Virgin Mary, suffered under Pontius Pilate, was crucified, died, and was buried. He descended into hell; the third day He rose again from the dead; He ascended into heaven, sitteth at the right hand of

judicare vivos et mórtuos. Credo in Spiritum Sanctum, sanctam Ecclésiam cathólicam, Sanctórum communiónem, remissiónem peccatórum, carnis resurrectiónem, vitam aetérnam. Amen.

God, the Father, Almighty; from thence He shall come to judge the living and the dead. I believe in the Holy Ghost, the Holy Catholic Church, the communion of saints, the forgiveness of sins, the resurrection of the body, and life everlasting. Amen.

### Salve Regina

Salve, Regína, mater misericórdiae; vita, dulcédo et spes nostra salve. Ad te clamámus éxsules filii Hevae. Ad te suspirámus geméntes et flentes in hac lacrimárum valle. Eia, ergo, advocáta nostra, ilos tuos misericórdes óculos ad nos convérte. Et Jesum, benedictum fructum ventris tui, nobis post hoc exsilium osténde. O clemens, o pia, o dulcis Virgo Maria.

*V.* Ora pro nobis Sancta Dei Génetrix.

### Hail Holy Queen

Hail, Holy Queen, Mother of mercy! Our life, our sweetness and our hope! To thee do we cry poor banished children of Eve! To thee do we send up our sighs, mourning and weeping in this valley of tears! Turn then, most gracious advocate, thine eyes of mercy towards us; and after this our exile, show unto us the blessed fruit of thy womb, Jesus! O clement, O loving, O sweet Virgin Mary!

*V.* Pray for us, O Holy Mother of God.

*R*. Ut digni efficiámur pro-missiónibus Christi.

*R.* That we may be made worthy of the promises of Christ.

Oremus

Let us pray

Deus, cujus Unigéntius per vitam, mortem et resurrecti-ónem suam nobis salútis aetérnae praémia compar-ávit: concéde quaésumus; ut haec mystéria sacratíssimo beátae Maríae Vírginis Rosário recoléntes, et imitémur quod cóntinent, et quod promíttunt, assequá-mur. Per eundem Christum Dóminum nostrum.

O God, whose only begotton Son by His life, death, and resurrection has purchased for us the rewards of Eternal Life, grant we beseech Thee that meditating upon these mysteries of the most Holy Rosary of the Blessed Virgin Mary, we may imitate what they contain and obtain what they promise. Through the same Christ, Our Lord.

*R.* Amen

*R.* Amen

## Magnificat

## Canticle of the Blessed Virgin Mary
(St. Luke 1:46-55)

Magnificat ánima méa Dóminum. Et exsultávit spír-itus méus in Déo salutári méo. Quia respéxit humilitá-tem ancillæ súæ ecce enim ex hoc beátam me dícent ómnes

My soul doth magnify the Lord; and my spirit hath rejoiced in God my Savior, because He hath regarded the humility of His handmaid for behold

generatións. Quia fécit míhi mágna, qui pótens est: et sánctum nómen éjus. Et Misericórdia éjus a progénie in progénies timéntibus éum. Fécit poténtiam in bráchio súo: dispérsit supérbos ménte córdis súi. Depósuit poténtes de séde, et exaltávit húmiles. Esuriéntes implévit bónis: et dívites dimísit inánes. Suscépit Israël, púerum súum, recordátus misericórdiae súae. Sicut locútus est ad pátres nóstros, Abraham et sémini éjus in sǽcula. Glória Pátri, et Filio, et Spirítui Sáncto. Sicut érat in princípio, et núnc, et sémper, et in sǽcula sæculórum. Amen.

from henceforth all generations shall call me blessed, because He that is mighty hath done great things to me, and holy is His Name, and His mercy is from generation unto generation to them that fear Him. He hath shown might in His arm; He hath scattered the proud in the conceit of their heart. He hath put down the mighty from their seat, and hath exalted the humble. He hath filled the hungry with good things, and the rich He hath sent empty away. He hath received Israel, His servant, being mindful of His mercy. As He spoke to our fathers, to Abraham and to His seed forever. Glory be to the Father, and to the Son, and to the Holy Ghost. As it was in the beginning, is now, and ever shall be, world without end. Amen.

## Sancte Michaël Archéngele | Prayer to St. Michael the Archangel

Sancte Míchaël Archángele, defénde nos in prælio; contra nequítiam et insídias diáboli esto præsídium. Imperet illi Deus, súpplices deprecámur: tuque, Princeps milítiæ cæléstis, Sátanam aliósque spíritus malígnos, qui ad perditiónem animárum pervagántur in mundo, divína virtúte in inférnum detrúde. Amen.

Saint Michael the Archangel, defend us in battle; be our defense against the wickedness and the snares of the devil. May God rebuke him, we humbly pray: and do thou, O prince of the heavenly host, by the power of God thrust into hell, Satan and all evil spirits, who prowl about the world seeking the ruin of souls. Amen.

## Fatima Prayers

O my Jesus, forgive us our sins, save us from the fires of hell, and lead all souls to heaven, especially those who are in most need of Thy mercy! (Nostris, O Jesu débitis indúlge, érue nos ab ígnibus inférni, coelíque portas univérsis pande, miséris praesértim. – This prayer is added to the rosary after each Gloria.)

My God, I believe, I adore, I hope, and I love Thee. I ask pardon for those who do not believe, do not adore, do not hope, and do not love Thee.

Most Holy Trinity, Father, Son, and Holy Ghost. I adore Thee with the most profound humility, and I offer Thee the most Precious Body, Blood, Soul, and Divinity of our Lord Jesus Christ present in all the tabernacles of the world in reparation for the outrages, sacrileges, and indifferences by which He is offended. Through the infinite merits of His most Sacred Heart and the Immaculate Heart of Mary, I ask for the conversion of poor sinners.

O Jesus, it is for the love of Thee, for the conversion of sinners, and in reparation for the sins committed against the Immaculate Heart of Mary.

---

## Litany of the Holy Face[†]
### Approved for private use by Pope Pius IX
### Jan. 27 1853

O Jesus, whose adorable Face Mary and Joseph worshiped with profoundest reverence, *have mercy on us.*

O Jesus, whose adorable Face is the masterpiece of the Holy Ghost, in which the Father was well pleased, *have mercy on us.*

O Jesus, whose adorable Face ravished with joy the angels, shepherds and Magi, in the stable at Bethlehem, *have mercy on us.*

O Jesus, whose adorable Face wounded with a dart of love the aged Simeon and the Prophetess Anna in the temple, *have mercy on us.*

O Jesus, whose adorable Face was bathed in tears in Thy holy infancy, *have mercy on us.*

O Jesus, whose adorable Face at the age of twelve astonished the doctors in the temple, *have mercy on us.*

O Jesus, whose adorable Face is white with purity and ruddy with charity, *have mercy on us.*

O Jesus, whose adorable Face is more beautiful than the sun, brighter than the moon and more brilliant than the stars, *have mercy on us.*

O Jesus, whose adorable Face is lovelier than the roses of spring, *have mercy on us.*

O Jesus, whose adorable Face is more precious than gold, silver and gems, *have mercy on us.*

O Jesus, the charms and grace of whose adorable Face wins all hearts, *have mercy on us.*

O Jesus, whose adorable Face is most noble in Its heavenly features, *have mercy on us.*

O Jesus, whose adorable Face is the admiration of Angels, *have mercy on us.*

O Jesus, whose adorable Face is the sweet delight of the saints, *have mercy on us.*

O Jesus, whose adorable Face was the delight of Thy Virgin Mother and of Thy holy father, St. Joseph, *have mercy on us.*

O Jesus, whose adorable Face is the ineffable mirror of Divine perfections, *have mercy on us.*

O Jesus, the beauty of whose adorable Face is ever ancient and ever new, *have mercy on us.*

O Jesus, the modesty and mildness of whose adorable Face attracted both just and sinners, *have mercy on us.*

O Jesus, whose adorable Face appeases the Divine wrath, *have mercy on us.*

O Jesus, whose adorable Face is the terror of evil spirits, *have mercy on us.*

O Jesus, whose adorable Face is the treasure of graces and blessings, *have mercy on us.*

O Jesus, whose adorable Face was exposed to the inclemency of the weather in the desert, *have mercy on us.*

O Jesus, whose adorable Face was scorched by the sun and bathed in sweat on Thy journeys, *have mercy on us.*

O Jesus, the expression of whose adorable Face is wholly Divine, *have mercy on us.*

O Jesus, whose adorable Face gave a holy kiss and blessing to the little children, *have mercy on us.*

O Jesus, whose adorable Face sorrowed and wept at the grave of Lazarus, *have mercy on us.*

O Jesus, whose adorable Face was brilliant as the sun and radiant with glory on Mount Tabor, have mercy on us.

> *V.* The light of Thy Face has been shed upon us, O Lord,
>
> *R.* Thou hast given joy to our hearts.

### *Let us pray*

I salute Thee, I adore Thee, I love Thee, adorable Face of Jesus, my Beloved, noble seal of the Divinity! With all the powers of my soul, I apply myself to Thee, and humbly pray Thee imprint in us all the features of Thy Divine likeness. Amen.

# Litany of the Holy Face

## II

O Jesus, whose adorable Face is worthy of all reverence, veneration and worship, *have mercy on us.*

O Jesus, whose adorable Face grew sad at the sight of Jerusalem when Thou didst weep over that ungrateful city, *have mercy on us.*

O Jesus, whose adorable Face was bowed to the earth in the Garden of Olives because of the burden of our sins, *have mercy on us.*

O Jesus, whose adorable Face was bathed in bloody sweat, *have mercy on us.*

O Jesus, whose adorable Face was kissed by Judas the traitor, *have mercy on us.*

O Jesus, the power of whose adorable Face smote the soldiers to the ground in the Garden of Olives, *have mercy on us.*

O Jesus, whose adorable Face was struck by a vile servant, derided by enemies and desecrated by their unholy hands, *have mercy on us.*

O Jesus, whose adorable Face was defiled with spittle and bruised by blows, *have mercy on us.*

O Jesus, the Divine look of whose adorable Face wounded Peter's heart with love and sorrow, *have mercy on us.*

O Jesus, whose adorable Face was humbled for us before the tribunals of Jerusalem, *have mercy on us.*

O Jesus, whose adorable Face preserved Its serenity and dignity when Pilate pronounced the death sentence, *have mercy on us.*

O Jesus, the brow of whose adorable Face was crowned with thorns, *have mercy on us.*

O Jesus, whose adorable Face was covered with bloody sweat, and fell to the ground under the Cross, *have mercy on us.*

O Jesus, whose adorable Face the pious Veronica wiped on the way to Calvary, *have mercy on us.*

O Jesus, whose adorable Face was lifted up on the torturous Cross, *have mercy on us.*

O Jesus, the eyes of whose adorable Face shed tears of blood, *have mercy on us.*

O Jesus, the mouth of whose adorable Face was tormented with vinegar and gall, *have mercy on us.*

O Jesus, the hair and beard of whose adorable Face were plucked out by the executioners, *have mercy on us.*

O Jesus, whose adorable Face was disfigured like to that of a leper, *have mercy on us.*

O Jesus, the incomparable beauty of whose adorable Face was disfigured by the sins of the world, *have mercy on us.*

O Jesus, whose adorable Face was overcast by the mournful shadows of death, *have mercy on us.*

O Jesus, whose adorable Face was washed, anointed and wrapped in a shroud by Mary and the holy women, *have mercy on us.*

O Jesus, whose adorable Face was laid to rest in the grave, *have mercy on us.*

O Jesus, whose adorable Face was resplendent in beauty on the day of Thy resurrection, *have mercy on us.*

O Jesus, whose adorable Face was radiant in glory on the day of Thy ascension, *have mercy on us.*

O Jesus, whose adorable Face is hidden in the most Blessed Sacrament of the Altar, *have mercy on us.*

O Jesus, whose adorable Face will appear in the clouds at the end of the world with great power and majesty, *have mercy on us.*

O Jesus, whose adorable Face will be the terror of sinners, *have mercy on us.*

O Jesus, whose adorable Face is the joy of the just in heaven, *have mercy on us.*

*V.* O Lord, show us Thy Face,

*R.* And we shall be saved.

### *Let us pray*

We beseech Thee, O almighty and merciful God, grant us and all who venerate the Countenance of Thy dearly beloved Son, all disfigured by our sins, the grace to behold It throughout eternity in the glory of Its majesty, through the same Jesus Christ our Lord. Amen.

( † This is another version of the Litany of the Holy Face, as found in the second part of this book.)

## Prayer to the Holy Face

Composed by Saint Therese of the Child Jesus and of the Holy Face
"The Little Flower of Jesus"

O Jesus, who in Thy cruel Passion didst become the "Reproach of men and the Man of Sorrows," I worship Thy Divine Face. Once it shone with the beauty and sweetness of the Divinity; now for my sake It is become as the face of a leper. Yet in that disfigured Countenance I recognize Thy infinite love, and I am consumed with the desire of loving Thee and of making Thee loved by all mankind. The tears that streamed in such abundance from Thy eyes are to me as precious pearls which I delight to gather, that with their infinite worth I may ransom the souls of poor sinners.

O Jesus, whose Face is the sole beauty that ravishes my heart, I may not behold here upon earth the sweetness of Thy glance, nor feel the ineffable tenderness of Thy kiss. Thereto I consent, but I pray Thee to imprint in me Thy Divine likeness, and I implore Thee so to inflame me with Thy love, that it may quickly consume me, and that I may reach the vision of Thy glorious Face in heaven. Amen.

---

# Veneration of the Thorn-Crowned Head of Our Savior

"And platting a crown of thorns they put it upon His head ... They began to spit upon Him, and they gave Him blows. Others smote His Face and said: 'Prophesy, who is it that struck thee?' "

O Holy Redeemer! Thou art clothed with a scarlet cloak, a reed is placed in thy hand for a scepter, and the sharp points of a thorny crown are pressed into Thy adorable head.

My soul, thou canst never conceive the sufferings, the insults and the indignities offered to our Blessed Lord during this scene of pain and mockery.

The impious mock Thee, O Jesus; I salute Thee and offer Thee supreme homage as King of heaven and earth, the Redeemer of the world, the Eternal Son of the living God.

O my afflicted Savior! O King of the world! Thou art ridiculed as a mock-king; I believe in Thee and adore Thee as the King of kings and the Lord of lords, as the supreme Ruler of heaven and earth.

O Jesus! I devoutly venerate Thy Sacred Head, pierced with thorns, struck with a reed, overwhelmed with pain and derision.

I adore the Precious Blood flowing from Thy bleeding Wounds. To Thee be all praise, all thanksgiving, and all love forevermore!

O meek Lamb, victim for sin! May Thy thorns penetrate my heart with fervent love, that I may never cease to adore Thee as my God, my King and my Savior.

*V.* Behold, O God, our protector,
*R.* And look upon the Face of Thy Christ.

*Let us pray*

O my beloved Savior, at the sight of Thy most holy Face disfigured by suffering, at the sight of Thy Sacred Heart so full of love, I cry out with St. Augustine: "Lord Jesus, imprint on my heart Thy Sacred Wounds, so that I may read therein sorrow and love; sorrow, to endure every sorrow for Thee; love to despise every love for Thee." Amen.

# Ecce Homo!

"Jesus therefore came forth bearing the crown of thorns and the purple garment. And Pilate saith to them: 'Behold the Man.' "

Hasten thither, my soul, and behold Thy Savior; behold in how pitiable a condition He is presented to the people.

Behold, how the glory of the Eternal Father, the mirror of His splendor, has become disfigured.

Behold your Redeemer, the crown of thorns upon His head, the blood streaming down His Face; His hands, swollen and cut by the cords, holding a reed instead of a scepter; the mock-mantle saturated by the bleeding wounds of His torn and mangled body!

O bleeding Jesus! to what an agonizing state Thou art reduced. Thou, the most beautiful of the children of men, hast become a man of sorrows.

Hail, adorable Face, worthy of all respect, veneration and worship! O worshipful Face, whose brow is crowned with thorns, whose eyes are filled with blood!

We venerate Thee, O adorable Face, into whose mouth is poured vinegar and gall, whose hair and beard are painfully torn out.

*V.* Show us Thy Face,
*R.* And we shall be saved.

*Let us pray*

Almighty and merciful God, grant we beseech Thee, that whilst reverencing the Face of Thy Christ, disfigured in the Passion because of our sins we may merit to contemplate It shining forever in celestial glory; through the same Jesus Christ our Lord. Amen

---

# O Sacred Head

O Head, all gashed and gory!
O'erwhelmed in woe and scorn;
O Head, the Angels' glory!
Yet pierced by many a thorn.
Far other fate should meet Thee,
Far other be Thy crown;
A thousand times I greet Thee,
While tears of love flow down.
Thy cheeks are wan and faded,
Thy lips are ghastly white,
Thy beauty quite o'ershaded
In death's obscurest night.
Yet tender love is lighting
E'en still Thy Sacred Face,
Poor sinners still inviting
To undeserved grace.
Ah, Lord, the thorns Thou wearest
Should pierce my guilty brow;
Beneath the Cross Thou bearest
My guilty back should bow;
The cruel whips that tore Thee,
Mine, mine alone should be;
Yet Jesus, I implore Thee,
Turn not Thy Face from me.
When my last hour is knelling
Forsake me not, I pray;
But shades of death dispelling
Be Thou my light, my stay.
O Face, now gashed and gory!
What joy it is for me,
To hope one day in glory
Thy gracious smile to see.

———————

# Prayer to Our Lord on the Cross for a Happy Hour of Death

My crucified Jesus, mercifully accept the prayer which I now make to Thee for help in the moment of my death, when at its approach all my senses shall fail me.

When, therefore, O sweetest Jesus, my weary and downcast eyes can no longer look up to Thee, be mindful of the loving gaze which now I turn to Thee, and have mercy on me.

When my parched lips can no longer kiss Thy most sacred Wounds, remember then those kisses which now I imprint on Thee, and have mercy on me.

When my cold hands can no longer embrace Thy Cross, forget not the affection with which I embrace it now, and have mercy on me.

And when, at length, my swollen and lifeless tongue can no longer speak, remember that I called upon Thee now.

Jesus, Mary, Joseph, to Thee I commend my soul.

---

## Prayer to the Eternal Father
For the Conversion of Sinners and Salvation of the Dying

Eternal Father, we offer Thee the adorable Face of Thy beloved Son Jesus, for the honor and glory of Thy most Holy Name, for the conversion of sinners, and the salvation of the dying.

---

# The Holy Face Medal

Less than 100 years after the revelations and mission given to Sister Marie de Saint-Pierre (the Carmelite of Tours by Our Lord to establish a worldwide devotion to His Holy Face, Our Lord and Our Lady entrusted another mission to the spread of this devotion to Bl. Mother Maria Pierina de Micheli (Congregation of the Daughters of the Immaculate Conception).

In 1938, Our Lady appeared with a scapular in hand. On one side was the image of the Holy Face with the words "Illumina Domine Vultum Tuum Super Nos" around it, and on the other side the Sacred Host surrounded by rays of light with the following words around it, "Mane Nobiscum Domine." That is, "O Lord, may the light of Thy countenance shine upon us" and "Stay with us O Lord." Then the Blessed Virgin Mary spoke the following words to Bl. Mother Maria Pierina,

*"Listen to me very carefully and refer everything with exactness to the Father confessor. This scapular is a weapon of defense, a shield of strength, a pledge of love and mercy which Jesus wishes to give to the world in these times of sensuality and hatred against God and the Church. Diabolic snares are being laid to tear the faith from men's hearts, and evil spreads. True apostles are few, a Divine remedy is necessary, and this remedy is the Holy Face of Jesus. All those who shall wear a scapular\* like this, and will make, if possible, a visit to the Blessed Sacrament every Tuesday, in reparation for the outrages that the Holy Face of my Son Jesus received during His Passion, and which He receives each day in the Eucharistic Sacrament, will be fortified in the faith, made able to defend it and to overcome all difficulties within and without: and in the end will have a happy death under the loving gaze of my Divine Son."*

\*In 1940, the first medals of the Holy Face were made based on the image from the Holy Shroud. The fact that medals were made instead of scapulars caused doubt in Mother Maria Pierina. However Our Lady dissipated any doubts, *"My Daughter, be calm because the scapular is replaced by the medal. The medal carries the same promises and favors."* Pope Pius XII approved both the devotion and the medal of the Holy Face.

In November of 1938, Our Lord appeared bleeding and in sorrow to Mother Maria Pierina.

*"Seest thou how I suffer? And yet so few understand. How much ingratitude on the part of those who say they love Me. I have given My Heart as the sensible proof of My great love for man, and I give My Face as the sensible object of My grief for the sins of mankind and I desire that it may be honored by a special Feast on Tuesday of Quinquagesima, a Feast preceded by a Novena in which all the Faithful will make reparation with Me, thus uniting and participating in My grief."*

In 1958, Pope Pius XII established Shrove Tuesday as the Feast of the Holy Face (Tuesday of Quinquagesima or the Tuesday before Ash Wednesday).

For additional information with respect to this devotion, one may read more on the life of Sister Marie de Saint Pierre and the life of Bl. Maria Pierina de Micheli. The information on the medal and the Feast of the Holy Face have been included in this section, as they are directly tied to reparation and the salvation of souls.

# Chaplet of the Holy Face

The third part of this book contains information on the Chaplet of the Holy Face. This section provides some additional meditation points, and additional guidance on how to say the chaplet.

Along with honoring the five senses and the five wounds of Our Lord, a total of seven Glorias are said during the chaplet in which we honor and can meditate on the Seven Last Words of Our Lord, and the Seven Sorrows of Our Lady.

St. Athanasius relates that the devils, on being asked what verse in the whole Scripture they feared the most, replied: "That with which the sixty-seventh Psalm commences: Let God arise, and let His enemies be scattered; let them that hate Him flee before His Face." They added that it always compelled them to take flight.

On the Crucifix

> Deus in adjutorium meum intende. Domine, ad adjuvandum me festina. (O God, come to my assistance. O Lord, make haste to help me.)

On the first large bead

> Glory be to the Father, and to the Son, and to the Holy Ghost. As it was in the beginning, is now, and ever shall be; world without end. Amen.
> My Jesus, mercy.

On the second large bead

> Announce the first sense (touch) Gloria Patri...
> My Jesus, mercy.

Arise O Lord, let Thy enemies be scattered.
Let them that hate Thee flee before Thy
Face. (repeated on each small bead)

On the third large bead
Announce the second sense (hearing)
Gloria Patri...
My Jesus, mercy
Arise O Lord...(on each small bead)

On the fourth large bead
Announce the third sense (sight)
Gloria Patri...
My Jesus, mercy
Arise O Lord...(on each small bead)

On the fifth large bead
Announce the forth sense (smell)
Gloria Patri...
My Jesus, mercy
Arise O Lord...(on each small bead)

On the sixth large bead
Announce the fifth sense (taste)
Gloria Patri...
My Jesus, mercy
Arise O Lord...(on each small bead)

On the seventh large bead (recall all the wounds suffered
by Our Lord during His passion)
Gloria Patri...
My Jesus, mercy
Arise O Lord (on the last three small beads)

On the Holy Face medal
O God our protector, look upon us, and cast Thine
eyes upon the Face of Thy Christ.

## The Seven Last Words of Our Lord:

1. Father, forgive them, for they know not what they do.
2. Amen I say to thee, this day thou shalt be with Me in paradise.
3. Woman, behold thy son.
4. My God, My God, why hast Thou forsaken Me?
5. I thirst.
6. It is consummated.
7. Father, into Thy hands I commend My Spirit.

## The Seven Sorrows of Our Lady

1. The prophecy of St. Simeon.
2. Flight to Egypt.
3. Loss of the Child Jesus for three days.
4. Meeting on the road to Calvary.
5. Crucifixion and death of Our Lord.
6. Our Lord is taken down from the Cross and placed into the arms of Our Lady.
7. Our Lord is laid in the sepulchre.

---

# Seventh Part
# THE LIFE OF SISTER MARIE DE SAINT PIERRE

(The following version of the Life of Sister Marie de Saint-Pierre, is from the 1885 publication of *Sister Saint Pierre and the Work of Reparation with an Appendix of Prayers and Devotions for the Confraternities of the Holy Face.* The original prefaces have been included for historical context.)

# Preface

The following work is a translation of *The Brief Life of Sister Saint-Pierre*, which was published by the Rev. Father Janvier at Tours in 1882 with the approbation of his Archbishop. Her own account of her experiences, and remarkable manifestations of Divine favor, has been already given to the public by the instrumentality of the Carmelite Nuns of New Orleans.* This *Life*, collated and completed by means of her letters and the annals of her monastery, was published by the Rev. P. Janvier, Dean of the Metropolitan Church of Tours and Director of the Priests of the Holy Face. It bears the imprimatur of the Archbishop of Tours; and the English translation is approved by the Archbishops of Baltimore and New Orleans, and by other prelates.

The present work by the devoted Father Janvier is, as he explains in his preface, an attempt to give the principal facts of the life of the saintly Carmelite, with an account of the Work of Reparation to which the Confraternity of the Holy Face is consecrated. We think it will be read by pious Catholics for their edification and benefit. His Grace of Baltimore tells us that "her *Life* is intended to promote piety and edification, not only in cloistered institutions, but also in the ranks of the secular life."

The Archbishop of New Orleans warmly approves and recommends it, and declares "that he will be glad to see it rapidly spread among the faithful, who will find it a treasure of edification and instruction designed to inspire them with devotion to the Holy Face." The question of the virtues of Sister Saint-Pierre has not been raised at Rome, and the Holy See has thus far decided nothing in regard to the supernatural character of the revelations which she received. However, with the approbation of the Supreme Pontiff, the Confraternity of the Holy Face has been established, and there can be no reason to doubt the many miracles wrought through the instrumentality of M. Dupont, the Holy Man of Tours. The Confraternity of the Holy Face was established at St. Dizier in 1847, and at Tours in 1876, where now there is an association of priests especially devoted to its interests. It has been enriched by indulgences granted by Pope Pius IX of blessed memory, and Pope Leo XIII, gloriously reigning.

The brief of Pope Leo XIII dated December 9, 1884, recognizes the Confraternity at Tours as legitimately established, and, "in order that it may daily increase, opens the treasures of the Church to its members who shall perform the devotions recommended by the rule." These indulgences are also applicable to the souls in Purgatory. Indulgences, both plenary and partial, had been accorded by his Holiness Pius IX in 1847, 1848, and 1876. With this high sanction, the Confraternity has been erected in the United States.

This work, which now we recommend to the devout lovers of Jesus Christ, will fully, though briefly, explain the aim of the devotion to the Holy Face of our Lord. By exciting in our souls a stronger personal love for our Redeemer, it will lead us to a life more in union with Him. His Blessed Face, which represents to us not only all the sorrows which He endured for our salvation, but also all the sweetness of His Sacred Heart, will be before us to attract us more powerfully day by day. It will wean us from sin, from the love of the world, and even from our own foolish pride. Then, with true loyalty, we will be able to make reparation to Him by deeds and words which love prompts and sanctifies. If there be a blessed work on earth, it is that of reparation. If there be an affection which can have complete power over the heart and intellect, it is the love of our dearest Lord and Savior. We are convinced that the devotion to the Holy Face will be the means of sanctifying many souls, and that it is especially suitable to the needs of our day. The great Master and Teacher of Holiness will accomplish much in us, if we will only seek to live in His sight and obey the motions of His grace. May He, of His infinite mercy, deign to show us the light of His countenance, and to look with love and blessing upon our feeble efforts to extend His reign in the hears of men!

— T. S. P.    New York, April 12, 1885.

* *Life of Sister Saint-Pierre, a Carmelite of Tours. Written by herself. Baltimore: John Murphy & Co. 1884.*

## Preface by Rev. Fr. Janvier

This little book has long been earnestly desired. Friends of the Carmelites and readers of the *Life of Sister Saint-Pierre*, written by herself, have asked an abridgment of it which should be the counterpart of our notice on M. Dupont and the Work of the Holy Face. In responding to this desire we have neglected nothing which could render this pious history interesting and popular, and at the same time make it serve as a means of propagating the Holy Work of Reparation. In this we believe we are obeying the orders of our Lord transmitted to His servant. "The Lord," she said, "asks of France a Work of Reparation which will be for her the rainbow of mercy. Ah! If it were extended to all the dioceses, all the cities, I would be without uneasiness, for God is faithful to His promises.... I have always said, and I still repeat it; it is this which is to disarm the justice of God and save France. Happy if they know how to profit by this means of salvation!"

A pious and eloquent layman recently said: "The social edifice is falling into ruins. Humanly speaking, nothing can sustain it. Perhaps you rely on God? On God! — as individuals, granted; but as a nation? Has not France driven Him from her government, her laws, her morals? On God! — when everywhere His Name is blasphemed? On God! — when His Day is profaned and His Church attacked? All that is happening to us, is it not the expression of His just anger? Is it not precisely this anger that is first to be appeased? In truth, this accomplished, salvation becomes possible; 'for if God is for us who shall be against us?' Now, the sure means of softening His anger, and consequently the great means of salvation which God Himself, before reducing us to extremities, has deigned to recommend is REPARATION." *

O you who love the Church and France, read, and from the teachings of the pious Carmelite of Tours learn in what consists this Reparation, and in acting upon it, what you have to do.

— P. Janvier

Festival of the Finding of the Holy Cross, May 3, 1882

* *Allocution of General Foloppe, November 12, 1881*

# Sister Saint-Pierre

## Chapter I: Her Youth

It is to Catholic Brittany, strong in faith and great in heroic virtues, that we are indebted for having given us Marie de Saint-Pierre. She was born at Rennes on the 4th of October, 1816. At her baptism she was given the same patrons as her father and mother — St. Peter, Prince of the Apostles, and St. Francis of Assisi: Françoise-Perrine being derivatives of these names. Her father, Pierre Elnère, was a locksmith by profession. He married Françoise Portier, who bore him twelve children. This couple were fervent Christians. The father daily assisted at Mass, every evening visited the Blessed Sacrament, and during the day still found time to pray. Early on, he taught his little daughter the practice of the Way of the Cross, and her mother instilled in her a tender devotion to the Blessed Virgin Little Perrine was often sick and had a disposition difficult to manage. But, thanks to the guidance of her pious parents, she early learned to govern it and to overcome her faults. From childhood she had a deep abhorrence of sin, and bitterly reproached herself for the slightest imperfections. Her eldest sister, finding her one day in tears, asked her the cause of them. "I weep for my sins," she answered with simplicity.

Another day a poor blind man, miserably dressed, passed before the house. He had lost his way, and paused at the corner of the street waiting for some charitable hand to set him right. A secret instinct warned the child that here was an occasion to curb her pride and self-love. Suddenly darting out, she took his arm, and, giving him her hand, she led him whither he wished to go. Whenever anything disagreeable happened to her she checked her impatience, saying: "My God, I offer Thee this in expiation for my sins."

She had such a dread of evil that, having at the age of eight years an uneasiness with respect to a little storybook that had been loaned to her, she carried it to her parish priest and asked his advice. When she learned from him that, without being bad, it was a frivolous book, she immediately returned it without having read the first page. The remembrance of the sufferings of our Lord deeply affected her. She thought her sins the cause of His sorrows and pains; confused and contrite, she would say: "O my Savior! Didst Thou see even then, during Thy Passion, that I would one day be converted and belong entirely to Thee?" She often made the Way of the Cross, kissing the earth at each Station. But her chief attraction was mental prayer. At first, not knowing the method, she recited her prayers with great attention, waiting until God should make known to her this holy exercise. She had not long to wait. When she was but ten years old she heard a sermon on the subject which shed a bright light on her mind and heart, and soon made her proficient in this science of the saints.

At the age of twelve she lost her mother. Like St. Teresa at the same age and under similar circumstances, she ran in her wild grief to Mary, threw herself at her feet, and implored her to be a mother to her in the place of the one that had been taken from her. The Queen of Heaven adopted, in fact, this innocent soul, and gave her through all her life sensible proofs of her maternal care. As her father was burdened with a large family, he confided her to the care of two aunts, who were persons of great piety. They kept a large store for the sale of seamstresses' work, and had a number of young women in their employment. There Perrine made new progress in virtue, was a model to her companions, and even to several of them became a preceptress of the Interior Life, striving to make them love and practice mental prayer, in order to be more united to God.

She seized every opportunity of devoting herself to works of mercy, such as helping the poor and visiting and assisting the dying. Near to Mr. Elnère's house a poor family came to live, consisting of three members — the father (a day-laborer), his blind wife, and a little boy four or five years old. The young girl looked upon them as the image of the Holy Family of Bethlehem. She had a great affection for them, and spared no care to relieve their poverty; she often visited them, instructed them in their religion, made them approach the Sacraments, and when there was any disturbance, restored peace in the household. Soon after, she devoted herself to nursing a poor young woman who died in her arms. Receiving her last sigh, she hesitated not with her own hands to prepare her for burial, notwithstanding the fear she had of death, and to which she had never before been in such close proximity.

For a moment, however, this soul so pure was on the point of being seduced by the frivolities of the world She first relaxed her fervor and then had the misfortune to make a few concessions to vanity. God, in love and mercy, punished her. Pressed by remorse, and having, as a member of the confraternity, to prepare herself for a festival of the Blessed Virgin, she endeavored to make a good and serious retreat. She then felt the interior workings of grace, and came forth from these exercises completely changed, resolved more than ever to live for God alone. The desire for a religious life, which she had already experienced, developed itself strongly in her heart. It was the sole object of her thoughts, of her burning desires. For this end she imposed fasts on herself and made pilgrimages in honor of the Blessed Virgin and St. Joseph. She also addressed herself to St. Martin, the illustrious Bishop of Tours, for whom she had a great devotion, supplicating him to receive her as a religious in his diocese, though she did not then know that any

Carmelites were there.

Still she was distressed by perplexities. Her confessor, who was a man of God, wished to test her vocation. For five years he made her undergo numerous and painful humiliations. At the end of this time she was inspired to make a pilgrimage to a celebrated chapel of the Holy Virgin in the vicinity of Rennes — Our Lady of La Peinière. There she clearly perceived that God called her to serve Him by the practice of religious vows. All her yearnings drew her towards Carmel, while her confessor appeared desirous she should enter the order of the Hospital Sisters. But as she was returning from her pilgrimage our Lord, after Holy Communion, made her interiorly hear these words: "My daughter, I love you too much to abandon you any longer to your perplexities. You will not be a Hospitalière, but a Carmelite." The interior voice repeated this several times, "You will be a Carmelite." and she believed the last time was added, "Carmelite at Tours." In the meantime her confessor, without informing her of the fact, had proposed her as an applicant. Therefore what was her astonishment and joy when she heard him say: "My daughter, you are received among the Carmelites!" She left Rennes on the 11th of November, 1839, under the auspices of St. Martin, whom she had not uselessly invoked. Her virtuous father accompanied and presented her himself. She was then twenty-three years of age.

## Chapter II: Her Mission

In the Carmelite convent Perrine gratefully felt she was in her proper place. The fire of Divine love filled her soul. From the first, her companions recognized in her a solid judgment united with a cheerful, equable disposition; she was reserved and very discreet; she shunned all self-seeking and singularity; her modesty, mortification, and obedience were most exemplary. The candor and tranquility of her face mirrored the innocence and serenity of her soul. A sweet simplicity characterized this elevated nature, as may be judged by the following trait.

On the day of her arrival, during the hour of recreation, she was invited to sing. Without waiting to be urged, she at once began to sing a canticle which, she said, "I had sung in advance while awaiting the fortunate day of my entrance into Carmel; it commences with these words: 'Blessed be God, I am in a refuge.' . . . They were composed of some fifteen stanzas, and I sang them in so joyous a manner that no one thought of interrupting me." The new-comer did not seem disposed to leave one stanza unsung, when suddenly the Mother-Prioress, at first absent, came in. Finding one singing and the others attentively listening, she judged it a fitting opportunity for giving the new postulant her first trial. "Indeed, you have been in a hurry," said she to the latter, "to show off your little talent!" An embarrassing silence followed, which was broken only when the Mother-Prioress turned to the singer and said: "Let us see if you know any more." "Oh! Yes, Reverend Mother," she answered; "I have kept the best for you." And without betraying the least annoyance or ill-nature, she began anew. They knew then that the little girl from Brittany, by virtue and temperament, was not one ready to take offence or be easily depressed; that she possessed the cheerfulness which St. Teresa held as one of the proofs of a vocation to Carmel.

Her first interior attraction was a tender devotion to the Divine Infancy of Jesus. "I looked on myself," she said, "as a little servant of the Holy Family, and consecrated myself to them in that capacity." She mentions having still another ambition, which with a charming candor, she thus explains: "The Reverend Mothers were making their annual retreat, and during that time the postulants and novices took their recreation in the novitiate. One evening during recreation, when we were all collected before a picture of the Holy Family, I proposed to make a little Bethlehem for the Holy Family, each of us to especially consecrate ourselves to serve it in the capacity of that beast of burden which should fall to her lot; for instance, one would represent the donkey, another the ox, and so on. The proposal was unanimously adopted." The lots were drawn, and, to her great satisfaction, she was chosen to represent the donkey of the Infant Jesus. "Thus," she said, "I was His donkey in prayer, striving to warm Him by my love; and His little servant in my actions, imagining myself in the house of Nazareth, and performing as if for the Holy Family all the daily duties of my state of life."

She was inspired to honor the Infant Jesus each day of the month by meditating, one after another, on the different mysteries of this period of His life. Thus the thoughts of the Divine Child followed her in all her actions, and rendered every occupation easy and agreeable.

On the 8th of June, 1841, she made her profession. To the names which she had borne since her novitiate, and which placed her under the protection of the Queen of Angels and the Chief of the Apostles, her devotion for the Holy Family suggested an additional title. Henceforth Perrine Elnère will be known as Sister Marie de Saint-Pierre of the Holy Family.

The Prioress of the Carmelites of Tours at this time was Mother Marie of the Incarnation, a religious as eminent for her prudence as for her exalted virtues. She at once employed the newly-professed in different manual labors, and afterwards gave her the office of Portress. This office, so contrary to her natural inclinations, was the means Providence used to elevate her to the highest degree of perfection. The pious Sister dreaded its duties, fearing she would not be able to unite with them the spirit of recollection which was so dear to her. Respectfully she made known to the Reverend Mother-Prioress her distaste and fears; notwithstanding which the Mother-Prioress retained her in this employment, and she kept it all her life. This disposition was providential; for thus the humble daughter of the cloister in the performance of her duties frequently found herself in contact with pious secular persons who, later on, were not slow to aid her in her Work of the Reparation.

This mission, which grace was secretly preparing her for during the four years she had been in the convent, was to be conferred on her by our Lord Himself. It was the 26th of August, 1843, the day after the Feast of Saint Louis, King of France; in the evening the Sister was meditating at the foot of the cross, when the Savior said to her:

*"I have heard your sighs; I have seen the desire you have to glorify Me. My Name is everywhere blasphemed; even the children blaspheme! This frightful sin more deeply than all others wounds My Divine Heart; by blasphemy the sinner scorns Me to My Face, openly attacks Me, annihilates My Redemption, and pronounces his own condemnation and judgment. Blasphemy is an empoisoned arrow which wounds My Heart continually. I will give you a Golden Arrow, that with the delicious wounds of love you may heal the wounds of malice which sinners give Me."* And He dictated to her the following formula: *"May the most sacred, most adorable, most incomprehensible, and most ineffable Name of God be praised, blessed, loved, adored, and glorified in heaven, on earth, and in the hells, by all the creatures of God, and by the Sacred Heart of our Lord Jesus Christ in the Most Holy Sacrament of the Altar. Amen."*

Such was the Golden Arrow that the Lord gave to His servant, assuring her that every time she repeated this formula of praise she would wound His Heart with a wound of love. *"Be watchful of this favor,"* said He to her; *"I shall ask of you an account of it."* At that moment it seemed she beheld issuing from the Sacred Heart of Jesus, wounded by this arrow, torrents of graces for the conversion of sinners, which inspired her with confidence to say: "My Lord, dost Thou then give me charge of blasphemers?"

She did not fail to make known all this to the Mother-Prioress, who being as prudent as she was experienced, wished to prove and assure herself it was not an illusion. She consulted pious and learned ecclesiastics, and closely watched the conduct of the Sister. Far from encouraging her in this extraordinary way, she endeavored to turn her from it. She even forbade her to recite certain prayers which had been recommended. But several incidents which she could not but look upon as miraculous — among them her own cure, obtained by the prayers of the Sister in accordance with the order of our Lord, and in the manner He Himself willed — made her relax her severity towards her and to permit her at least to say the prayers of Reparation.

Our Lord continued to reiterate His orders to His servant. The poor Sister would sometimes exclaim: "Ah! If the Divine Master could suffer bitterness, He would be sorrowful unto death on beholding men; instead of making up for their failings by uniting themselves to Him and thus glorifying our Heavenly Father, they continually blaspheme His Holy Name and unite themselves with Lucifer and his reprobates. How satisfied, on the contrary, He would feel to see at least a few faithful and grateful children united to Him in order to love and bless the Name of that Father whom He so tenderly loves!"

The contemplation of this obstacle brought her to make a heroic act of entire abandonment. "I feel myself," she said, "interiorly urged to make to God the sacrifice of my whole being and all the merits which I can acquire." But she submissively awaited the consent of her Prioress.

On the festival of St. John of the Cross (one of the patrons of Carmel), our Lord made His spouse hear these momentous words: *"Until now I have only shown you in part the designs of My Heart, but today I wish to show you them in their entirety. The earth is covered with crimes. The violation of the first three Commandments of God has irritated My Father; the Holy Name of God blasphemed, and the Holy Day of the Lord profaned, fill the measure of iniquities. These sins have mounted to the throne of God and provoked His wrath, which will soon burst forth if His justice is not appeased. At no time have these crimes ascended so high. I desire, with an ardent desire, that there be formed an association, well approved and organized, to honor the Name of My Father."*

Here the object of the Work of Reparation is clearly indicated: it is to repair the violation of the first three precepts of the Decalogue, which include all crimes that have a special character of hostility against God and the profanation of the Lord's Day.

Amazed and confused, the humble daughter of Carmel hesitated. But our Lord said to her: *"Take good care; for if, wanting in simplicity, you put obstacles to My designs, you will be held responsible for the salvation of souls; if, on the contrary, you are faithful, they will embellish your crown."* In conclusion He said: *"And to whom should I address Myself, if not to a Carmelite, whose very vocation enjoins on her the duty of unceasingly glorifying My Name?"*

Thirteen days after, on the eve of the Immaculate Conception (7th of December), the Blessed Savior returned to the same subject, and this time the culpable nation is named. He made the Sister see how greatly He was incensed against France on account of her blasphemies. "He has declared to me," she said, "that He can no longer dwell in this France, which, like a viper, tears the bowels of His mercy. He still patiently bears the contempt shown Himself, but the outrages committed against His Eternal Father provoke His wrath. France has sucked unto blood the paps of His mercy; this is why justice will now take the place of mercy, and His wrath will burst forth with greater fury for having been longer delayed. Filled with terror, I tremblingly said: 'My Lord, permit me to ask, if this Reparation which Thou desirest be made, wilt Thou yet pardon France?' He answered me: *'I will pardon her once more; but, mark well, once. As this crime of blasphemy extends over the whole kingdom, and as it is public, so also must the Reparation be public and extend to all her cities. Woe to those who will not make this Reparation!'* "

What Frenchman's heart could be unmoved, hearing warnings so severe, so solemn? The reproach, alas! — is but too well merited, for the crime is evident and incontestable. Everywhere among us we hear uttered incessantly and with impunity that blasphemy designated by our Lord to His servant as a frightful sin. France is pronounced the most guilty of all nations, because she is the most highly favored by Heaven, the most loved of Christ, and the eldest daughter of the Church. Having become in Europe the principal center of the spirit of revolution by the practical atheism she professes in her laws and government, she exerts in regard to blasphemy a kind of universal proselytism, as baneful to individuals as it is to society. Is it astonishing, then, that she is especially threatened with the strokes of Divine Justice? After receiving this message Sister Marie de Saint-Pierre, as we learn from one of the other Carmelites, came from the choir in a state difficult to describe. She was deathly pale and bathed in tears; her countenance, usually so cheerful, bore an impress of suffering which it long retained. She appeared as if crushed, annihilated beneath the weight of Divine Wrath.

In the midst of her anguish a great consolation was bestowed upon her. She learned that the Sovereign Pontiff, Gregory XVI, had by a brief dated August 8, 1843, permitted the establishment of pious Confraternities for the Extirpation of Blasphemy. "I no longer doubted," she said, "that the work entrusted to me came from God. What particularly struck me and awakened my admiration was the following happy coincidence in this manifestation of Divine Providence: On the 8th of August the Sovereign Pontiff issued his brief at Rome, and on the 26th of the same month, and in the same year, the day after the festival of Saint Louis, our Lord revealed to an obscure little Carmelite this great Work in Reparation for blasphemy with which He wished to enrich France as a means of salvation, to snatch her from the hands of His offended and irritated justice."

# Chapter III: Her Revelations on the Reparation

On Christmas night of 1843, having obtained the permission of her Superiors, the Sister made, according to the reiterated demands of our Lord, "an act placing all her merits in the hands of the Most Holy Infant Jesus." As a reward she was favored with still more abundant lights and graces. "It seems," she said, "that I hear Jesus from the depths of the tabernacle addressing us these words: *'O ye My friends and faithful children, behold if there be any sorrow like unto Mine! My Divine Father and My Spouse, the Holy Church, the delight of My Heart, are despised and outraged by My enemies. Will no one rise up to console Me by defending them against those who attack them? I can no longer remain in the midst of this ungrateful people. Behold the torrent of tears that flow from My eyes! Can I find none to wipe them away by making reparation for the glory of My Father and imploring the conversion of the guilty?'* " "Ah!" cries the pious Sister, "if a king, or even his ambassador, be treated with indignity by a foreign power, how quickly the whole nation rushes to arms to avenge the insult! Troops are mustered, and the death of numberless soldiers is accounted as nothing. And yet the holy and terrible Name of the God of Hosts, of the King of kings, is despised and blasphemed, His Day is profaned by sinners in infinite numbers, and no one is troubled thereat, no one thinks of Reparation. Behold, our Lord Jesus, the Envoy and Son of the God of Armies, the Ambassador of the Kingdom of Heaven, demands a Reparation of Honor to His Eternal Father, or war will be declared against us and France will suffer the chastisements of His wrath. Will we pause to weigh the matter? Will we hesitate in our choice?"

The Archbishop of Tours, who at that time was Monseigneur (Mgr.) Morlot, wished to see and examine the writings of the Carmelite. We say her "writings," because the Mother-Prioress had required her to write all her revelations. The Prelate approved in this regard the wisdom of her Superiors, and authorized Rev. Pierre Aileron, Superior of the Carmelites, and at the same time pastor of Notre Dame La Riche, to establish in his parish an Association for the Reparation of Blasphemy. This was on the model of the one in Rome, approved by Gregory

XVI, August 8, 1843. Its members were thus enabled to gain the numerous spiritual advantages granted to the Roman association. The permission of Mgr. Morlot is dated March 15, 1844. The association, on being established, took for its patrons St. Michael the Archangel, St. Louis, King of France, and St. Martin. Those that belonged to it were to recite daily a *Pater, Ave, Gloria,* and the *Golden Arrow* aforementioned.

This, without doubt, was something — a first step towards the Work of Reparation. But more was required — namely, an Archconfraternity similar to that of Our Lady of Victory for the Conversion of Sinners. The Sister was very sorrowful. They saw her coming from her prayers pale, trembling, and bathed in tears. She continually offered herself in sacrifice to turn away the Divine scourges and obtain the salvation of her country. On learning that the usual prayer of St. Denis was "Give me souls!" she unceasingly repeated it, and begged the Sisters to do the same. In the meantime the Divine Master revealed to her more and more the enormity of blasphemy. *"You cannot understand,"* He said to her one day, *"the malice and abomination of this sin. If My justice were not restrained by My mercy it would instantly crush the guilty, and all creatures, even inanimate ones, would rise up to avenge My outraged honor."* After this, the Sister added, "He showed me the excellence of the Work of Reparation; how it surpasses all other devotions, is agreeable to God, to the angels, the saints, and is useful to the Church. Ah! — if you knew the degree of glory you acquire in making but a single act of Reparation for blasphemy, in saying only once in the spirit of reparation, 'Admirable is the Name of God!' "

She again wrote: "This work is within me as a consuming fire. I continually beg our Lord to deign to save France; to establish in all her cities His Work of Reparation, and to raise up apostolic men for this end. Thou seest, my sweet Jesus, that I, a poor unworthy creature, can do nothing; vouchsafe then, to enlighten the heart of him who can render Thee this service with the knowledge of all that I suffer."

The Carmelites, forced to leave their monastery, lived for two years in a secular dwelling where cloister enclosure was almost impossible. Sister Saint-Pierre, still in her office of Portress of the Interior, had much to suffer. Yet our Lord, in the very midst of the embarrassments and distractions of her charge, consoled her with new and consoling lights. In her great desire to comfort and strengthen those who came to her with their sorrows, she was inspired to communicate to them the devotion of the Gospel of the Circumcision, and of the Holy Name. Thus she writes of this devotion: "The demon uses all possible means to snatch from our Lord Jesus Christ the inheritance purchased by the cross, and he is ever seeking to rob this Good Shepherd of the lambs obtained at so great a price. To put this ravishing wolf to flight, Jesus has made known to me that He wishes His sheep marked with His Holy Name, by bearing on their person the Gospel which announces to all nations that the Incarnate Word was named Jesus. This amiable Savior has acquainted me with the virtue of His Sacred Name — that it would drive away the demon, and that all those placing themselves under its special protection would receive great graces." Her superiors permitted her to distribute printed sheets of this Gospel on which was stamped an image of the Infant Jesus. To this was added a piece of the palm blessed on Palm Sunday. These sheets were folded and enclosed in a little square sachet, marked upon the outside with the Sacred Heart and the instruments of the Passion. It was to be worn on the person in the same way as a medal attached to a scapular, etc. The pious Carmelite had thus in view the glorification of the Name of Jesus. Numerous graces came to confirm her faith and make her rejoice in the devotion. Every one wished to have these little sachets. On the sheets, beneath the Gospel, these words were inscribed:

"When Jesus was named, Satan, vanquished, was disarmed."

"Our Lord has revealed to me," said the Sister, "how glorious it is to Him to have His victory celebrated by these words, for they make the demon tremble with rage; that He will bless all who wear this Gospel, and will defend them against the attacks of Satan."

On the 17th of June 1845, the Divine Master resumed His great design, and encouraged His servant to address the Archbishop personally. The Prelate very kindly visited the holy Carmelite, whose virtues he held in the highest esteem. Ushered into his presence, she knelt, kissed his feet, and humbly asked him to deign to accomplish the work he had so happily begun in authorizing the Association of Notre Dame La Riche; and she disclosed to him how strongly our Lord had urged her to request the official establishment of the Work of Reparation in the metropolis of Tours, formerly the center of so many graces for France. In the kindest manner the Prelate answered: "My child, with all my heart I desire to establish the Work and give it all necessary and well-deserved publicity; but there are obstacles in the way which are difficult to overcome. It is a hard task for us to incite our people to follow the ordinary practices of piety. Might not the proposal of new and additional devotions provoke the wicked to still greater blasphemy?" Nevertheless he reassured her by declaring he saw in her revelations no stamp of illusion, but recognized in them the *Seal of God*;

and he exhorted her to still pray and solicit new light on the subject. He permitted her to recite the Prayers of Reparation, and sometime after accorded permission to have them printed. He also approved of a little book against blasphemy entitled *Collection of Prayers Followed by Little Office of the Holy Name of God*, composed by M. Dupont.

"This little book," said the Sister, "authorized by the Archbishop, at once became very popular, and by this means in a short time more than twenty-five thousand Prayers of the Reparation were distributed. Tours received numberless applications for them from persons in various cities who wished to propagate this devotion to the Holy Name of God, and everywhere they were recited with the greatest fervor. Our Lord revealed to me that this new harmony appeased His wrath, but that He still wished to have an association established such as He had demanded."

# Chapter IV: Her Revelations of the Holy Face

Obeying the Archbishop's counsels, Sister Saint-Pierre began to pray with renewed fervor for greater light regarding the establishment of the Work of Reparation. But it pleased the Divine Master to lead His servant once more through the path of interior trials. She was assailed with fears and doubts; terrible temptations met her at every turn; all sensible consolations were withdrawn; she felt that her soul had lost even sanctifying grace, and in her agony she hardly dared receive Holy Communion. One day, while awaiting the hour of Mass, and hesitating as to whether she should approach the Holy Table, she thought that this Bread of the Strong would infuse courage. She seized with renewed faith her crucifix, and, recalling to mind that Jesus had said that the Act of Praise called the *Golden Arrow* delightfully wounded His Heart, she pronounced this formula ten times in succession and resolved to receive Holy Communion in Reparation for blasphemy. Nothing more was needed to touch the Heart of the Heavenly Spouse. This fervent, loving soul was filled with consolations, and the Mystery of the Sorrowful Face of Christ was suddenly revealed to her. She felt herself transported in spirit to the road to Calvary. "There," she said, "our Lord vividly portrayed to me the pious act of Veronica, who with her veil wiped His most Holy Face, covered with spittle, dust, sweat, and blood. This Divine Savior made me understand that the impious at present, by their blasphemies, renewed the outrages formerly inflicted on His Holy Face. All the blasphemies hurled against the Divinity, whom they cannot reach, fall back, like the spittle of the impious (during the Passion) upon the Face of our Lord, who has offered Himself a victim for sinners. Then He told me I must imitate the zeal of the pious Veronica, who so courageously braved the crowd of His enemies to reach Him, and He gave her to me as a protectress and model. By promoting the Reparation for Blasphemy we render Him the same service as did this heroic Jewish woman, and He looks upon those who act thus, with the same gratitude as when He gazed upon her on His way to Calvary." The purpose of the Reparation begins with this seed, and we see its growth with successive revelations.

Henceforth the Sister applied herself to rendering homage to the Holy Face. "I believe," she said, "I am under the special protection of the pious Veronica; I am continually occupied in adoring the august and most Holy

Face of the Divine Savior. This adorable Face is the mirror of the perfections contained in the Most Holy Name of God." "I comprehended" she said, "that as the Sacred Heart of Jesus is the sensible object offered to our adoration, to represent His boundless love in the Most Holy Sacrament of the Altar; so in the Work of the Reparation, our Lord's Face is the *sensible* object offered to the adoration of the Associates, to atone for the outrages of blasphemers, who attack the Divinity, of which it is the mirror and expression. By virtue of this adorable Face presented to the Eternal Father we can appease His just wrath and obtain the conversion of the impious and blasphemers." Our Lord favored His servant with still other lights. He made her comprehend that the Church is His Mystical Body, and religion the face of that Body. "He then showed me," she said, "that this Face is today a butt for the enemies of, His Holy Name; and I saw, by means of this Divine Light, that the impious, by wicked words and blasphemy against the Holy Name of God, spit upon the Savior's Face and cover it with mud; that all the blows given to Holy Church and religion by sectarians are a renewal of the numerous buffets which the Holy Face of our Lord received, and that these wretches, in striving to annul the infinite merits of its sufferings, cause, as it were, the sweat of this most Holy Face."

"After this vision," continued the Sister, "the Blessed Savior said to me: *'I seek Veronicas to wipe and honor My Divine Face, which has few adorers.'* Additionally, He made me understand anew that all who would devote themselves to this Work of the Reparation would thereby perform the office of the pious Veronica. After which He addressed these words to me: *'I give you My Face as a recompense for the services you have rendered Me. They are slight, it is true; but your heart has con-*

ceived great desires. *I therefore present you this gift in virtue of the Holy Ghost, in the presence of My Father, the angels and saints, through the hands of My Most Holy Mother and St. Veronica, who will teach you in what manner It should be venerated.'* He moreover added: *'By My Holy Face you will perform wonders.'* " The Sister understood that this precious gift was not for herself alone; that it was to become in the Work of Reparation a distinctive sign and powerful means of action. But this grace was for her, after that of the Sacraments, the greatest she could receive. *"Now,"* added the Lord, *"if any do not recognize in this My work, it is because they close their eyes."*

"Two days after, having taken for the subject of my prayer," the Sister said, "the betrayal of Judas, I sorrow-fully considered the outrage the Face of our Lord had received in the kiss of His perfidious disciple, and it seemed to me that the Divine Master invited me in a spirit of reparation to kiss most fervently the image of His Holy Face (See Brief of Pope Leo XIII). After obeying the inspiration, I felt that this amiable Savior willed to instruct me on the excellence of the gift He had presented me in His adorable Face, and He had the goodness to accommo-date for the feebleness of my mind the following simple comparison: *'As in earthly kingdoms,'* said He, *'one can obtain what he wills with coin stamped with the king's effigy, so with the precious coin of My sacred Humanity, whose effigy is My adorable Face, one can obtain in the Kingdom of Heaven all that he desires.'* And He promised me, besides, that all who, by words, prayers, or writings, would defend His cause in this Work of Reparation, He would defend before His Father, and would give them His Kingdom."

Following these communications on the Holy Face, the next day Sister Saint-Pierre had an interior light on the same subject, which she expressed in the following prayer:

"Remember, O my soul! — the instructions which Thy Heavenly Spouse has this day given thee concerning His adorable Face. Remember that the Divine Head represents the Eternal Father, who is unbegotten; that the Mouth of this Holy Face represents the Divine Word, begotten of the Father; the two Eyes, the reciprocal love of the Father and the Son, for these Divine Eyes have but one light, one identical knowledge, and produce the one same love which represents the Holy Ghost. Contemplate in His flowing Hair the infinite perfections of the Most Blessed Trinity. Behold in this Majestic Head, the precious portion of the Sacred Humanity of the Savior, the image of the Unity of God."

A series of other communications soon revealed more clearly additional consoling truths. On the 3rd of November, in order to show more plainly how fitting was the choice He had made of His Holy Face as the principal object of the Adoration, our Lord declared to Marie de Saint-Pierre that He gave it to her *"to be wiped with her homages and perfumed with her praises,"* and He added: *"According to the care you will take to make reparation to My Face, disfigured by blasphemy, I will take of your soul, disfigured by sin. I will re-imprint My likeness upon it, and make it as beautiful as when it came forth from the baptismal font. There are men skilled in restoring health to the body, but I alone am the 'healer of souls,' I alone can renew in them the image of God, effaced by sin."* Hearing these words, the pious Sister in transports exclaimed: "I salute Thee, I adore Thee, and I love Thee, O adorable Face of Jesus, my Beloved, Noble Seal of the Divinity. With all the powers of my soul I apply myself to Thee, and I most humbly pray Thee to imprint in all of us Thy image, disfigured by sin."

"What a mystery of love!" continued our Carmelite, "Man is invited to repair the outrages made to his God, and in a loving return He promises to restore His image in our souls! Let us, therefore, wipe the august Face of the Savior, soiled with the spittle of blasphemers, and He will wipe our soul, soiled with the spittle of sin."

## Chapter V: Her Prayers for France

The year 1846 had dawned on the world, and yet there was no outward indication that the ardent wishes of Sister Saint-Pierre would be realized. On the 23rd of January she was favored with a message, which she hastened in tears, to make know to the Mother-Prioress. These are the fearful words the Divine Savior used: *"The face of France has become hideous in My Father's eyes, and she provokes His justice. To obtain mercy for her, offer Him the Face of His Son, in whom He takes delight. Unless this is done, she will feel the weight of His wrath in well-merited chastisements. The Holy Face of her Savior is her salvation. Behold the proof of My goodness to France, who only repays Me with ingratitude."* Henceforth, docile and frightened, the pious Sister began to say this prayer, which she continually repeated:

"Eternal Father, we offer Thee the adorable Face of Thy well-beloved Son for the honor and glory of Thy Holy Name and for the salvation of France."

It was now with great anguish that she received new lights. Those warnings of God, and the apparent impossibility of seeing His commands obeyed, filled her with sorrow and desolation. "My poor heart," she said, "is pierced by a sword of grief. Again our Blessed Lord has centered all the faculties of my soul upon His precious thorn-crowned Head and His adorable Face, which is made a butt for the outrages of the enemies of God and His Church. Again I have heard His sorrowful pleas, 'that He seeks souls to atone for the outrages inflicted upon Him, and to heal His Divine Wounds by applying to them the wine of compassion and the oil of charity.' "

Four days later, the Divine Master made known to His servant that two persons had rendered Him signal service during His Passion: the first, as already mentioned, was the pious Veronica, who glorified His humanity by wiping His adorable Face on the painful road to Calvary; the second was the "good thief," who from his cross, as from a pulpit, openly defended the Savior's cause and confessed His Divinity, blasphemed by the other thief, and the impious. He presented both as models in the Work of Reparation — Veronica to those of her own sex who are called to defend His cause, not by preaching, but by wiping His Holy august Face with the veil of prayer, praise, and adoration; and the "good thief" as the special model of men and the ministers of His Church, who are called upon to publicly defend the honor of God and to proclaim His glory before those by whom it is outraged. To St. Veronica our Lord gave the impression of His Divine features; to the "good thief" an immediate entrance into His celestial Kingdom. And He promised the Sister to be no less munificent to those who by their "prayers, words, adorations, or writings defended His cause; He will defend their cause before His Father in Heaven and give them His Kingdom." And He enjoined her to make these promises known to all, adding: "If you keep these things hidden, without speaking of them, you will commit an injustice." In another communication the Lord urged her to offer herself as a victim for the sins of France.

*"Pray for her,"* said He; *"immolate yourself for her. I give you anew My Face: offer It to My Father to*

*appease His justice. Ah! — if you but knew Its power, Its virtue. And wherefore? Because I have taken upon My Head all the sins of mankind, in order that My members may be spared. Therefore offer My Face to My Father, for this is the means of appeasing Him."* And He added: *"I desire the Work of the Reparation; rest assured it will be firmly established, but the fruit you bear is not yet matured."*

In the mission assigned to the daughter of Carmel, we see the salvation of France closely linked with the Work of Reparation; hence for both, our Lord offers the same exterior signs, the same efficacious means — namely, the devotion of His adorable Face. Such is the subject of the following message: *"My daughter, I take you for My steward and anew I place My Holy Face in your hands that you may unceasingly offer it to My Father for the salvation of France. Use to advantage the Divine gift, which in My Holy Face, I entrust to you. By so doing you will obtain the conversion of many sinners. Nothing that you ask in virtue of this offering will be refused you. Ah! — if you but knew how pleasing to My Father is the sight of My Face."* Again, showing her the boundless treasures of the infinite merits of His life and Passion, the loving Savior added: *"My daughter, I give you My Face and My Heart, I give you My Blood, I give you My Wounds; draw from them and pour out upon others; buy freely, for My Blood is the price of souls. Oh! — what sorrow for My Heart, to behold the remedies which have cost Me so dearly despised by men. Ask of My Father for as many souls as I have shed drops of blood in My Passion."*

The prayers of Reparation seemed to the Sister a wall which protected France against the shafts of Divine Justice; a hundred times daily she offered to God the adorable Face of Jesus.

On the 27th of January 1847, another message bound together two excellent devotions, which occupy an essential place in the Work of Reparation. "Our amiable Savior," said the pious Carmelite, "has made me hear His sighs upon His unappreciated love in the Most Blessed Sacrament of the Altar, from the lack of faith among Christians, and He has happily bound my heart and mind at His feet, in order that I may keep Him company in this abandonment, by adoring His Most Holy Face hidden under the Eucharistic veil. Yes, it is by this august Sacrament that Jesus, our Savior, wishes to communicate to souls the virtue of His most Holy Face, which is there more dazzling than the sun. And He has promised me anew to imprint on the souls of those that honor It, His Divine Likeness."

Then suddenly our Lord conveyed to her mind, a clear sense of the connection existing between His Most Holy Name and His adorable Face. "He made me under stand," said she, "by a comparison as simple as it is appropriate, how the impious, by their blasphemies, attack His adorable Face, while the faithful glorify it by the homage and praise they render to His Name and His Sacred Person."

"Behold a man, distinguished for his name and merits, in the presence of his enemies; they do not lift a hand against him, but they heap insults upon him, treat him with contempt, and call him by injurious epithets instead of the titles that justly belong to him. Observe now the face of this injured man; does it not seem that all the opprobrious words uttered against him by his enemies are reflected there, and make him suffer a veritable torment? See how his face burns with shame and confusion. Is not the ignominy inflicted upon it harder to bear than physical tortures in other parts of his body? This is a faint picture of the Face of our Lord outraged by the blasphemies of the impious!"

"Let us observe this same man in the presence of his friends, who, hearing of the insults he has received, hasten to console him by treating him according to his dignity, paying homage to the greatness of his name, and addressing him by all the titles due his exalted rank; does not the face of that man express the sweetness of these praises? Happiness rests upon his brow and beams on his radiant countenance, joy sparkles in his eyes, and a smile is on his lips. In a word, his faithful friends have cured the burning anguish of that face outraged by his enemies; glory has taken the place of opprobrium. This is what the friends of Jesus do by the Work of Reparation; the glory they render to His Name rests on His august brow and delights His most Holy Face in a special manner in the Blessed Sacrament of the Altar."

In our days the crimes which most outrage our Lord in His Sacrament spring from secret societies. They are designated to the Sister under the general name of Communists, as being the greatest enemies of the Church and France. "He has commanded me," she said, "to make war against these wicked men, who for the most part were born in that Church of which they are now the declared enemies. He has given me to combat them the arms of His Passion, His Cross, and the other instruments of His tortures. *'My daughter,'* said He, *'they have dragged Me from My Tabernacles, they have profaned My Sanctuaries and laid hands on the anointed of the Lord. Have they not committed the crime of Judas? Have they not sold Me for money? Let not this knowledge be without fruit. I make it known to you in order to animate you for the combat. March towards them with the simplicity of a child and the courage of a valiant soldier.'* " And the virgin of the cloister repeated with the prophet: "Let God arise and His enemies be dispersed, and let all that hate Him flee from before His Face."

This was in 1847. The governments of the period did not appear to be uneasy about the plots of these enemies of social order who have since overturned thrones and brought confusion to Europe. "Alas!" said the pious Carmelite, unable to restrain her tears, "days of wrath are approaching, and yet this Work of the Reparation, which I have borne for nearly four years under sorrows, that God alone can know, has not appeared. O my God! — arise; it is Thy cause as well as ours; we pray Thee to defend France with the protection of Thy Holy Face, and grant her mercy for the glory of Thy adorable Name. Yes, enlightened from on high, I firmly believe that on this Work of Reparation depends the future of France. I see it always linked to France as the means of salvation that God in His infinite mercy has chosen for her. Wherefore, I would give the last drop of my blood to obtain its establishment, for then the Lord would be appeased and innumerable souls would be saved."

# Chapter VI: The Archconfraternity of the Reparation

The 7th of March, 1847, our Lord said to His faithful servant: *"Rejoice, My daughter; the hour approaches when that most beautiful work under the sun is to appear."* As the Sister was much troubled concerning the many obstacles to be overcome, the Divine Savior said to her: *"These obstacles are only the mist of a morning ushering in a fine day."*

A point emerges here, regarding the Work of Reparation through the Holy Face. Without doubt the Redemption wrought upon the Cross is, and always will be, the masterpiece of Divine Wisdom and Divine Love; but the Reparation asked of Marie de Saint-Pierre by the Savior is so intimately connected with the Redemption of man, so identified with the expiation of Calvary, that we may truly consider it an application of the same; and thus, notwithstanding the feebleness and unworthiness of the instruments employed, it is in reality "the most beautiful of works, the most necessary for the needs of the age in which we live."

The day, in fact, was fast approaching when this Work would be definitely established. The Confraternity, having not been instituted at Tours in the manner the Lord wished, resulted in the Holy Virgin of La Salette coming in person on the 19th of September to begin it. Sister Saint-Pierre had solicited the intervention of Mary, and Mary, Our Merciful Mother, announced it. "Since his Grace," said Sister Saint-Pierre, "having not come to a decision, I appealed to Mary. I clearly saw there was no hope but in her intercession; daily I recited the chaplet to obtain the establishment of the Work. I longed to proclaim it throughout France and make known to my country the misfortunes which threatened her. Oh! — how I suffered in being the sole depositary of so important a thing!" "Holy Virgin," she again exclaimed, "appear in the world, make known to someone that which has been communicated to me concerning France." When the pious Sister heard that the august Queen of Heaven had spoken to the little shepherds of the Alps, Maximin and Melanie, she cried with joy: "O Virgin Mother of my God! I thank Thee for having given me these two little shepherds as sounding trumpets to echo from the mountain to the ears of France all that has been revealed to me in solitude." And again: "The voice of my dear little associates has been heard throughout the world. Let us pray, let us weep for our sins. The time is not far distant when France will be shaken to her foundations. But she will not be engulfed if the Work of Reparation appears before the eyes of the Lord. She, who was to be utterly destroyed, will be only lightly chastised."

In fact, in less than a year after — and perhaps to this we owe our continued existence — the Work was earnestly begun  Mgr. Parisis, Bishop of Langres, having heard of the proposed Work, took a lively interest in promoting it as much as possible. His zeal for the Holy Name of God made him labor with much ardor for the establishment of the Association; his efforts were crowned with success. He wrote to Mgr. Morlot, Archbishop of Tours, who, still judging that it was not the right time to announce an opinion, left the initiative of the Work to the Bishop of Langres, being all the more willing to do this as Langres was his (Mgr. Morlot's) birthplace. A Confraternity of Reparation was then canonically established at St. Dizier in the church of St. Martin of Lanoue. Reverend M. l'Abbe Marche, its pastor, was sent to Rome to solicit, in behalf of the Association, the title of Archconfraternity, together with some indulgences. Pope Pius IX received the petitions with the most ardent enthusiasm, and it was on this occasion he made use of the words that have been so often quoted: "Reparation is a work destined to save society." He granted the requested indulgences, and by a brief dated July 30, 1847, raised the Association of Reparation established at St. Dizier to the dignity of an Archconfraternity, with the right of aggregating through-out the Catholic world similar associations; and his Holi-ness requested that his name should be the first subscribed on the register of membership — a signal privilege, which was to be the seed of wonderful benedictions.

The Confraternity of the Reparation answered so well the need of our times, and was so evidently the work of God, that from its very commencement it spread like a fire among dry reeds.

Nevertheless, it had for its center only the second parish of a small town, in a diocese far from the place where the revelations had been made. Besides, the episcopal ordinance of Langres had made no mention of the devotion of the Holy Face indicated as the sensible object of the Reparation. Consequently, though the canonical erection of the Archconfraternity of the Reparation filled the pious Sister with joy, she yet said, "My heart is not entirely satisfied; for in this work the Church of Tours, the heritage of the great St. Martin, still remains inactive. When will it bring forth the fruit which has been conceived in its midst?"

She was not to see the fulfillment of this legitimate desire; her earthly pilgrimage was drawing to a close. Still the future welfare of her country was ever before her, and she ceased not to pray most earnestly for its salvation. On the 2nd of December our Lord appeared to her covered with wounds. "He made me," she said, "hear these sorrowful words: *'The Jews crucified Me on Friday; but the Christians crucify Me on Sunday. Ask them in My name, at least for this diocese of Tours, the establishment of the Work of Reparation, in order that My friends may embalm My Wounds by pious expiations, and obtain mercy for the guilty. My daughter, the storm is already threatening, but I shall keep My promise if My wishes be accomplished. Speak with humility and at the same time with holy liberty.'*"

The storm of which the Savior spoke was indeed at hand. Two months later it was to burst forth in all its fury. The Divine Master clearly announced this to His servant in a communication on the 13th of February.

"Our Lord," she said, "has made known to me in these words the terrible woes impending over us: *'The Church is threatened with a fearful tempest Pray, pray!'* " "It is impossible," she adds, "to describe the touching and impressive accents with which this charitable Savior said to me, *'Pray, pray!'* "

This prediction was, indeed, verified in 1848, in the epoch usually called *Days of February*, by an unexpected Revolution which hurled Louis Philippe from his throne, made France a Republic, and shook all Europe, particularly Rome, which Pope Pius IX was obliged to leave and seek refuge in Gaeta.

The soul of the Sister was in anguish. "Ah!" she cried, "the Lord has long asked of France a Work which would be for her a *rainbow of mercy*. Happily, the work has been inaugurated, and its influence is being felt; but it is yet too feeble to arrest the wrath of the Omnipotent. Ah! — if it were but extended to all the dioceses I should be without uneasiness, for God is faithful to His promises." She adds: "Oh! — how I wish to make known to all the bishops this consoling truth, and entreat them in this great crisis to aid in the Work of Reparation. I have always said it, and I again repeat it: *It is this Work which is to disarm the justice of God and save France and the world!* Happy if they know how to profit by this means of salvation!"

"Nothing," she further said, "is more efficacious to disarm the irritated justice of God than to offer Him this Most Holy Face, which has taken upon Its head the thorns of our sins, and has exposed Itself to the strokes of that same justice. It has canceled our debts, It is our security;

whence our amiable Savior has commanded me, notwithstanding my unworthiness, to keep myself constantly before the throne of His Father, offering Him this Divine Face, the object of His contentment. And this tender Savior has made me the consoling promise: *'Every time you offer My Face to My Father I will open My mouth to demand mercy.'* The good Jesus has also promised to have pity on France. Let us, then, have great confidence; His all-powerful Name will be our buckler, and His adorable Face our rampart. And He made me also understand that He wished this devotion to His adorable Face rapidly and widely extended. O good Jesus! Hide us in the secret of Thy Holy Face, that it may be for us an impregnable tower, a fortress against the attacks of our enemies." One day after Holy Communion our Lord appeared in the interior of her soul as He is represented in the *Ecce Homo.* "He at first attracted my attention," she said, "upon the contemplation of His Holy Face. Soon He directed it to the reed He held in His Hand, and presented it to me to combat the enemies of the Church, promising me they would feel my blows. He made me understand that this feeble reed was the figure of my soul. Yes, I am only a feeble reed, but in the hand of Jesus Christ, my Spouse, becoming most powerful against His adversaries, I shall say with faith and confidence: 'O malice of the demon, vanish before the reed of Jesus Christ!' "

"Eternal Father, I offer Thee the most Holy Face of Jesus. It is a mysterious coin of infinite value which alone can cancel our debts. Eternal Father, I offer Thee the most Holy Face of Jesus to appease Thy wrath. Remember It has borne the thorns of our sins, and the blows of Thy justice, of which It still bears the marks. Behold those Divine Wounds of whose voice I wish to be the echo; they incessantly cry, 'Mercy, mercy, mercy for sinners!' "

With these words she bowed her face to the earth, saying, "Lord, I merit only hell!" The Good Master answered: *"I have applied to your soul the virtue of My Face, to restore therein the image of God. Those who will contemplate the wounds of My Face on earth shall one day contemplate it radiant with glory in Heaven."*

"At that moment," said the Sister, "I was on Tabor and would fain have repeated with the apostle St. Peter: 'Lord, it is good to be here. Let us make three tabernacles for the three powers of my soul, that it may always enjoy this sweet repose which infinitely surpasses all the pleasures of earth.' But our Lord made me understand that His true spouses should prefer the heat of combat to the repose of contemplation, and should not shrink from throwing themselves into the conflict to defend His glory."

It was after these Divine consolations that Marie de Saint-Pierre composed, as by inspiration, those beautiful invocations of the "Adorable Face of our Lord" improperly called the "Litany." They are jets of light, cries of love, a kind of spiritual poem to the glorification of the Holy Face, which she is pleased to consider under its different aspects — joyous, sorrowful, glorious, merciful, and terrible. At the end of her writings, in a hymn of thanksgiving, she particularly thanks our Lord "for having made her the gift of His Divine Face, so suitable to appease the justice of the Celestial Father, and from which flows a precious Blood which assures us of eternal life." She adds: "O blessed, holy angels! Thank Jesus and Mary for me, who have heaped favors upon me, and draw me to heaven, in order that I may, notwithstanding my unworthiness, sing eternally with you a hymn of gratitude for all the graces I have received from my God, and, above all, for the Work of Reparation which His mercy has established in France."

# Chapter VII: Her Virtues

It is time to speak a few words of the virtues of our dear revered Sister. We shall only mention those which were the most characteristic.

Above all, she possessed charity in an eminent degree; the glory of God and the conversion and salvation of sinners were the sole objects of her thoughts and the motive of all her actions. The loss of souls made so vivid an impression upon her that she could not repress her sorrow. More than once she was heard weeping and sobbing. Her tender and solid piety also inspired her with a great zeal to relieve the souls in purgatory, especially those that were the most forlorn.

Her heart expanded with love for our Lord; she honored His Sacred Humanity in all its mysteries, but those of His Birth and hidden Life had for her inexpressible charms. Her devotion to the Divine Infancy and to the Holy Family was manifest on all occasions. Being Portress, it was a source of joy to her to open the door to carpenters, whose occupation reminded her of the labors of the childhood of Jesus and St. Joseph. One day a wagon drawn by a donkey entered the courtyard of the monastery. Approaching the animal, the good Sister began to tenderly stroke it in remembrance of the service rendered Jesus and Mary by the humble beast in their flight into Egypt. At Christmastime she showed her joy and piety in various ways; she contemplated with a radiant countenance the statue of the Infant Jesus in the crib, took it in her arms, lit tapers before it, and sang for the Divine Babe her sweetest songs of praise; sometimes, even, like David before the Ark, she began to dance, inviting her companions in the Novitiate to do the same. The Mother-Prioress expressed astonishment and warned her against dissipation. "Oh! — no, Reverend Mother," she answered, "I do it to honor the Infant Jesus, and to make amends for all the guilty dances that offend Him."

Her affections were also directed to Jesus in the Eucharist. In the choir, before the Blessed Sacrament, the expression of her face, her manner, her looks, made it seem that, piercing the Eucharistic veil, she really saw Jesus on the altar. Quitting the sanctuary, she left there her heart; and in whatever part of the house she happened to be, she turned towards it, transported with joy when she could catch a glimpse of the altar. She reached a rare degree of humility. She sincerely believed herself the least in the community, the most miserable, an unworthy sinner, and reproached herself for the slightest imperfections as if they were grave faults. One day a Sister found her weeping and asked the cause. Sister Saint-Pierre reminded her of a fault she had committed the day previous in her presence. The Sister assured her she had not noticed it, it was so very trifling. "Nevertheless," she answered, "God may have been offended, and that is the cause of my tears." Although she sincerely confessed it, conceit was never in her mind. Once when she was still a novice, the Mother-Prioress asked her during recreation to sing for a newly-arrived postulant the canticle, "Blessed be God, I am His spouse." She did so with so sweet a voice and so lively an accent of piety that her young companion was delighted. When she had finished the Mother-Prioress said aloud: "Eh, well, my Sister Saint- Pierre, how many thoughts of vanity had you whilst singing?" Lowering her eyes, she modestly answered: "If I have had any I have banished them."

Her obedience was prompt, implicit, and perfect. She complied in the simplicity of a child with all that was required, stimulated thereto by the example of the Child Jesus at Nazareth. The words of the Gospel, "*He was submissive to them*" were ever on her lips. She rendered a blind obedience not only to her superiors, but to the

Sisters upon whom she was dependent, and, in fact, to all, regarding them as her mistresses and making it a duty to acquiesce in their wishes, just like a child who has no will but that of its guardians. Thus she was able in her last sickness to say in all truth and candor: "It is my consolation in death that I have always been obedient."

Her recollection was so profound that merely to see her was sufficient to raise one's thoughts to God. She seemed unconscious of what was going on around her, so much so that even after her Profession she was ignorant of the various places assigned the different nuns in the choir and refectory. One of the nuns, whose cell was so situated that she had an opportunity of seeing her when she thought herself unseen by human eyes, assured us that during the time she occupied this cell, which was for several years, she never saw her raise her eyes from her work but to cast them on the little statue of the Infant Jesus which she always kept near her.

After any supernatural communications she would appear pale, trembling, and bathed in tears — especially when they concerned the impending woes for France. Then her tears flowed, calmly and silently. She would then appear so absorbed in recollection that it was difficult to draw her therefrom; and this would last for hours, though without hindrance to the performance of her duties. Her union with God was intimate and continual; she never lost sight of Him, and, according to her expression, her soul, closely united to our Lord, was "happily bound at His feet." But this life, apparently so heavenly and sweet, was not exempt from interior trials and sufferings. The Mother-Prioress was convinced that these were so great that, whilst serving to purify her soul, they shortened her days in this world.

She also possessed, in an eminent degree, that sweet liberty of spirit which distinguishes a true Carmelite.

She knew how to blend perfectly the practice of the most honorable virtues, the charms of charity, and even joyfulness. One day a friend brought to the convent, as a present, a piece of cake. Sister Saint-Pierre, then Portress, was very much fatigued. On receiving the cake she immediately carried it to the Mother-Prioress and presenting it to her, said with her usual simplicity: "What a providence — the donkey of the Infant Jesus is hungry!" The good Mother smiled, and gave a piece of the cake to her little Portress, who, giving thanks to God, happily partook of it.

During recreations she spoke but little, always preferring to listen; nevertheless she was cheerful and amiable, expressing herself to the point and taking part in all that was said, though it was often necessary for her to make extremely violent efforts to break off her interior converse with God. Her companions loved to be near her, because they always found it to their spiritual benefit. Her reserve was especially noticeable in matters pertaining to charity; she excused everyone, palliated their defects, and did so cordially and with tact.

During her last illness, having passed a night of extreme suffering, she said to a nun who was from the same part of the country as herself: "You remember that in Brittany our little excursions ended with a feast, each person furnishing his or her share, one paying for the cream, another for the sugar. The good Jesus, last night, assigned me the furnishing of the sugar by making me suffer very much."

When, in 1848, she fell sick, it was at the time of the government elections, and the Carmelites had more than one worry. One day the Mother-Prioress said halfjestingly: "Since you cannot pray anymore, you will be the spiritual drum, and whenever you hear the National Guard beat the call to arms, you will call the holy angels to our assistance." She accepted her new mission, and the next day presented the Reverend Mother with a little drum, upon which was inscribed the Holy Name of God and that of each of the choirs of holy angels. Unable to make vocal prayers, she would take the little drum on her bed, and, striking it with her fingers, thus call the heavenly militia to their aid. The world may laugh at this trait of childish piety, but those not of the world will see in it the admirable simplicity of a soul transformed by the science of the crib and the virtue of obedience. This drum, after the death of the Sister, was sent to a friend of Carmel as a plaything to amuse his little boy. Instead, the family richly encased it under a glass globe and is preserved as a precious relic.

Until the last, our dear Sister cherished a special devotion to the Divine Infant Jesus and the cares which at that period of His life He received from His august Mother. She was richly rewarded by the ineffable communications graciously given to her concerning the Divine Maternity, whence she drew greater and greater confidence for the triumph of the Church and the salvation of France.

## Chapter VIII: Her Last Sickness and Her Death

The mission of the Sister was accomplished. According to the designs of God, there remained for her only to perfect the sacrifice which she had so often made of herself. Already her health was beginning to fail. At the close of Lent in 1848, she entered upon those sufferings which, uniting her more and more to Jesus crucified, were to crown her pure and holy life by an admirable death.

On Good Friday, at three o'clock, while prostrate on the ground adoring Jesus Christ dying on the Cross, it was revealed to her that the Divine wrath about to descend upon men. Immediately, renewing her act of perfect abandonment, she offered herself to God as a victim to appease

His irritated justice. It seemed as if the Lord had awaited this last and generous offering before immolating His courageous victim, for immediately she developed that long and painful sickness which caused her final dissolution. She was consumed by a burning fever; her throat became ulcerated; her tongue and mouth felt as if they were incessantly pierced by cruel thorns — a noticeable fact, since our Lord had told her she must pray and suffer for blasphemers. Night after night she was unable to take the slightest repose; each change of position on her bed became a new martyrdom; ulcers were formed, which added to her sufferings. This frightful state for human nature she bore without the least injury to her interior disposition; her patience never waned, her union with God was continual, her spirit of sacrifice entire and without reserve, her docility, innocence, and simplicity like that of a child.

Early in June she received the Holy Viaticum and Extreme Unction with a fervor and rapture that made it seem that she already had a foretaste of the eternal joys in store for her. On Friday, the 16th of June, they thought her dying, and began the *Prayers for the Agonizing.* Perfectly conscious, she united with the pious nuns by making frequent aspirations. Suddenly she entered into a supernatural state, the effects of which were very apparent. When, after the commending of the departing soul, they pronounced these words, "Maria, Mater Graticae, Mater Misericordiae" she impulsively threw up her arms toward Heaven with the eagerness of a child at the sight of its mother. She remained a long time in this position, although a few moments before so weak and stiff were her arms that they seemed immovable. Afterwards she extended them in the form of a cross, in order to expire as a victim. When the dear nuns attempted to prevent it she said: "Leave me thus; for me it is a duty." Alternately taking her crucifix and the little statue of the Infant Jesus which never quitted her, she covered them with kisses and pressed them to her heart. Then, holding the little statue as high as possible, she pronounced in a low, solemn tone these words: "Eternal Father! — once more I offer this adorable Child, Thy Divine Son, in expiation of my sins and those of the human race, for the needs of the Holy Church, for France and the Reparation. Amiable Jesus, I abandon this work into Thy hands; for it I have lived, for it I shall die." Then, placing the statue on her head, she said: "Divine Child, cover my criminal head with the merits of Thy precious Blood; renew in my soul grace and innocence; clothe me in Thy purity and the spirit of Thy humility. Oh! — hasten unto me! When shall I leave earth? Come, O my Jesus, and delay not! Mary, my tender Mother, come for my soul!"

She said to the Mother-Prioress: "My work is finished, as our Lord has made known to me; for the Work of Reparation which is to save France is established. It was for this God placed me on earth. Now I have but to suffer; it is necessary for the accomplishment of His designs. Ah! — how true it is that He has means of satisfying His justice unknown to man."

Her agony was long and painful. As death approached she recollected that our Lord had promised to restore to her soul at the last hour the image of God, and she wished to renew her baptismal vows; as a symbol of the grace she desired to receive, she asked for some holy water, made the sign of the cross upon her head, and pronounced these words: "Child, I baptize thee in the Name of the Father, and of the Son, and of the Holy Ghost." Then, joining her hands, she added: "I renounce Satan and all his works and pomps; I desire to belong forever to Jesus Christ." After this little ceremony her face assumed such an expression of heavenly beauty that one might readily have imagined her a child just from the waters of Baptism or an angel about to re-ascend to its celestial home. From that moment till her last sigh she never ceased praying. The sweat of death covered her brow, its chill had already benumbed her pain-worn frame, and yet the cold, livid lips continued to murmur: "Jesus, Mary, Joseph! Come, Lord Jesus! *Sit Nomen Domini benedictum!*" These were her last words. Soon her eyes closed, and as a last trail of resemblance to her Divine Master, she uttered a cry, and sweetly expired. It was on Saturday, a day consecrated to Mary. The mortal remains of this admirable daughter of St. Teresa have been, through the care of M. Dupont, deposited within the enclosure of the Carmel of Tours, in the Chapter-Hall, which is on the right of the entrance of the chapel. A mural stone near the holy-water font bears this simple inscription:

*Here rests Sister Marie de Saint-Pierre*
*of the Holy Family,*
*A Professed Religious of this Monastery,*
*Who died July 8th, 1848, aged 31 years and 9 months,*
*Having been a Religious 9 years and 8 months.*
*Lord, Thou wilt conceal her in the secret of Thy Face.*

# Chapter IX: The Confaternity of the Holy Face

After the death of Sister Saint-Pierre, two works closely allied in spirit to the Reparation and the Adoration of the Holy Sacrament, came from her virginal tomb like two miraculous flowers — the Congregation devoted to Perpetual Adoration, founded by Mademoiselle Dubouché (in religion Mother Mary Teresa); and the Nocturnal Adoration by Men, instituted by the celebrated Jewish pianist, Hermann (later Father Marie-Augustine, of the

Order of Discalced Carmelites). But it was M. Dupont who, in the designs of God, had the special mission to carry out and develop the work shown to the Carmelite of Tours for the salvation of France: the Work of Reparation for Blasphemy and the Profanation of Sunday by the Devotion of the Holy Face.

Towards the close of the Lenten season of 1851, he exposed in his private oratory an engraving of the sorrowful Face of our Lord, an authentic facsimile of the Veil of Veronica preserved in the Vatican Basilica. Miracles soon began to manifest. The man of God rejoiced, because he believed them proof of the truth of the revelations made to Sister Marie de Saint-Pierre. To the end he hoped the life and writings of the venerable Sister would be published. Understanding their worth, he knew how much good they would do. His hope was realized. In 1876, before his earthly career ended, he learned that the Archbishop of Tours, Mgr. Colet, had issued orders that insured their being presented to the world. With a radiant face he blessed God, and with his gaze turned towards the Carmelite convent, he peaceably expired on the 18th of March. On his death, his oratory, where for twenty-five years the Holy Face had been honored, was at once transformed into a public chapel. Mgr. Colet officiated on the occasion of its dedication. At the same time he established in this sanctuary the Confraternity of the Reparation for Blasphemy and for the Profanation of Sunday, affiliating it to that of St. Dizier already erected. Using his power as Ordinary, he gave to this Confraternity of Tours a distinct character, and made of it, properly speaking, a Confraternity of the Holy Face, which was really the embodiment of Sister Saint-Pierre's inspirations. Finally, to minister to the new chapel and attend to the spiritual wants of the pilgrims who flocked from all parts thither, the worthy successor of St. Martin instituted under the title of "Priests of the Holy Face," a society of regular clergy living in community in the house formerly occupied by M. Dupont, and who, following in his footsteps and under his auspices, would devote themselves to all the Works of Reparation.

Since then the Oratory of the Holy Face has become a center of prayers and expiations to which the gaze and hearts of numbers turn, not only from all parts of France, but, in truth, from all Christendom.

It was not long before other Confraternities of the Holy Face, similar to the one founded at Tours by Mgr. Colet, were established in many cities. Letters from all parts of the world are received soliciting pictures of the Holy Face like the one so long venerated by M. Dupont, which was an authentic facsimile of the Veil of Veronica. It would be impossible to calculate the number of the holy pictures exposed in various places (and nearly always with a lamp burning before them) — in cathedrals, parish churches, public chapels, private houses and oratories, in hospitals, and in the enclosure of religious communities. The Priests of the Holy Face at Tours have charged themselves with the pious duty of obtaining these pictures (the facsimile of Veronica's Veil) from Rome and facilitating their distribution, or rather, we should say, supplying the demand for them, which is a consequence of the recognition of the wants of our age; so natural is the idea of Reparation, so befitting and salutary, so powerful in attracting souls.

This need of Reparation is urgent; all Catholic hearts welcome its appearance. If it be true that France, God's privileged nation, the Eldest Daughter of the Church, is the most guilty because "much shall be demanded from her to whom much has been given," and that blasphemy in her midst is more audacious and profanations of God's Holy Days more perverse; should not every generous Christian soul feel called upon to labor zealously in establishing and propagating this Work of Reparation so urgently demanded in our Lord's Name by the Carmelite of Tours? What is more natural and just than to unite our efforts in repairing what impiety and hatred of God have combined to corrupt and ruin? The Work revealed to the admirable virgin whose history has been related, is as she herself said, "a necessity of justice and a pledge of mercy." Let our efforts be in common, let us unite ourselves in striving fervently to appease Divine Justice; then it will be our consolation to experience only the effects of mercy, which will be as abundant as our reparation is prompt and fervent.

# Source Materials & References

*Devotion to the Holy Face.* (1954). Clyde, MO:
    Benedictine Convent of Perpetual Adoration.

Janvier, P. (1887). *Manual of the Archconfraternity of the
    Holy Face followed by the Little Office of the Holy
    Name of God.* Tours: The Oratory of the Holy
    Face.

Janvier, P. (1885). *Sister Saint Pierre and the Work of
    Reparation with an Appendix of Prayers and
    Devotions for the Confraternities of the Holy Face.*
    New York: The Catholic Publication Society Co.

Rigamonti, M. I. (1958). *Missionary or Messenger of
    the Holy Face: Sister Maria Pierina de Micheli.*
    Great Britain: King Bros.